MEMORIES

MEMORIES

BY

C. KEGAN PAUL

" . . . *At the last shall come old age,*
Decrepit as befits that stage;
How else wouldst thou retire apart
With the hoarded memories of thy heart,
And gather all to the very least
Of the fragments of life's earlier feast."
            —R. BROWNING, *The Flight of the Duchess.*

" . . . *New measures, other feet anon!*
My dance is finished."
            —R. BROWNING, *A Grammarian's Funeral.*

ARCHON BOOKS
1971

First published 1899
by Kegan Paul, Trench, Trübner & Co. Ltd.

This edition first published 1971
by Archon Books
995 Sherman Avenue
Hamden, Connecticut, 06514

ISBN 0 208 01157 9

Printed in Great Britain

CONTENTS

		PAGE
Foreword		vii
I.	*Childhood, 1828–1836*	I
II.	*School-days—Ilminster, 1836–1841* . .	36
III.	*Eton—The Fellows and Masters, 1841–1846*	61
IV.	*Eton—School Life, 1841–1846* . .	108
V.	*College Life at Oxford, 1846–1851* . .	135
VI.	*Clerical Life—First Experiences, 1851–1854*	173
VII.	*Conduct of Eton and Master in College, 1853–1862*	201
VIII.	*Vicar of Sturminster Marshall, Dorset, 1862–1874*	243
IX.	*Publishing—Holidays Abroad, 1874* .	270
X.	*Friends in London, 1874* . . .	315
XI.	*The End of Wandering, 1890* . .	364
	Bibliographical Note	378

FOREWORD

IT is perhaps a pity that this reprint of Kegan Paul's *Memories* appears over the name of his old publishing company (or the modern form of it) because somebody may interpret the gesture as a kind of advertising. He was a publisher only at the end of an attractive intellectual life, and it would be hard to recall another book so filled with entertaining stories of country and parish life, school and nursery in the high Victorian years. It has the calm style of a civilized mind, and deserves its place among candidates for reissue.

His tales are always pleasant and quietly told—whether he describes nursery remedies, or the decapitation of a miner who fell down a shaft and hit his neck on the returning bucket. Then there was the curious schoolmaster at his father's parish of Wellow "who objected to flogging, but when further questioned as to what method of punishment he used, had replied, 'I hangs them up by their thumbs'." And one can see enjoyably the undergraduate episode in the rooms of his friend Hopkins of Balliol:

One day I was engaged to lunch with **Hopkins** of Balliol, an old Eton acquaintance, whose rooms were decorated in the most ecclesiastical manner. I found him stripping texts from the walls in wild haste, and appealing to those of his friends who had arrived to help him to shove under the bed a large crowned figure of the Blessed Virgin. It appeared that he had just heard that his father, a Berkshire squire, whose contempt for ecclesiastical millinery, etc., was most pronounced, was in Oxford, and even then on his way to Balliol. The transformation was effected, and the meeting between father and son was unbroken by storms. I was spending a few days in Berkshire with Hopkins some years ago, and was amused to find this very figure of the Blessed Virgin presiding over a well in the grounds, set in a little niche against a tree. But she is there purely for decorative and in no degree for devotional purposes.

It would be unfair to quote other examples, because discovering them is a pleasure of this book. The picture through it all is in far perspective of a time when shades of religious attitude governed the world in which he moved. Many of these pages are about Eton, where Kegan Paul went as a boy and returned later as master in College. But mild doubts and statements from his religious position made it necessary for him to leave, and when a suitable parish became available the Bishop of Salisbury "wrote to know if it were possible to keep a heretic out of his diocese."

Kegan Paul wandered under the influence of Comte towards Unitarianism, and out into the world of publishing. He was a singularly admirable publisher, keeping commercial value in its place behind conviction, good taste and truth to God. Our managerial claptrap was distant from the range of his vocabulary. He cared very much about typography, and in one essay looked to the day when Mr. William Morris might design a type face and turn his attention to reform of the printing world. Some of his editions of poets in the late eighteen-seventies and the eighties are excellent examples of Victorian elegance before the much-praised "revival of printing." Twelve numbers of the journal *Bibliographica*, begun in 1895, are notable instances of fine printing under the influence of Herbert Horne.

When he went over finally to Rome, his reasons are moving and a little surprising; as that his attention was directed "to the cure of Pascal's niece of a lachrymal fistula, by the touch of the Holy Thorn preserved at Port Royal," which convinced him "that the Thorn must, from its effects, have been one that touched the Sacred Head." Such a happening made Bible miracles credible, and "it was on the testimony of a living Church that I would accept the Scripture."

In these matters and his conscientious social care—extending to moral doubt as to whether he should call on George Eliot—and the span of his life, he was a complete Victorian. This book was written in the last years, after a carriage accident had forced him to retire from activity. He had been born near Ilminster in 1828, at White Lackington where his father was curate in sole charge, and lived for two years into the new century.

COLIN FRANKLIN

MEMORIES

I

CHILDHOOD

1828–1836

ON April 17, 1883, the premises of Messrs. Kegan Paul, Trench & Co. at No. 1 Paternoster Square, E.C., were wholly destroyed by fire. In them was burnt a volume in which, for a few years past, I had been writing my reminiscences from time to time, and I have felt some disinclination to work at them again. I wrote then with the feeling that, whether I published or not, my children would like to read the record, when they too begin to live more in the past than in the future : I write now, intending to publish, since I have taken interest in the narratives of several men I have known, and am inclined to

think that the careful memories of the somewhat varied life I have lived may prove in the
same manner entertaining to others. These
pages will not pretend to tell everything. The
morbid self-analysis of Rousseau needs all, and
more than all, his genius to make it tolerable,
and if it be pleasant reading under any circumstances, it is unprofitable. I will try to
write without undue self-blame or self-praise.

I was born on March 8, 1828, at White
Lackington, near Ilminster, Somerset, of which
village my father was curate in sole charge. He
was also incumbent of Knowle St. Giles's hard
by, a very small village with no parsonage.

My father was born December 20, 1802,
and came of a Scotch stock, but I know nothing
whatever of his family beyond my grandfather,
who was a West India merchant, and also
owned an estate in St. Vincent, West Indies.
My father's mother was Mary Warner of
Bequia, a small island near St. Vincent. She
was very many years younger than her husband,
and was his god-daughter, a spiritual relation
which would have stood in the way of their
marriage had they been Catholics. My father's
childhood was mainly spent in London, as

whenever his parents happened to be in the West Indies he lived with his father's partner. He was educated at the Charterhouse school, for which he always had a great affection. It will serve to show the growth of London within the present century to say that the two houses at which he mainly spent his holidays were Mr. Charrington's, the brewer's, in Stepney, and his father's partner, Mr. Innes's, 51 Guildford Street. Mr. Charrington's house was approached from London through country fields, and stood in a park wherein were deer and a good trout stream, for the sake of which stream the brewery was probably there established; while the north side of Guildford Street was unbuilt, and the south side looked north over trees and hedges with an unbroken prospect of Hampstead Hill.

Thence my father went to Caius College, Cambridge, and was intended for the law, but his health failing after he began to keep terms in London, he went to join his father in St. Vincent, of which island Mr. Paul was then Lieutenant Governor. On my father's return to England, it appeared to some of his friends that they could aid him to Church preferment,

which would give him a fixed profession.
Therefore, though he had considerable means
from West Indian property, he took Orders, with,
no doubt, a determination to do his duty, but
without the high ideas of self-devotion which
all men are supposed to have, and many really
have, in these days. No West Indian difficulties had then begun, and both at College
and in his early married life my father had an
ample, even a large income, and my mother
was considered to have done well for herself
in a worldly sense.

Though my mother was also West Indian,
and from the same island, the families had
never met or been known to each other in
those parts. Kingston Park, my grandfather
Paul's estate, was on the coast and on the out-
skirts of the main town of the island ; my
grandfather Horne's estate was on the further
side of the mountain slopes. But when Mrs.
Paul, my grandmother, was left a widow she
came to England and settled in Bath, where
my father and mother met.

My mother, Frances Kegan Horne, was born
in St. Vincent in July 1802. Her family was
old Colonial, having been settled in St. Vincent

for some generations. They had come originally from Holland, claiming kinship with the Counts Horn, so well known in the history of that country. My maternal grandmother was Mary Kegan, of Irish descent. I only mention these facts because they show in particular, what we all know in general, how very mixed a race we English are. I am English by birth, residence, education, and prejudice, but racially I am wholly and solely Scotch, Dutch, and Irish.

I print here a copy of a document which I found in type among my mother's papers, as showing the care with which her grandfather, Mr. Kegan, recorded the births and god - parents of his children, and also for the curious fact that one of her aunts was christened Peter — a thing more common in those days in Catholic than in Protestant countries.

JOSEPH KEGAN, *Anguilla*, was born 22nd *September* 1735, Old Stile.

MARY VIRCHILD, *St. Christopher's*, was born 27th *November* 1739. Died 7th March 1797.

JOSEPH KEGAN and MARY VIRCHILD were married 28th *October* 1758, by the Rev. Mr. *George Paul*.

SUSANNAH REBECCA KEGAN, *St. Martin's*, was born 19th *November* 1761. Baptized by the Rev. Mr. *Jonathen Flemen; David Hendry, Mathew Larton, Johanna Gumbes*, and *Rachael Carley Wright* being Sponsors. Died 21st August 1792.

CHARLES KEGAN, *St. Martin's*, was born 22nd *April* 1763. Baptized by the Rev. Mr. *John Runolds;* Mr. *John Runolds, John Thomen, Mary Dogget*, and *Margaret Virchild* being Sponsors.

MARGARET VIRCHILD KEGAN, *St. Martin's*, was born 4th *September* 1765. Baptized by the Rev. Mr. *Howinch; Patrick Willson, Edward Gumbes, Kizia Leverock*, and *Ann Willson* being Sponsors. Died 27th August 1807.

MARY KEGAN, *St. Vincent*, was born 4th *August* 1767. Baptized by the Rev. Mr. *Robertson; Jeremiah Pinniston, James Manwaring, Mary Jane Pinneston*, and *Mary Dogget* being Sponsors.

FRANCES RACHAEL KEGAN, *St. Vincent*, was born 24th *October* 1769. Baptized by the Rev. Mr. *Robertson;* Mr. *Hunt*, Mr. *Oliver*, Mrs. *Hunt*, and Miss *Elizabeth Ashe* being Sponsors. Died March 16th 1796.

PETER ELIZABETH KEGAN, *St. Vincent*, was born 26th *October* 1771. Baptized by the Rev. Mr. *Robertson; Ashton Warner Byam*, godfather, *Keziah Leverock* and *Susanna Kegan*, godmothers. She departed this life, 25th *June* 1772, by the smallpox.

JOSEPH LAMBERT KEGAN, *St. Vincent*, was born 5th *May* 1773. Baptized by the Rev. Mr. *Finletre; Robert Gent* and *Peter Duhon*, godfathers, *Mary*

Dogget and *Susanna Kegan*, godmothers. He departed this life 31st *December* 1774.

JOSEPH KEGAN, *St. Vincent*, was born the 8th *February* 1775. Baptized by the Rev. Mr. *Finletre*.

JOSEPH KEGAN sen. departed this life, 3rd *August* 1775 in the 40th year of his age.

My mother and her sisters were sent home for education, and the younger ones made their home, after the death of their parents, with their eldest sister, Mrs. Keating, who married early (literally from school) the brother-in-law of her uncle, Mr. Kegan, a retired Indian civilian. I mention this lady by name, because she is a link with a state of things which has not only passed away, but has been almost wholly forgotten. In speaking of the West Indies we are apt to consider only the White Settlers, the Creoles, *i.e.* those of pure, un-mixed, European blood, and the Negroes, originally imported as slaves to the Planta-tions, whose descendants were still slaves when my parents were young. We do not take into account the Caribs, the original inhabitants, a yellow race of savages, who, as the islands were colonized, had gradually retreated to the mountains, and remained in great numbers in some of the wilder islands. They were for the most part unnoticed and ignored, but now and then became dangerous enemies hovering on the borders of civilized life, like the North American Indians described so well in Fenimore Cooper's romances. The war between France and England at the end of the last century, when so many of the West Indian islands changed hands, stimulated risings in various places. My aunt was born in 1792, and her earliest recollection was of being taken from her cot, when she was about four years old, to flee to a place of shelter nearer the coast, as a band of armed Caribs were coming from the mountains against the inland planters and their estates. There was some slaughter and much damage, but the planters rallied and retaliated ; the Caribs were thereafter treated as wild beasts, and I suppose have now absolutely ceased to exist.

About ten years later, and within my mother's memory, occurred the great eruption of the volcanic mountain La Souffrière, which probably helped to complete the discomfiture of the remaining Caribs. The catastrophe is well known to the students of earthquakes and volcanoes, and wrought vast havoc in the island. My grandfather and his family again had to flee by night, amid showers of stones, while a stream of lava descended on his estate, and the whole industry of many years was so utterly destroyed that the very trace of where cultivation had been was effectually blotted out. Dust from the volcano fell on the decks of ships one hundred miles away, and these were driven so far from their course that their officers and crew believed they had sailed over the very place where St. Vincent had been. A sea captain, a friend of the family, called on Mary Horne, then a girl at school in Kensington Square, to tell her that St. Vincent had disappeared, and she wore mourning for her family for a considerable time, till reassuring news arrived. It may be understood that, strong-minded woman though she became, her recollections and thought of the West Indies were curiously compounded of aversion and terror. My mother's recollections of the flight in the darkness from the volcano were that the whole thing, if alarming, was exciting and even amusing.

While I am speaking of those days, I may

venture to give one word to old Mr. Christopher Keating, my aunt's father-in-law, because it gives also my own earliest recollection,—that is, of my being sent round the breakfast table by the old man, who was crippled and could not move from his chair, to see that the spoons had been driven through the lower ends of the eggs which had been consumed, " lest the witches should ride in them." Mr. Keating had few superstitions, and I suppose few prejudices, on the subject of religion. In India, as a civilian, he had had for many years a native companion, as was the almost universal custom ; the bond being persistent and abiding, in fact a morganatic marriage. The lady in his case was a Mohammedan, and even in those lax days, Mr. Keating, high in station and a most able official, was severely blamed and well-nigh dismissed, for building a mosque to her memory when she died. Yet he had this one superstition, partly playful, but still more serious, about the eggs, and it made so strong an impression on me that I do not even now like to see any one finish an egg without thrusting the spoon through the bottom, and am always careful to do it myself.

When my father and mother married in May 1827, weddings were wont to take place at a very early hour, and the breakfast was really what it was called, little later than the normal time. According also to the simple fashion of the day, my father drove his wife home in his own carriage to Lackington, about thirty-five miles, stopping at Wells to dine. I was little more than two years old when we left Lackington; therefore, though I knew the place well in later years, it need hardly be said that I have no personal recollections of our residence in the little tumble-down cottage which then served as a Rectory-house. But some tales pertaining to that time made a strong impression on me as I heard them in after days.

One was of a very ghastly murder, still undiscovered, and never probably to be discovered in this world, of a Mr. Stuckey, who was, I think, a land agent in the neighbourhood. My father and mother were driving home in the late twilight of a summer evening, when the horse shied violently, and my father saw that he had done so at three men crouching in the hedge, evidently trying to avoid observation. There was no attempt to stop the carriage, my father whipped up the horse, and the incident seemed over. Next morning, however, Mr. Stuckey, who would have passed that spot very shortly afterwards on his return from Crewkerne market, was missing; his pony arrived at his door without the master, of whom nothing was heard for several months. A gentleman in the neighbourhood kept bloodhounds, which were called into requisition, and the whole country-side was searched, without effect. In August, however, at harvest-time, the reapers came across Mr. Stuckey's body in a field close to the spot where my father had seen the men, where also the ineffectual bloodhounds had endeavoured to track them. The man had been murdered, but I think not robbed: no clue to the assailants was ever found, nor any reason for the murder suspected.

Soon after I was two years old, my father, retaining his living of Knowle, took the curacies of Writhlington and Foxcote, about eight miles from Bath. We lived at Writhlington for ten years, and all my childish recollections are connected with it. In spite of several collieries, seen from the drawing-room windows, it was a pretty and attractive home; the country people were simple and friendly; we children were left a good deal to ourselves, and we roamed where we would and when we would. I still seem to see a hedge of Roses de Meaux (do such roses exist now?) which formed a fence to our field, and to smell the syringa in the shrubbery, to taste the peppermint bull's-eyes, which our neighbour the farmer, whose suitable name was Mattick, used always to produce from his breeches-pocket, and am sure there were never such fruit-trees as the quince, the medlar, and the Siberian crab which grew upon the lawn.

But to persons of riper years there were drawbacks; church restoration was as yet un-dreamed of, and the fabric of the church was disgraceful. As very few of the congregation could read, the services were almost entirely confined to a duet between the parson and the clerk. The Communion table was a plain four-legged piece of carpentry, without a cover, such as might have stood in our kitchen; the whole service, when there was no Communion, was read in the desk; the Holy Communion was administered about four times a year, but always on Good Friday as well as on Easter Sunday; the surplice was a full white gown, unrelieved by any stole or scarf. My father's reading of the prayers was grave and dignified, his doctrine old-fashioned and orthodox, his sermons moral essays far over the heads of his congregation, his parochial ministrations above the average of those days. I never remember seeing a baptism performed in the church during my childhood, or a woman churched during the service. Each of these offices took place in private, generally on Sundays after the rest of the congregation had left church, or on any week-day when the clergyman happened to be at home and could come to the church. It is curious, however, that certain pre-Reformation customs were always kept up. Both men and women bowed or genuflected to the altar, on entering church, though, had they been asked, they would probably have thought that the custom was directed to the squire's pew. Women always carried a prayer-book, whether they could read or not, wrapped up in a clean pocket-handkerchief; and this I believe to have been a reminiscence of the Housel cloth that was carried by individuals when not spread over the altar rails at the

time of Mass. The only attempt to give any
instruction was at the Sunday-school, and this
was held in the chancel.

Nearly all the colliers belonged to the village
club, and the funeral of a member was always
largely attended by his fellow-clubmen. We
had a very old green parrot, allowed to wander
at will about the house and garden. The
creature on one occasion climbed to the top
of a high fir-tree in the garden which over-
looked the churchyard, and seeing a very large
assemblage at a funeral below, screamed out
in most distinct tones: " O Lord, what fun !
what fun ! O my eyes, what fun !" This,
indeed, was an accident, but there was a
general want of decorum about the Church
services in those days.

But to return to the fabric. In the chancel
were monuments to the Goldfinch family, in
whose possession the old Manor-House had
once been, and in the vaults below were their
coffins mouldering to decay. On the walls was
an ominous green slime. The floor of our old
pew had several holes, and a frowsy smell
ascended to my sisters' and my noses, as we
were nearer to the floor than our elders. If

the day chanced to be very fine, a ray of light struck from the window through the said holes to the bulging coffins and showed us their nauseous state. Probably some faint attempt had been made at embalming, for the odour was not unbearable in those pre-sanitary days. Now, however, I place to the account of those dead Goldfinches a bad typhus fever from which we children suffered, leaving its traces in a rash on our heads. I only mention this unpleasant circumstance for the sake of the old-world remedy which was applied—bell oil, after some village recipe—the stale, dirty, and rancid oil used for the clappers of the Church bells, to make them swing easily, with which we were for some time anointed night and morning.

Our residence at Writhlington was once broken early in our stay there, and perhaps that, next to the egg-shells, is my earliest recollection. My father went to St. Vincent when West Indian affairs began to go wrong, to settle matters connected with the estate. Labour began to be dear when slavery was abolished ; crops were insecure, land went out of cultivation. Slavery was always hateful, and though the actual slave-trade had ceased, the memory rankled. My mother remembered with a shudder seeing a very aged negro take up her young brother in his arms, and mention casually that he, before leaving Africa in his early youth, had often helped to eat such another plump piccaninny. On the estates of my two grandfathers the negroes had been exceptionally well treated ; but indeed, throughout the islands of which I have known any particulars, there was little to complain of in actual condition of living, apart from the fundamental abomination that man was the chattel of man. But undoubtedly emancipation was ill managed, and the slave should have been obliged to pass through a feudal and intermediate state before complete freedom. We all know the ruin and disaster which fell on West Indian properties, perhaps justly, in punishment for slavery, extravagance, absenteeism, and racial contempt, but the ruin was hard to bear at the time. Under the light-heartedness of the negroes there was at work the feeling of class hatred for all that had gone before. I remember a snatch of a song I heard in my youth, as having been sung in

the islands about the time my father went out
to see if anything could be done.

> " But 'Mancipation come, ha, ha !
> Den me wear Massa's coat, ha, ha !
> Me kiss him wife,
> Me steal him knife
> And cut him ugly throat, ha, ha ! "

My father, however, was in those days a man
of buoyant spirits, and he was able to throw
off the following epigram, which I found years
afterwards in an old commonplace book belonging to my mother.

> " ' No sweets without their bitters,' few
> To prove this proverb fitter
> Than poor West Indian planters, who
> Find even sugar bitter."

My father's voyage was made by sailing ship
from Bristol, and it was more than three weeks
later than the intended date before the vessel
could leave the port, on account of contrary
winds.

When my father returned we went back to
Writhlington from Bath, where we had spent
the time of his absence, and shortly after this
one of my mother's brothers, with his **wife**
and family, arrived from St. Vincent to **stay**

with us. Never was such consternation and
amaze as Black Ann, the nurse, created in the
Somerset mining village. I seem to see her
now as she sallied forth to church on the
morning after her arrival ; low dress, bare arms,
a turban of flaming colours, her flashing eyes
and gleaming teeth set off by a skin blacker
than any collier's. Her absolute disregard of
her mistress's wishes was astonishing, and dis-
organising to our household. Peal followed
peal of the bell which sounded in the kitchen,
while she "turned her eyes tail up," and remarked languidly, "Let um ring again, and den
I come."

There are not many things during childhood
which seem worthy of record as I look to those
days, except such as show the advance in
comfort and in the decencies of life. There
were no lucifer-matches, and nurseries for the
most part were illuminated at night by rush-
lights, which, or rather the edifice in which
they were burnt, are described by Dickens in
Pickwick. They were terrifying things to a
child ; the light through the holes used to
elongate itself on the walls and take strange
shapes as the night wore away, and the rush

candle burned low ; then as day dawned the whole thing would go out with a splutter and a stink, perhaps before the nurse had the wakefulness or the presence of mind to leap from her bed and light the fire in winter. If she did not, she had to turn to the tinder-box, with its flint and steel, and hammer away till a chance spark fell on the tinder and kept a feeble glow to which a sulphur match could be applied. This was often a long process, and the maid shivered in the cold while the sparks refused to fall and the tinder would not take fire.

We, and our elders also, slept on feather beds, and with curtains tightly drawn round to keep out every breath of air. It is wonderful that we survived the frowsy atmosphere in which we were put to sleep. The morning tub was unknown after infancy : a foot-bath occasionally, and a general wash once a week, was all that was deemed needful or even wholesome. But all sanitary matters were little considered, and we lived in and bore with smells that now would breed a pestilence.

There was no fire-damp in the Somerset coalmines, and the colliers used to go about with tallow candles stuck in a little socket in front of their caps. They were a pleasant, kindly set of men, and on the best terms with us children. The way of going up and down the mine was a sort of barrel at the end of a rope, called a hutch, and the upper edge of this was very sharp, generally bound with iron. While we were at Writhlington a man fell down the shaft, and met an ascending hutch, which all but filled the shaft. His neck struck on the edge, and he was decapitated, his body falling to the bottom of the shaft, while the head reached the surface in the hutch.

The first visit to London that I remember was made before I was eight years old. We posted all the way, sleeping at Marlborough. In London we stayed in Guildford Street; our hostess was, of course, engaged about her own avocations ; my mother was not with us, and my father was absent most of the day on the business which had brought him to town. I could not go out alone, and was turned loose on the books in the library. I remember getting through the whole of *Camilla*, with interest, though probably with little understanding of what I read. I understood *Gulliver's Travels* better, and the edition I read was entirely unexpurgated. So also were the *Arabian Nights*, and I am still of opinion that the only way to render harmless the Bible, Shakspere, the *Arabian Nights* and all other books dealing with matters difficult and delicate, is that a child should read them at an early age, when all that is improper passes by with the harder words ; the sense of the whole is grasped, but not that of each component word. A charming and pure-minded old lady spoke to me a few years since, somewhat to my astonishment, of the wit of *Candide*. I assented and did not discuss. But when one of her daughters, a mature and married woman, fell upon the book, and came with horror and confusion to protest, the good lady could only say : "I daresay it may be very bad, my dear, but I read it when I was twelve, and if it was improper I did not understand it ; all I know is that it was very amusing."

About the same time I devoured all the poetry I could get hold of, and strange to say Falconer's *Shipwreck* was the poem which made on me the greatest impression. My father had a fair modern library, and before I was eight years old I had read the Waverley

novels, many of the volumes of an excellent
series called the *Family Library*, and, singularly
enough, a good deal of Theology. What I am
now saying about my reading may be taken
as applying to the age of twelve, so far as
my home life is concerned, since it is scarcely
possible to date each stage in intellectual
development. I suppose I was about ten
when I lighted upon a book called *Downside
Discussions*, which I read with profound interest, if with little real understanding. Some
Protestant controversialist had challenged the
Downside Benedictines to a public argument
on the points of difference between Rome and
the Protestant Churches, and strange to say,
the challenge was accepted : a public dis-
cussion took place, and the matter ended as
such encounters usually end, without apparent
result. I do not remember any details, but it
was clear to me that the Protestant champion
had not answered all that was said on the
other side.

About the same time two books fell in my
way which would have done much to make me
a Catholic had there been any to guide me,
as it was the impression made on me by them

was quite indelible. One was the well-known tale, *Father Clement*. In the life of Mr. Philip Gosse, the naturalist, his son, Mr. Edmund Gosse, tells us that the reading of that work gave his father the strong abhorrence of Rome, which remained with him throughout his life, and no doubt such was the effect intended by the author.

On me the influence was quite the reverse; the Protestant clergyman in the book, a Presbyterian, but put forward as a type of a Protestant minister, is asked where was his Church before the Reformation. His answer is at once so evasive, and so fatuous, that it was, to me, impossible to accept it for a moment, while the practices of piety inculcated on the young Papists, and held up to scorn, such as veneration for the Saints, fasting, the sign of the Cross, &c., seemed to me meritorious, or at least perfectly innocent. And in so far as the hero, Father Clement, had Protestant leanings, he appeared to be leaving the more for the less worthy cause.

The second book was *The Nun*, published anonymously, but known to be written by Mrs. Sherwood, the author of *The Fairchild Family*,

Little Henry and his Bearer, and other books of a vehemently Protestant character. It is of high literary merit and far more true to fact than *Father Clement.* Subtracting certain absurdities as to nuns kept in dungeons for heretical opinions, and secret meetings in underground chapels, in which the Bishop urges putting a recalcitrant nun to death— "When a limb is affected with gangrene, my daughter, no ideas of false compassion should prevent our cutting it off,"—convent life is not ill described, as seen through distorted spectacles.

The book had been given to my mother by her dearest friend, and for that friend's sake it always lay on a table in her room. I read it for its literary charm, till I knew it almost by heart, and here my sympathies were wholly with the orthodox nun Annunciata, with the Abbess and the Bishop, who were not, I was sure, guilty of the deeds attributed to them, rather than with Angelique and Pauline, who escape in the Revolution troubles to become wives and mothers. But there was no one to deepen these vague impressions; Roman priests and nuns, however interesting, were much like the characters in fairy tales, denizens of a world into which I never expected to enter. I was then but vaguely conscious of a dignified Church beyond the Anglican, and no mere body of Dissenters. I began to be aware of the fact, when my mother went one Holy Thursday to the *Tenebræ* service at Prior Park, and gave me an account of it. She had made acquaintance, how I do not know, with a certain Father Logan, who preached the Three Hours' devotion on that occasion. I think my mother went to Prior Park from time to time for some years, and all that she told me impressed me deeply.

I trace my real awakening to the meaning of literature, my intellectual "conversion," so to speak, to the autumn in which I was twelve years old. I had nearly died of scarlet fever, and when convalescent went with some relatives to Teignmouth for change of air. They left me alone for one long day, while they were absent on an excursion. I read a play of Shakspere for the first time. It was *Antony and Cleopatra*, which entranced and delighted me, so that I became a diligent reader and student of the greatest English poet.

This was the new birth, from which I date my true mental life. I ought also to except the Bible, my knowledge of which was considerable, chiefly from those nightly readings with my mother of which I have already spoken. I can conceive no better mode in which a mother can know her children and gain their affection than by visiting them after they are in bed; more confidences come in that peaceful hour than at any other, and even after the lapse of fifty-five years, when I am alone in my bedroom, I miss the gentle presence, and think that I listen for a step which I can never hear again.

We were wont to move for the winter into the neighbouring city of Bath, where we attended the Octagon Chapel, later Margaret's Chapel, and, on rare occasions, the Abbey. I believe my elders found something in the services which aided their piety, but I remember nothing which increased my own. I loathed church-going, though I was not an irreligious child.

In Bath there were still persons who retained some tradition of the High Churchism of Queen Anne's time, and we learnt from them that it was an old and pious use to attend Services on

Wednesday and Friday. There was even one chapel, attached to a hospital for old men, which retained daily prayer. There also lingered the tradition that it was well to practise some self-denial in Lent. An old physician who was very kind to us children then gave up snuff, and it was the only season in which we could approach him without sneezing.

Another reverent custom prevailed in the churches in Bath, which has now gone out of use or nearly so. Whenever the Lord's Prayer occurred in the second lesson for the day, in the Church Service, the whole congregation rose and stood during the reading of it.

The first person who made much impression on my childhood was James Brooke, afterwards Rajah of Sarawak, who was and remains to me the type of a grand and heroic nature. He had been sent by his father from India, to my great-uncle Mr. Kegan's care, and was almost brought up with my mother. She was his confidante in all his earliest troubles and scrapes ; to her were written many of his earliest letters when he went to India. When I, as a boy, knew him, he had returned from his first Indian expedition, and was full of that charm which drew to him so many young men in his adventurous life.

James Brooke's *Life* was written by the late Miss Jacob, sister of the Bishop of Newcastle, and contains a very fair estimate of the man. The earlier part was contributed by me. James Brooke never married, and during his life, he made over the government to his nephew, John Johnson, the son of his sister; but being dissatisfied with that gentleman's policy, he returned to the East to set aside his previous choice, and put in the place of the second Rajah his younger brother Charles, who also took the name of Brooke, and is now the third Rajah.

Another friend of my mother was Mrs. Thomas, widow of an Archdeacon of Bath, and a daughter of Dr. Harrington, a descendant of Sir John, the author of *Oceana*. Her recollections went back to the days when Bath was in its old-world glory, and she used to tell how gentlemen and ladies were wont to bathe together in the hot baths, in long gowns, the ladies with their hair dressed, the gentlemen in their wigs. Each lady had with her a little floating bowl of wood, in which she carried her handkerchief, fan, and sometimes a snuff-box.

These two and a Mr. Staples, whom I was taken to see in London, were the only persons who made much impression on me in my childhood. Mr. Staples was one of the few Englishmen who remained in Paris all through the Terror, had seen the king taken to execution, and many other of the absorbing events of that time. He gave me the first interest in that great uprising of the New Age. Very many years afterwards, when I was writing the *Life of Godwin*, I read for the first time the remarkable letter which Mary Wollstonecraft wrote on having seen the king pass to his trial.

"About nine o'clock this morning (Dec. 26, 1792) the king passed by my window, moving silently along—excepting now and then a few strokes on the drum, which rendered the stillness more awful—through empty streets, surrounded by the National Guards, who, clustering round the carriage, seemed to deserve their name. The inhabitants flocked to their windows, but the casements were all shut; not a voice was heard, nor did I see anything like an insulting gesture. For the first time

since I entered France, I bowed to the
majesty of the people, and respected the
propriety of behaviour, so perfectly in unison
with my own feelings. I can scarcely tell you
why, but an association of ideas made the
tears flow insensibly from my eyes, when I saw
Louis, sitting with more dignity than I expected
from his character, in a hackney coach, going
to meet death where so many of his race have
triumphed."

As I read this I seemed to have heard it
all before, and then recollected what Mr. Staples
had told me as a boy. He too had seen that
strange and terrible procession, and the practical
identity of the two accounts was a witness to
their fidelity, and an evidence of the power
with which the scene had graven itself on the
memory of those who were eye-witnesses.

One more early recollection is connected with
Mary Wollstonecraft, or rather with her daughter
Mary. My aunt, Mrs. Keating, told me that in
1814 she went to London with Mrs. Kegan,
that the latter might consult the great surgeon,
Sir Anthony Carlyle. He placed them in a
boarding-house, or rather in what would now
be called a private hospital kept by a lady

whom he had trained to watch such cases, as was hers, for him. This lady was a friend of the Godwins, and all their set, and my aunt vividly remembered her landlady coming to their sitting-room in strong agitation to say that Mary Godwin had eloped with young Mr. Shelley, that Jane Claremont had gone also, and that Mrs. Godwin had started in pursuit.

Our country neighbours were few, and the roads atrocious, so as to prevent much communication. But I have recollections of rare dinner-parties at home, in fine weather, and when there was a moon ; and of an occasional visit with my father and mother to country houses. The one thing that stands out prominently is that it was by no means uncommon for a country gentleman to be the worse for liquor after dinner, not drunk, but in the condition Miss Austen describes "stuffy uncle Phillips, breathing port wine."

Our nearest doctor was in the village of Chilcompton, six miles off, and the ordinary doctoring of the village was done by my mother from her own medicine chest, a real chest, full of large bottles. From this also the doctor made up his prescriptions, when he came, for us and for the poor. The amount of calomel, jalap, and other violent medicines then used was frightful, while the lancet was called into play for almost every ailment. People were regularly let blood every spring and fall, and women especially during every month of their pregnancy. When the cholera first appeared in England many people fell ill with fright, and there was one awful evening, when the wind blew a hurricane, with torrents of rain, that our cook made sure she had cholera, rejected all domestic remedies, and made the groom go off on horseback for the doctor. He arrived drenched to the skin, inspected the woman, and then weighed out a dose of jalap, such as even in those days my mother had not dreamed of. " But it will kill the woman," she objected. " No," said Mr. Leech—his real name —" it will not kill her, for she is strong, but as there is nothing whatever the matter with her, it will cure her of fancying she has cholera again."

As far as I remember there was one dame's school in the village, of course under no sort of control or inspection, and a Sunday-school held in the chancel of the church, in which as soon as I could read myself, I took a class. The smell of Sunday corduroys, onions eaten for breakfast, peppermints to be sucked in church during the sermon, and "boys' love" stuck between the leaves of prayer-books, is never to be forgotten. Sunday observance for the elders of the parish was mainly confined to washing, and it was difficult to recognise our collier friends in their unaccustomed white skins. A very small percentage came to church. There were, however, a few who "got religion," as the phrase was, and unable to find vent for their fervour in the then chill services of the Church, became Primitive Methodists, or Ranters, as they were termed. In fine weather they met on the open down, where the believers from two or three small villages could come together. Once as my father was riding from Writhlington to Foxcote on Sunday to take an afternoon service, they very civilly but firmly barred his progress, then, holding his horse's bridle, knelt down and prayed for his conversion; placing him in a somewhat embarrassing position. Totally devoid of education, they used in their prayers words of sonorous power, but no meaning. While waiting outside a cottage door, after knocking, my father once heard these words spoken inside: "O Lord, look down upon our forefathers and warm their cold hearts." This was a prayer for the dead with a vengeance !

It was not at Writhlington, but at another village with which I was well acquainted, that the "Ranters," when they fell to prayer, took the precaution of expelling the devil from their midst. They prayed vehemently, and in their petitions shouted so as to scare him ; then feeling sure no devil could have resisted them, closed all windows and doors fast, plugging the keyhole with paper, and as it was summer and no fire on the hearth, blocked the chimney with a potato sack, and then prayed again in security. But suddenly an excited woman exclaimed: "He baint gone ; I seed 'en, I seed 'en." "Wheer ? wheer?" cried the assistants. "I seed 'en look out of the nozzle of the bellows." The devil had taken refuge in them. Then the bellows were carried to the door, the paper was removed from the keyhole ; and the evil spirit being whiffed through, all went well to the end of the exercise.

II

SCHOOL-DAYS—ILMINSTER

1836–1841

WHEN I was eight years old it was settled that I should go to school. My mother's health was failing, and for more than a year her eyes gave her great trouble, so that she lived chiefly in a darkened room, and could take but little charge of her children. She had had the main care of my education up to this time, my father only teachng me Latin and the Greek alphabet. The school chosen for me was Ilminster, an old foundation in the town close to my birthplace. Though in after years I knew it so well that every tree and stone in the neighbourhood seemed to have been familiar to me from earliest infancy, this was of course my first conscious introduction to the place. My father and mother drove to Lackington, spent a night at the parsonage, and left me the next day to be taken to school by Mrs. Johnson, the parson's wife, sister of James Brooke. I cried myself to sleep in the evening, and my window facing the east, whereas our nursery at Writhlington looked north, the morning on which I went to school is the one on which I remember first seeing the sun rise. It was a glorious October morning, warm and bright as April, but the sunrise was no true omen. That day was the sunset of my childish ignorance, innocence, and happiness : I was going to a school which was, to me at least, a hell, and where life was one long misery.

My box had been sent to Ilminster by carrier, and soon after breakfast, Mrs. Johnson, Charlie (the present Rajah of Sarawak), his sisters, and I set out for our two miles' walk, or less, through Dillington Park, to the town. I remember the rustle of our feet in the fallen leaves, and the large bright horse-chestnuts we picked up under the trees ! The old house at Dillington was in process of demolition, to make way for the new quasi-Elizabethan edifice, which would have been so much better had Mr. Hanning-Lee waited but a few years longer, for the revival of architecture.

The Head-Master of Ilminster was the Rev. John .Allen, whom my father and mother had known in Lackington days. My parents had liked the Allens, knowing nothing of their relations to the boys they undertook to educate.

I looked forward happily enough to entrance into school life, for the town and neighbourhood were full of friends who were sure to notice me for my mother's sake. They did so. I still look back with pleasure to holidays spent at Mr. Leathes', a wine merchant in the town, whose wife showed me much affection ; and at the Mules's, one of whom was vicar of the place, another the doctor who had helped to bring me into the world. It was a day of great delight in each summer when Mr. Hoskins, rector of North Perrott, father of Admiral Sir Anthony Hoskins, whose boys were at the school, would drive over and take half-a-dozen of us to a picnic at the top of Herne Hill. He used to bring a delicious pie called a crowdy pie, enclosed in a crust, top and bottom alike, to save the danger of a broken dish. But better still were the rare

occasions on which I gained leave to visit the
Cotterells, the relations of my mother's maid
Jane, who lived with us from my baby days
till after I went to Eton. Cotterell was a
master carpenter, who lived in a delightful
old-fashioned house in Ilminster with stone
mullions, and behind his house was a large
walled garden sloping to the south, producing
such fruit as I have never known since—figs,
apples, pears, filberts, medlars in inexhaustible
profusion as it seemed to me. The red Quar-
renden apple especially has never been so red
and so large since. But these days were mere
oases in the desert.

Allen and his wife were, I think, of all
people with whom I have ever had to do, the
least fitted to train the young. Allen was
a little wiry, energetic man, with a keen
eye, sharp-cut features, and short hair like a
blacking-brush, combed straight up from his
forehead, with perhaps the thought, not in
his case fallacious, of adding to his stature.
He was an able man, and for clever and
advanced boys was a good teacher, witness
such pupils as he turned out in the Rev.
Spencer Northcote, afterwards head of St.

Mary's Oscott, and the Rev. Canon Macmullen, long the Catholic priest of Chelsea. These two, going straight from Ilminster, gained scholarships at Oxford, when very young. So too the able Church historian, Canon Perry, Sir George Cox, Canon H. Percy Smith, and others, traced to Allen the foundation of the good superstructure of learning they afterwards raised. But those were boys who would have succeeded anywhere, and they all entered the school at a greater age than I, a child of eight, who was necessarily left to under-teachers. There was an ignorant fellow named Sellick, who afterwards, I believe, became a sort of clerk to the school at Marlborough. I am told that at Marlborough Sellick was bursar's clerk, and managed the distributions of school-books, and weekly pocket-money. He is remembered there as 'Slug,' a name more suited to his appearance than his temper, for, unlike most very fat men, he was extremely irascible. There was also a miserable little usher named Tweed, to whom we boys, ill-treated ourselves, but not by him, showed, I grieve to say, every possible indignity, and who taught us nothing; a person named Coates, who set long punishments to poor little fellows who could hardly write; and Dr. Routledge, *Daddy*, of the London publisher's family, who was I believe a sound scholar, but could not teach. He was a good and kindly man, but living away from the school with his family, and with boarders of his own, knew nothing of the devilry of the school-house except the floggings. But with these he could not be expected to interfere, for in those days all education was driven in with the cane.

So far as I came under Allen, I learnt, and to him I certainly owe something of what little I know. But the text-books used were bad, the facilities for private preparation of lessons were non-existent; we children were never helped to learn for ourselves; we never heard a word of kindness or encouragement; furious flogging for the majority, the grossest favouritism for a few, appeared to be the only discipline known or imagined.

The mode in which the floggings were carried out was an ingenious piece of cruelty. The head-master sat on a sort of dais at the end of the room, at a high desk, in which he kept his papers. The space between the dais and the walls was filled by two closets open at the top, so that, though gloomy, there was still light enough to see, and even to read, unless the day were dark. Just within the door was a cupboard containing the canes used for flogging. The canes were a trifle longer than the cupboard, so that, when a little door about four inches square was opened, a cane started out like Jack-in-the-box, ready to the hand. This box was connected with a spring in the master's desk, some six feet distant. When a boy was to be punished—and there were few days, perhaps few lessons, without such an occurrence—Allen used to fling his gown behind him on his chair, and with a lithe bound spring to the cupboard, having first touched the spring in his desk ; the ominous click which answered within the cupboard was heard over the hushed and expectant room. Then driving the miserable child before him, he shut the door, swung the victim across his knee, and with the waxed cane ready to his hand, he flogged till he was tired, and then locked the boy in for an hour or two to recover himself as best he might. I have felt, and seen on others as well as on myself, the weals caused by the cane, as thick as a finger, while all between each stripe was livid, broken, and bleeding. I have known the black-and-blue bruises still on the skin for more than a month after the flogging. I believe that with one exception, his own son, a boy of my age, Allen hated me above all others, and I do not think that in either case there was reason or justice for it. Withal he was a pious person, and was said to preach good sermons. He became a High Churchman when that phase of faith grew into fashion, and I believe he died regretted, except by those who had known him as well as did his victims.

The one charm of the man was his voice. He was a finished singer, not the least like an amateur, but trained in all the best methods of the best professional artists. His voice was a vibrant sympathetic tenor, and both in singing and speaking he used it with marvellous skill. It charmed even boys not usually sensitive to "fine shades" of this kind. I have been called to account by Allen for some trifling misdemeanour, and his voice has moved me like the pathetic tones of a violin. I have felt myself a sinner, and repented bitterly that which needed no repentance. Only after I had left him did the truth assert itself, and I felt I had been tricked by the magic of musical sound.. My mother understood in after years what Allen was, and what we had endured ; but her sister, who was devoted to music, and who had been charmed by Allen's voice, could never be brought to believe that he who could sing and speak so divinely was brutal to his boys. No doubt, however, she believed with her whole heart that the devil had once quoted Scripture. Neither women nor men are always logical.

Allen read as well as he sang, with a strong Somersetshire accent, but I am by no means an advocate for eliminating all *nuances* of pronunciation from our speech. He always gave the Somerset aspirate before the letter R, and pronounced " read " as hread, " rabbit " as hrabbit. He made his pupils read well also. All those I have named as his pupils were exceptionally good readers, and almost every boy educated at Ilminster was at least a fair elocutionist.

Mrs. Allen, though still young, was the fattest woman I ever saw, and the hottest.

She would go out on frosty days into the garden unbonneted, unshawled, in the hope of getting cool. In her disposition she was hard and coarse. No grain of motherly kindness, no passing gleam of tenderness for the child victims of her husband's floggings, ever softened the asperities of our life. Her household was ill conducted and her servants were profligate and immoral; the food supplied to the boys was bad, we were insufficiently warmed—one small stove in the school-room round which the elder boys clustered was all the fire we ever came near—and cleanliness was impossible. There was indeed a solemn function once a week when our feet were washed in hot water, and Mrs. Allen herself attended to our heads with a small-tooth comb, but for the rest, all that came between head and feet, we washed only in the holidays. The scanty supply of basins in which we dipped our head and hands in the morning hardly counts among the possibilities of true cleanliness. Occasionally on "washing days" a jug of rhubarb was handed round and drunk out of wine-glasses, much in the fashion of Mrs. Squeers's brimstone and treacle; and the school could take but little cow beef at dinner next day. It always *was* cow beef, for I remember that some of the boys considered a slice of the udder·as a delicacy.

Mrs. Allen took some of the teaching, not in the school of course, but in the private dining-room. She gave Sunday lessons in *Crossman's Catechism*, a book of which I have never heard since and do not know the doctrine—and in French. She was certainly a good teacher. She had been educated in France, had an admirable accent, gave us a good selection of books to read, and when I went to Eton, the French master told me I had been excellently grounded.

As may be supposed with such people at the head, the moral influences of the school were nought, and the tone of the school horribly low. We hated the place and its ways, but fell into these with facility. I must always except from this general statement such excellent people as my dear dead friend, Percy Smith, who could walk through hell without the smell of fire passing on him, and Frank Churchill Simmons, always, boy and man, living the noblest conceivable life, and, as was natural, hated by Allen at Ilminster. Percy Smith, however, was a favourite, perhaps as being the nephew of Allen's old master, Bedford, at Twyford, to whom he had been an assistant, and who had taught him to flog.

The social condition of the hundred or more boys at Ilminster was very varied. On the one hand we had the sons of the upper landed gentry, short of the aristocracy, in Devon and Somerset — Spekes, Pagets, Hoskinses, Fursdons, Mallocks, and also the sons, as day-boys, now and then as boarders, of the small tradesmen. Then there were a few people who settled in Ilminster, because there was a cheap school.

Friendship rarely exists among bullied boys. There are few whom I recollect with pleasure, save one or two I have named and a few others—Arthur Paget, bright, affectionate, impulsive, rash, who died too early, when, his wild oats having been sown, he might have settled down in his home at Cranmore, and let his great talents have fair-play; Frank Simmons and Arthur Paget were the friends who were more than brothers, in those young days and always. Percy Smith was a grave and reverend senior to us, as was a certain big Irish boy named Whelan, who was kind to me. Almost the only other lad I remember with affection besides my cousin, Edmund Cox, is a certain Tom Larcombe, the son of a widow who let lodgings in the town. I have never seen Tom since, but have heard of him as a flourishing ironmonger at Exeter.

In some respects the manners of the school were curiously different from those of our own days, when schools are more luxurious. Little boys slept two in a bed, £5 a year extra being charged for the privilege, which happily was mine, of a single bed. Pudding at dinner always came before meat, on the days when it was given at all, and was usually either a heavy suet, or an equally heavy batter pudding, which diminished appetite at a very cheap rate.

In the outfit which every boy was required to bring with him to school, nightcaps formed an item, and a large portion of the school wore them. It shows a curious change in toilet requirements, that while these were specified, there was no mention of sponge or sponge-bag. The nightcaps were a part of the régime which made people exclude every breath of night air from the bed, between the sheets of which, if the night were chill, a warming-pan was passed. Readers of *Pickwick* will remember that Mr. Pickwick wore a night-cap and that a warming-pan was among his luxuries. Their use began to die out about the time I went to school; though the demand, uncomplied with, for nightcaps lingered in school-lists for many a year afterwards.

Men of my age, looking back to their school-days, will remember that almost every other boy had warts on his hands. No doubt bodily ailments have their times and seasons, and increased cleanliness among school-boys is probably not the only reason that warts are almost unknown in the class of society of which I speak. I mention the circumstance because the "charming" of warts was extremely common, and the charms, from whatever cause, seemed to have efficacy and power. One was cruel enough. A slug was taken on a spring evening, and rubbed over the warts; it was then spitted firmly on a black-thorn, and left to die, rot and vanish away. The thorn and the slug were visited each day, and as the corpse diminished so did the warts. There were other charms, some connected with verbal incantation, which I have now forgotten. Many years afterwards, when I was living in Dorset, the station-master at a little village professed to "charm" warts. There was a poor fellow with whom warts had grown into a regular skin disease. Not only were his hands so covered with these excrescences that he could hardly do a stroke of work without making them bleed, but his whole spine was set with them, and his face not free. The station-master charmed them, and in a few weeks every trace of them had vanished, without any application even of the slime of a slug. Of course this only tends to prove how largely the body is dependent on the mental condition, on imagination and faith.

With differences which may be gathered from what I have said of the master, "*Vice Versa*" gives a fair picture of life at private schools fifty years ago. The one good thing I brought away was love for English poetry, encouraged in us by the great quantity we had to learn by heart. Our school-book on the subject was an admirable one, long since out of print, called *Readings in Poetry;*

certainly the best of its class I have known.
I was always a great reader both at home and
at school, chiefly, as I think best for boys,
of poetry and fiction. I do not remember
many books, however, which made a great impression on me at Ilminster, beyond Fenimore
Cooper's novels.

In 1839 my father became Vicar of Wellow,
five miles from Bath and about four from
Writhlington, and pending the enlargement and
partial rebuilding of the Vicarage, we went to
live for a year at Westfield Villa in Weston,
near Bath, whence my father rode backwards
and forwards to Wellow. In 1840 we removed
to Wellow, and the first entrance into our new
home was saddened by disaster and sorrow.
The disaster was the final and complete failure
of the West Indian property, which had been
languishing ever since the slave emancipation.
However, there had always been some income
from the estate till the time of which I speak,
when the supplies failed wholly, and money
also was wanted to keep the estate going at
all. My father determined to take pupils, and
was fortunate in finding as many as he wanted
for some years. It was not a pleasant experi-

ment, my mother never liked it, and her health was very unfit to cope with the situation, even if she had not soon been saddened by the loss of children. My father, though he taught fairly well, as I believe, had not the smallest sympathy for or understanding of boy nature, and pupils had the effect, as is generally the case, of breaking up our home life.

The sorrow was caused by the deaths of two little brothers, one an infant, the other, who died very suddenly, a promising boy of six. With this child all the light and joy died out of my mother's life for a long time to come.

I had left Ilminster the previous Christmas, having been for some time laid up with a bad knee, injured in jumping over forms in the school-room.

Before, however, I pass to the record of public school life, it may be well to chronicle some points in which manners and customs were different from those which now obtain.

In my early school-days all travelling was done by coach and private conveyance. On more than one occasion, my uncle and aunt, who then and for many years travelled with their own fat and leisurely horses, came to take

me from school; at other times we went to
Bath by coach. Allen always used to end a
speech which he made at the end of each
term by saying, "And now, gentlemen, the
Bath coach is waiting for its passengers;"
though of course it never waited, nor would
it have done so had we not been ready. Two
incidents of these journeys are very vividly
impressed on my memory; one of a June day
when we drove into Ilchester, starting from
Ilminster after an early breakfast to find the
London mail, which had travelled all night, had
just arrived, and the tradesmen were putting
up their shutters on the news of the death of
William IV. The second was that the driver
of the stage-coach, on one of my journeys home,
drew up his horses in the chill morning at
the request of his passengers that they might
see a man hanged at Ilchester jail. We were
on the bridge, a good distance off, and the sight
was not very curious or indeed very terrible,
but the black figure swayed to and fro, and
the passengers were silent for some little time
afterwards.

I was interested in the execution, if not
horrified, for we boys at school not long

before had taken a very deep interest in the murder of Lord William Russell by his valet, Courvoisier, whose last dying speech had been amongst the most popular, though not the most edifying literature of the term.

Travelling by coach may seem pleasant in these days, when a fine day is chosen for a jaunt to Hampton Court or Dorking, and if the day turn out ill, the train is always available for the return journey; but it was painful work outside, or even inside, in bad weather, when the journey was long, and cramp took hold of the chilly limbs kept long in one position. "Shall we change legs?" was the recognised phrase for altering the position, when legs were dovetailed into legs of those who sat face to face on the back seats of the coach, or inside.

Perhaps the first indication to my young mind that the Church of England was a house divided against itself came from a conversation in the Bath coach. Two old gentlemen, full of curiosity, put me through a long catechism as to what Church my family attended in Bath, what books we read on Sundays, what clergymen my father invited to his house, and

the like. Then for the first time I heard the
words Evangelical and Orthodox, with the
decision, "Oh, Orthodox, yes, certainly Orthodox," as the summing up of the opinions held
by my family. It was then the name for the
party which soon became known as High
Church, Puseyite, or Tractarian, though my
father and my family in general strove to hold
the mean and not belong to any party.

If my relations avoided party in Church
matters, they by no means did so in politics.
They were all Tories of the highest kind, and
every one who was not so was beyond the
pale of salvation in this world and probably in
the next. How men had voted was published
in a pamphlet, and the Blues would not deal
with the Yellows, and *vice versa*. My mother,
however, did not share this feeling, and went
to what seemed the best shops. Therefore on
one occasion she bought a dress at Jolly's,
the Radical haberdashers in Bath, and ordered
it to be sent to her brother-in-law's house,
where she was staying. Late in the evening
inquiry was made for a parcel from Jolly's.
"Oh," said my uncle, "a boy from Jolly's came
to the door, as I was coming in. I sent him

back with a message that it must be a mistake, since no one here could possibly deal at that shop." The same relative once discharged his coachman at a moment's notice, not even allowing him to finish grooming the horse on which he was engaged, because as he entered the stable he heard the coachman observe to the groom, "Well, says I, Roebuck for ever."

Though in recent days, since the Home Rule agitation set in, there has been even in London society some little friction in social life, nothing that I have seen in later years has at all reminded me of the time of which I speak ; the different parties never met, and even religious creeds divided less than political.

Among the neighbouring clergy there were some singular characters. One was the Rev. Thomas Jolliffe, .who never wore braces, but buttoned his trousers over his waistcoat like the old pictures of charity-school boys. In this attire he attended a fancy ball in the neighbourhood, and the reporter for the county paper put him down as "The Rev. Thomas Jolliffe, Fancy Dress." It was not at all unusual in those days to see middle-aged clergymen frequent attendants and dancers at the public balls in Bath, just as they had been in the days of Miss Austen. Very different from these, however, was the Rev. Thomas Spencer, Rector of Hinton Charterhouse. I do not know what were his special religious views, though I think he would have been called an extreme Low Churchman; but he was a tee-totaller when no one else was so, a vegetarian, and a Chartist, any one of which facts was enough to set his neighbours against him. I think my father's house was almost, if not quite, the only one belonging to any one of his class or caste which was open to him.

Education in the villages was at a very low ebb. One of my father's first works at Wellow, after the restoration of the church, was to build a National school, to supplant a private venture by an old man who objected to flogging, but when further questioned as to what method of punishment he used, had replied, " I hangs them up by their thumbs." Though our migration had been so short a distance we had completely left the colliery district, and were among a purely agricultural population. It was a wonder to me to find that the colliers, who had always been so kind and friendly, were considered by the peasants as a lawless and dangerous crew. It was scarcely a surprise to the village when a man came into it one morning and represented that he had been robbed by colliers. They had carried out their work with completeness, for he walked up to the first house, which was the old schoolmaster's, without a single rag upon him, the assailants having taken all his clothes. He said he was an American, of Polish parentage, recently landed at Bristol. The schoolmaster wrapped him up in an old flannel dressing-gown, which barely reached his knees, and brought him to the Vicarage. There my father believed his story and clad him in a whole suit of clerical broadcloth, with accessories such as shirt and shoes. Indeed it is difficult to see what else could have been done with him in a remote village, even if no one had believed in him. The schoolmaster wanted his dressing-gown, which indeed was his scholastic robe of office. The victim went off clothed and fed, and in the afternoon his own tattered garments were discovered under a hedge about a hundred yards from the house to which he had first gone. It is curious that, so far as I know, no other tramp has ever adopted this ingenious if audacious mode of fraud. My father happily had a sense of humour which softened the loss.

There was much to feed that sense among the Somerset poor, and I wish I could record half the curious experiences which fell to him. Here, however, is a fair specimen. A small farmer named Dagg came one evening to beg that the Vicar would go to see his wife, who was very ill. On arriving at the farm, my father went to his ministrations in the sick-room, leaving the poor husband a prey to the deepest sorrow in the kitchen. "Well, sir, what do 'ee think of her?" he asked, when the parson returned. The answer could only be that he must prepare for the worst. "Oh, sir, 'tis hard to lose a wife again," he said; "you see, sir, she's my third." And then he went on with a sudden and indescribable change of tone and manner; "I shouldn't wonder if I were *to shoe the horse all round.*" He did; but in the few months that elapsed, the farm had gone to rack and ruin, for the third wife had been a good manager, and the man, always unthrifty, was quite unable to shift for himself, and had kept one horse and cart only from the general sale of his effects. He had become a "tranter," doing odd jobs, haulage of manure, and the like. He came by night once again to say that he wished his banns cried next Sunday, but would parson remit the fees, which he could not afford to pay. My father pointed out that this was an unthrifty beginning and a bad precedent, which he was not inclined to make. Dagg was crestfallen for a minute, and then remembering that the Vicar had employed him with his horse and cart for sundry small services, his brow cleared, he slapped his thigh with cheerful emphasis, and said, "Suppose we take her out in a load of dung?"

III

ETON—THE FELLOWS AND MASTERS

1841–1846

I KNOW not how it came about that I was to go to Eton. My cousin George Cox had gone to Rugby, and my dear friend Frank Simmons was to do the same. I rather think the fact that Arthur Paget and one or two other Somerset boys at Ilminster were to go to Eton, decided the matter, and decided also the choice of a tutor, Goodford, afterwards Head-master and Provost, himself a Somerset man.

Those were the days of nomination to college, and one could have been obtained for me without difficulty. But it was just at the time when "college" was at it lowest ebb, in comforts, morals, and numbers. My uncle and aunt driving from London to Bath, in the summer before I went to Eton, paid a visit of inspection, and I remember a phrase in one of my aunt's letters, that the "worst ward in the worst hospital" was preferable to Long Chamber. And those were the days of unreformed hospitals ! The number of scholars had dwindled from seventy to forty, simply because boys could not be found to submit to the hardships which awaited them ; but those who did, and had any sort of ability, were certain of scholarships, and ultimately of fellowships, at King's College, Cambridge. Some therefore were always found to avail themselves of the King's foundation, and the pick of these returned to Eton as masters, but it was whispered that some boys were admitted as payment for bills owing to their fathers, tradesmen in Windsor, and one was the son of an ex-valet of George IV. So I was to go as an Oppidan into Goodford's house. It was in some ways unfortunate, for "college" was reformed in a degree the very year I went to Eton.

So far as I remember, the day I went to Eton was the first time I travelled in a railway train. The Great Western Railway was opened in a piecemeal fashion. Not very long before we had gone as a family to lunch at Twerton Rectory, now destroyed, but then quite close

on the line, to see the first passenger train
pass between Bath and Bristol, and as it went
at full speed, I need hardly say there was little
to see. In the spring of 1841, we went to
Wootton Bassett by coach, and thence to
Slough by train. The short-sighted opposition
of Eton College, and I think of Windsor Castle
also, had the effect, as at Oxford, of keeping
the railway far from the sacred precincts.
Brunel had planned his line to pass through
Windsor and Oxford : it was many years before
there was a branch to Oxford from Didcot, and
at Slough the trains stopped for setting down
and taking up passengers, but there was at
first no regular station. My father went with
me to the house of his brother-in-law, Major
Bent, Wexham Lodge, near Slough, and the
morning after our arrival took me to be entered
at the head-master's house, then the Rev. E. C.
Hawtrey, D.D. As Hawtrey grew to be an old
man, his astonishing plainness was toned down,
and he gained in dignity, but in middle life it
was scarcely possible for a man to be more
grotesquely ugly. But he was kindly and
courteous. At Woodside, outside Windsor
Park, lived Mr. Parks, an old friend of my

father, who had married a cousin of Dr. Hawtrey, and as I rose towards the top of the school, he and Miss Hawtrey were so kind as now and then to take me in their carriage when I dined at Woodside.

It was at this house, I remember, that on one occasion, a child, looking up from a picture-book, asked the inconvenient question, "What is the difference between a bull and an ox?" The head-master answered at once, "The bull is the calf's papa, the ox is his uncle." It is much to have a ready wit on such emergencies! The late Sir John Awdry, once an Indian Judge, replied to a child who asked, "Do cocks lay eggs?" "Oh yes: when he has laid one, he is called a *cocoon;* when he has laid two, he is called a *cockatoo;* when he has laid three, he is called a *cockatrice.*" To go back to Hawtrey, I remember little else of him at that time, except that in one of the drives to Woodside, he expressed his strong disapproval of the picture of Eton life in Disraeli's *Coningsby*, which was just published. He appeared to take the extremely narrow schoolmaster's view, and was angry that Disraeli had not made himself ac-

quainted with the length of time that a boy
might be away from Eton without having his
name called over at "absence." He, however,
showed from time to time, that he had wit in
other things than in the repartees to a child,
witness his epigram, perhaps now forgotten,
when the Bishop of Tuam's charge, published
in 1845, was discovered to have been taken
without acknowledgment from that of the
Archbishop of Canterbury, published in 1841.

> "*Cantuariensis.*
>
> "Privatam monitus relinque chartam,
> Meamque improbe pone concionem.
> Quæ scripsi mea sunt.
>
> "*Tuamensis.*
>
> "Tuam requiris ?
> Frustra glorier hoc Episcopatu,
> Tuam ni liceat Meam vocari."

At Eton, however, the head-master is not
the supreme authority. Above him in those
days were the Provost and Fellows, these last
being with few exceptions drawn from the
Eton masters. They came with little or no
special training, imbued with the old traditions,
from the same set among whom they had been
school-boys, from a College which was out of

the University competition, and in which there was little general reading. It was strange they should have done as well as they did, under the singular circumstances in which they had been pitchforked into their enormous responsibility.

Let me endeavour in a very changed world to give some notion of the College and school authorities. I here reprint almost unchanged what I wrote about the College on the occasion of Mr. Wilder's death in 1892. He, when I went to Eton, was the junior Fellow, and my tutor had succeeded to his house. He was the last survivor of the old régime.

Fifty-one years ago, when the Great Western Railway was opened to Slough, Eton ceased to be a sleepy country village, where the great school lay under the protecting shade of the Castle walls, where the Court and Eton boys, and Cabinet Ministers in Windsor uniform, mixed on the Castle terrace with a friendly feeling of intimacy, which necessarily vanished so soon as it took no longer to go from Paddington to Windsor than from Charing Cross to Paddington. The railway extinguished

"Montem," a mediæval fête, half ecclesiastical, half the gambols of a band of mummers; and turned the 4th of June fancy-dress procession of boats into a mere suburban regatta.

Coincidently almost with the advent of the railway, Hawtrey became head-master, and, strange as it may seem to those who knew him in his later days, he began his career by being a decided reformer, to whom are owing most of the changes by which Eton differs from what it was made so soon as it emerged from the fire of the Reformation, and ceased to be a mediæval school.

When Hawtrey appeared as head-master in a college cap, dropping the extraordinary cocked hat always worn by Keate, and before him by Goodall, perched on the top of a large wig—when Hodgson, the Crown nominee, quite out of touch with Eton traditions, became Provost—the two men set themselves to carry out reforms in the housing of the scholars as well as in the teaching of the school. But the Fellows, living apart in the seclusion of the cloisters, gave for the most part but a languid assent to reforms they could not resist, and despite of railways, of the fact that arithmetic and

Euclid were made part of the school-work, and that the Ash-Wednesday pig-fair in the College Street was abolished, remained a community the like of which the world is not likely to see again. Mr. Wilder, just elected, and not yet fossilised into College ways, alone was eager for reform. He even declared that the new buildings should be warmed by fires in the boys' rooms rather than by hot water. Hawtrey, however, insisted on facings of Caen stone, and comfort gave way to what was supposed to be superior architecture.

Of those who knew the Fellows, who indeed had but little communication with the boys, few had opportunities of verifying their recollections in after life, or hearing from the lips of those who had known a still older generation than theirs, stories of old Eton days. But to me, who had such opportunities, all is fresh and vivid as yesterday.

Now that the College is a mere governing body sitting in London, the school is all in all, except in so far as the management of the revenue is concerned. But it was far otherwise in the time of which I am speaking. The College had been founded mainly as a

community of priests to say masses for the
founder's soul; and attached to this was a
school of seventy scholars, with a head and
lower master belonging to the foundation.
The education thus given gradually attracted
others, "town boys," most of them in "Dames'"
houses, to share it; these necessitated other
"assistant-masters," who by degrees took
boarders into their houses. The Rev. Thomas
Carter, of whom more hereafter, was the first
to make the innovation, and Dames' houses
are now things of the past, though from old
habit boys still speak of mathematical and
science masters, not being their tutors, in
whose houses they board, as "My Dame."
But the assistant-masters had no real standing
as belonging to the College. It is true that
when a vacancy occurred among the Fellows
it was usually filled from among the assistant-
masters, but that was because, as former
scholars of Eton, and Fellows of King's, they
had already belonged to the Royal Foundations
of Henry VI., not because they were recognised as assistants by the College; yet in so
small a community everything was known with
the greatest minuteness, even if it was ignored.

In the thirties Provost Goodall asked Mr. Eliot, then a young assistant, just appointed, who had only one pupil, to dine with him at very short notice. This was always understood as a sort of royal command, but Mr. Eliot did not so take the invitation, and declined it on the ground that he " had pupil-room," the technical phrase for preparatory work with pupils. The Provost, when his guests were assembled, stood on the rug, with Mr. Eliot's open note in his hand, and said, " I am sorry that we are one gentleman short ; Mr. Eliot is unable to come, because he has pupil-room. Dear, dear, what a clucking a hen makes when she has only one chick ! " The same gentleman drew some year or two later another wise saw from the Provost, and one which has a far-reaching application. The chapel windows were broken by a catapult or sling, within a definite hour, when the boys were in school. The windows were commanded by one house only, and there at that time were two boys who were " staying out "—that is, absent from school as not being well. The tutor, in defence of his lads, before they were questioned on the matter, objected that these could not be the culprits, because they were such good boys. "Have you yet to learn," said the Provost, "that it is the very best boys who do the very worst things?"

But a year or two later, when we come within the limits of our fifty-one years, Goodall and his wig were gone, and Keate was a Canon of Windsor. Provost Hodgson reigned in Goodall's stead, and we who then read Byron with deep delight and sympathy could not understand how the fussy, plethoric, uninteresting little man could have been the object of Byron's enthusiastic friendship, to whom he wrote in poetry, and had lent out of his own then scanty means a thousand pounds. Ah me! We who read poetry in those days have become prosaic enough since then, and ourselves the givers and the recipients of no less devoted friendship, have either forgotten, or seem to have forgotten, all the romance of school and college days.

Hodgson preached a course of sermons on the Prayer-Book, which ran on during his "residences" for five years, and possibly a good deal longer. We never attended to them, indeed could scarce hear a complete sentence but the text, and the constant recurrence time after time of the words, " I will pray with the spirit, and I will pray with the understanding also," was wont to send the whole school into a fit of giggles. But if he was a failure as a preacher, no Eton Colleger ought to forget that to his enlightened sway is due the whole reform in the management for the boarding of the King's scholars. It is almost inconceivable that the same precise state of things should have existed down to 1841 or 1842, which had obtained in the reign of Queen Elizabeth, and was then scarcely changed from much earlier times. It is true that before " college " was reformed under Hodgson, glass had been introduced into the windows, but it was quite a modern innovation. Well into the present century the windows were closed only at night by heavy wooden shutters, and the late Vice-Provost, the Reverend Thomas Carter, father of " Tom " Carter of Clewer, and of " Billy " Carter, the present Bursar, has assured the writer that he had never slept so comfortably as when the snow drifted under the shutters on to the beds. The Duke of Cumberland, after Culloden, gave the boys new green cloth quilts, which, greatly prized, and used only for a few weeks at election time each year, remained even to within my recollection. They were called Culloden rugs, and were accidentally destroyed by fire some twenty-five years ago. Queen Elizabeth had increased the boys' commons, and the grateful inscription yet remains in the Hall, cut by some hungry urchin at the time,

Queene Elizabetha ad nos gave October X
2 loves in a Mes [sic].

In old days the whole life of the boys was spent in Long Chamber, except that meals were taken in the Hall. By degrees the need of privacy was felt, and the upper boys had each their room or lodging in the town, each being also assigned to the dame of one of the boarding-houses chosen by his parents or tutor, who looked after him, more or less, in case of sickness. By a series of reforms extending over many years, " college " was rendered as comfortable as a tutor's house, proper servants and a resident master were appointed, but though these were only completed in more recent times, the initiative was due to Provost Hodgson.

The sixth-form boys maintained the privilege of taking their supper in Long Chamber, rather than cross the schoolyard to the Hall, and this only ceased when the new buildings were erected. Successive assistant-masters in college, whose rooms were at the end of what had been Long Chamber under the old system, complained of a musty smell in the study, rising where decay in the oak boarding of the floor testified to a certain amount of damp. In the summer holidays of 1858, the floor was removed, and two large cartloads of bones, chiefly of necks of mutton, were removed from between the floor and the ceiling of the rooms below. How they came there was explained by Mr. Carter, then Vice-Provost. He told me that when the sixth-form boys took their supper in "Chamber" the rats were wont to come out of holes in the floor and wainscot to feed on the bones which were flung to them. When these animals from time to time became a nuisance by their numbers, a fag was sent round while the rats were feeding, to insert long stockings in the holes, with the apertures carefully open. The modern sock was then unknown. When this was done an alarm was given, the rats on rushing to their holes were trapped in the stockings, which were then drawn out, and the rats were banged to death against the beds. "And you went into school next morning in the same stockings, sir?" "Of course, of course," was the reply, "we could not get clean stockings when we pleased." Mr. Carter went among the boys by the name of "Old Shoes," and died at the very advanced age of ninety-four. He was a steady-going average old gentleman, with a great power of placing his relatives in college offices and livings, and a plentiful lack of imagination. He greatly amused us as boys by taking as his text the words, "My sins are more in number than the hairs of my head," his own pate being as free from hair as an egg or a billiard ball. In his tenure of office as Vice-Provost there was talk of a new pulpit for the college chapel, and some sanguine man vainly hoped to persuade the authorities that it ought to be designed and erected by Mr. William Morris, then just becoming known as an artist, who had an office in Queen's Square. Mr. Carter walked therefore into Mr. Morris's studio with the words, "Do you keep pulpits?" as though he had been asking for tape or buttons. The pulpit remained unchanged, a piece of furniture as commonplace as the sermons ordinarily delivered in it.

It was an evil day for Art at Eton when the mania for church restoration invaded the minds of the respectable old gentlemen who had the care of the fabric. Before the Reformation, the chapel had never been properly finished. King Henry the Sixth had built the walls with their great buttresses to carry a vaulted stone roof like that of the sister chapel at King's, but it was unfinished when the Wars of the Roses broke out ; the building was roofless, and the east wall with its great window was still incomplete. When Edward the Fourth was in want of funds for the college he was himself endowing at Windsor, he bethought him of the unfinished buildings at Eton, and desired to confiscate the Eton revenues, on the ground that the buildings were incomplete. The Provost and Fellows set to work with a will, and it is said that in six weeks the reproach had ceased to be true, and the college fabric stood practically as it was until Allestree built, about 1666, the Upper

School, soon to be taken down and replaced by
the present building ; and until the chapel was
fitted up, tradition says by Wren, very much
in the style of the choir of St. Paul's.   If
any one will take his stand in the Brewhouse
Yard facing west, he will see the history written
in stone and in brick.   Before him is the great
east window, springing clear and clean until it
reaches the final arch, then huddled together at
the top, out of the line of any true curve, the
stones at the top of the window holding together as a mere pierced wall.   The wooden
roof is modern, succeeding a former wooden
one of the most temporary and haphazard description, plainly not that intended to be sup-
ported by the great buttresses.   Though the
chapel was thus finished in a scramble, the good
intentions of the college did not wholly succeed.
The foundation was not suppressed indeed, but
jewels, bells, and furniture were carried off to
Windsor.

On the spectator's right is the Hall, of which
the oriel window, projecting into the Brewhouse
Yard, has been still more incongruously finished,
the stone supplemented, and the upper mullions
filled in with coarsely built brickwork, but this

was not done till the seventeenth century, the completion of the chapel having served its end for the time.

When all had quieted down, after the interruptions of the Wars of the Roses, the neglect of Edward the Fourth, the brief period of prosperity under the Tudors, the intrusion of Provost Rous, Speaker of the Barebones Parliament, a church reaction set in. Wren's fittings, if indeed they were Wren's, required no destruction of what had gone before, and were not too sharply incongruous with the Gothic fabric, Renaissance though they were. There were in fact next to no previous fittings to displace, and if they hid a fancy carving on the wall of a man being hanged, done by some poor lad who winced under the tedium of a Puritan sermon, no great harm was done, nor were some frescoes on the walls any serious artistic loss. Wren's great pillared canopy over the altar, his black and white marble floor, his stately pews and stalls, all disappeared to make way for second-rate Gothic canopies, and a frigid uniformity about the chapel now renders any better work impossible, while much of the history of the place is swept away.

But the flood of light which invaded Wren's dark corners removed some abuses scarcely congruent with the decorum expected in a school chapel. Till the Restoration all boys with titles sat in the stalls among the Fellows. There was a custom that if during the "half" any one was elevated to this dignity, by the succession of his father to a peerage, which made him "honourable," or the death of his father which made him a baronet, the new occupant of the stalls had to provide half-a-crown's worth of almonds and raisins, to be consumed in Church, under the very noses of the Fellows, who looked discreetly the other way. This was called "Church sock." It is recorded that when Dr. Goodford, then Provost, went to the thanksgiving service at St. Paul's for the recovery from sickness of the Prince of Wales, he had provided himself with a paper of sandwiches, and offered a portion to his neighbour with the words "Church sock!"

In those old days when fat Provost Hodgson closed the procession into Chapel, he was preceded by Mr. Bethell, a tall, dignified, stately person, very handsome, in a rubicund, aquiline-nosed style; and as stupid as handsome men are wont to be. He had been Shelley's tutor, and nothing more grotesquely incongruous than this relation of pupil and tutor was ever devised. There was a tradition that when he took a class in school he simply called up boy after boy to construe, and when the lesson was finished just went over it again till the hour of release struck, making no comments, offering no illustrations. But to this there had been in the years of his mastership two exceptions. A lad translated the words "duplice ficu," "with a double fig." "Right," said Mr. Bethell, "a kind of fig that was double." So, again, to one who translated "postes aeratos," "brazen door-posts," he said, "Right! probably so called because they were made of brass."

In school at this day, when a boy writes a Latin or Greek exercise his tutor looks it over privately, comments on it, suggests and makes improvements, signs it with or without a note of approbation as "fair," or "well"; the boy then copies it out and presents it in school, with the "foul copy." Of old, the fair copy only was presented, and the change is due to Mr. Bethell. "I wish," said Dr. Keate to him one day, "you would be more careful about

your pupils' exercises. A copy of Greek
Iambics shown up to me this morning had in
it eleven false quantities." "Ah!" said Bethell,
"I dare say there were; *you should have seen
'em before I looked over 'em.*" And for the future
Keate did see, and drew his own conclusions.

He was the last man who wore a "spencer,"
an over-jacket, which allowed the tails of what
we now call a dress coat, but which then was
worn both in morning and evening, to appear
below it, and he had a sonorous voice, with
which he imposed on his audience—quite unintentionally, for he was a simple-hearted and
modest man, who, though he seemed to do so,
hardly deserved the epigram on his sermons :

> "Didactic, dry, declamatory, dull,
> Big burly Bethell bellows like a bull."

When he was made a Fellow, and for the
first time raised his voice in Chapel to begin
the Communion Service, with a sonorous "Our
Father" which rattled like thunder in the roof,
Okes, then a Master, afterwards Provost of
King's, turned to his next neighbour with the
remark "Paternoster *Row;*" and the boys were
wont to call him Papirius Bethell when he read

the Commination Service on Ash Wednesday, regardless of the fact that the surname of the Roman general "Cursor" had naught to do with cursing.

He preached once at the opening of a long disused chapel on the river, and a "cad at the wall," who was, as may be imagined, "parcus deorum cultor et infrequens," attended the service. His one comment was, "Lord! boys, you should ha' seen the spiders run."

He was a kindly man, whose one desire was to resist innovations. "You can't have a service without a Fellow, and you won't get me out of my bed at eight in the morning," was the unanswerable argument when early prayers in the College Chapel were proposed to him by a Conduct instead of a service at ten, at which the whole assistants usually were the Fellow, the Conduct, the Clerk, and Silly Billy, a poor idiot, who spent his time in running from St. George's Chapel in Windsor, to that of Eton College, so as to be present at four services on every day in the week.

But Mr. Bethell's eccentricities were as nothing compared with those of Mr. Plumptre, "Moses" as we called him, though none knew why. He was so staunch a Tory, so averse to all change, that none could imagine why he had ever married. It was obvious that when he was left a widower, after a few months of happy marriage, he would remain so to the end of a long life. With great self-denial he never moved from the worst house in the Cloisters, though he might have had the best, and took as his own room a small one which could scarcely hold two very large four-post bedsteads with a mere *ruelle* between them. His practice explained a difficult passage in *The Vicar of Wakefield*, wherein Dr. Primrose speaks of his only migrations having been those "from the blue bed to the brown." Mr. Plumptre, too, migrated every six months, not from bedroom to bedroom, but from bed to bed, taking that nearest to the window in summer, to the fire in winter, if, indeed, one can speak of distance at all in a room of some sixteen feet square. His father, Dean of Gloucester, had taken Hoadley's side in the Bangorian Controversy, and Mr. Plumptre, out of sheer conservatism, always used Hoadley's family prayers, despite of their alleged unorthodoxy, himself one of the most orthodox of men. This hatred of change was inherited. He was wont to tell a story of his father, the Dean, whose daughter, at the mature age of forty, ventured to differ from him. The Dean said gravely, as one who means what he says, " Tryphena, you are not too old to be whipped," and Miss Plumptre differed no longer.

The passing of the Bill for Catholic Emancipation was a great shock to Mr. Plumptre, both on religious and political grounds, and it is recorded that he and Mr. Briggs, a Fellow like-minded with himself, paced round and round the Cloisters the long night through, waiting the morning announcement of the division. They had sent a special messenger, who was to bring the tidings direct. They could not go to their beds while the fate of Protestantism was, as it seemed to them, trembling in the balance. Let us hope that where they now are, they are not excluded from the best Catholic society.

Very many years afterwards, about the year 1853–4, Mr. Plumptre called on Dr. Goodford, then head-master, to find an elderly relative of the latter staying with him. Dr. Goodford introduced them and said : " Now, Aunt, here is a gentleman with whom you will agree on politics." "I hope, sir," said the lady, "you disapproved of Catholic Emancipation." "The wickedest thing, ma'am, since the Crucifixion," was the immediate and startling answer.

As Mr. Plumptre's sermons were delivered in alternate shouts and gasps of almost total silence, both in the same sentence, it was difficult to carry away any real impression of what was said, but they were epigrammatic and racy, the selection of the text verging even on the comic. At Malvern, on the anniversary of the Queen's Accession, he preached on the single word "Shout"; at Windsor, to the Blue-coat Charity boys, on "She made him a little coat."

As he advanced in years he became rather deaf, but always heard exactly what he wanted to hear. When Edward Coleridge was made Fellow, and came into residence for his first course of sermons, Plumptre said: "When Green preaches I hear only one word, God; when Coleridge preaches I hear only one word, Devil," and in the epigram he hit off the characteristic teaching of the two men.

As master, Plumptre occupied the old red house at the north-east corner of what is now Keate's Lane; that in which Mary Wollstonecraft stayed with Mr. Prior in 1781, when she recorded that the sixth-form boys were obliged to receive the Communion once a term or pay a fine of a guinea. Mr. Plumptre's pupil-room being at once dark and small, he was wont to stand at a desk near the open window, and his pupils attended his "construing" in Keate's Lane.

Plumptre was one of the most generous of men, and his unobtrusive kindness to those from whom he differed very widely will never be forgotten by those who experienced it.

Mr. Dupuis was a Fellow who also lived to a great age, and will be remembered, if remembered at all, mainly by two sayings; one, that if a Royal Commission were sent to Eton, he would meet it at the college gates, and scourge it forth with dog whips; of course in the end he really met it with complete if grumbling acquiescence. The second was uttered on an occasion when one of the assistant – masters, with the aid of the head-master, borrowed nine volumes from the college library, on a special subject at which he was working, and was coming away with them under his arm. Mr. Dupuis met him, counted the volumes slowly and said : "Nine volumes in one day ; I have not taken out one volume in nine years."

Mr. Wilder was made Fellow in the year 1840, at the age of thirty-nine, and lived to the age of ninety-one. He was a dull, kindly, and hospitable man, who had some fine Lachryma Christi wine. He was wont to draw attention to this by offering his guests "some fine Italian wine, which unfortunately has a most distressing name." His munificence towards the chapel and other college buildings was considerable, but lacked discretion. He gave large sums of money to the windows, desiring to see them all filled with stained glass, but not enough to fill them all well; it would have been better to fill them by degrees, and to make each as perfect as possible. But such was not Mr. Wilder's way; uniformity and completeness, if in mediocrity, was a passion with him.

Luxmoore, Coleridge, Eliot, Durnford, W. Carter, Balston, and others well remembered by Eton men, all came after those of whom we have spoken, and had their own special and sometimes amusing peculiarities. But they were not like those in whose ranks there was no change for thirteen years, from 1840 till about 1853, when Hodgson died and Hawtrey became Provost. It was the pause before the great change, the calm flow of the cataract before it dashed into the stormy waters of reform. Peace to their memories. Would that we could still see the quaint procession passing across the schoolyard in their surplices to chapel, or on ordinary days in their gowns, Mr. Plumptre scorning a trencher cap, and wearing a tall beaver hat as M.A. of Cambridge. Or that we could see Mr. Bethell in spencer and gaiters striding up Windsor Hill to enter Layton's shop for lunch and say in those unforgotten tones : " Mock turtle soup for Mrs. Bethell and myself, and Parliament gingerbread for the young people." Or Hawtrey coming to the 4th of June Regatta in 1841 to recognise the ceremony for the first time. Till then the river had been out of bounds, and the masters were unable to ride or walk along the river banks because they might not witness the boating which was nominally forbidden. And year after year Dr. Keate, when asked that " Lock-up " on that day might be at ten o'clock instead of a quarter to nine, gave permission, but could not imagine why the boys wanted to be out so late. Nor did Provost Goodall understand why Mrs. Goodall dined at a different hour on that day.

Sir H. Maxwell Lyte has written a valuable history of Eton. The best passage therein, and this is no disparagement to the rest, was written by the late William Cory, and contains a kindly, if critical, account of Hawtrey. We wish some one could write a whole account of the inner life of Eton, and the real characters of the men who made it what it was. But the materials are scanty; there are few such pages as Mary Wollstonecraft's account of her visit to Mr. Prior, few such correspondences as the Paston Letters, though we trust some such may yet leap to light in the library of one of our country houses. To such a history these recollections may contribute in a faint degree.

Eton is reformed; the head-master is an athlete, also once Newcastle Scholar and Fellow of All Souls'; the French master can no longer describe himself, as Mr. Henry Tarver did to the Royal Commission, as an *objet de luxe*. French is part of the education of a gentleman, in spite of Dr. Balston's assertion to the contrary; science flourishes; and the Right Honourable T. H. Huxley was a member of the Governing Body, *vice* the Fellows superseded.

But that which in old days was mainly taught at Eton was how to learn. Plumptre, Keate, Hawtrey, Goodford taught this; they and others like them sent out Wellesley, Canning, Shelley; their traditions were alive when present statesmen and judges were at school; we have yet to learn what may be done by more varied teaching under the Governing Body, with certainly no less difficulties than of old in the Capua of a "summer half."

Among the masters, few need be recalled to memory. Edward Coleridge, a nephew of the poet, was one of the exceptions to the rule that assistant-masters should be King's men. He married a daughter of Dr. Keate, the former head-master, and occupied his house at the bottom of Keate's Lane. He was a handsome man of great energy, perhaps it may also be said of considerable pretentiousness, who impressed his personality on those who came in contact with him. His house was liberally conducted, and he had a remarkable

set of pupils, both in ability and in family;
though when he resigned it many years afterwards to become a Fellow, the discipline in
it was not found to have been so good in
fact as it was in seeming. The boys in his
house and form were disposed to doubt if his
scholarship was impeccable. Among his pupils
was a relative of his own, who died early,
affectionately remembered by all who knew him,
admired for the bright promise of his boyhood,
loved for the unselfishness of his character.
This lad had scant respect for his uncle. Once
in pupil-room he broke down in construing
Homer. "Not know your Homer, idle boy!"
thundered the tutor; "why, were I cast on
a desert island I should be content with these
only books, my Bible and my Homer!" "And
your Lexicon, sir?" said the pupil, impenitent
and unabashed. It need hardly be said that
he was "put in the bill," *i.e.* sent up to the
head-master to be flogged, for "impudence."

Coleridge adopted with all his heart the
teaching of the Oxford school, and was the
friend and correspondent of Pusey. Selwyn,
then a private tutor, and Abraham, an assistant, both afterwards Bishops in New Zealand,

were with him in this matter, and a moderate High Churchism was, on the whole, the tone of our teachers.

Cookesley, however, represented the extreme Low Church party. He was not an ornament to it, and was never a person who commanded respect. Late and unpunctual in school, disorderly in the pupil-room, lax in the discipline of his house, he was yet a thoroughly stimulating teacher in the short time he gave to his work. He was the first Eton master who discovered that there was a science of comparative philology, and though his incursions into that field would nowadays create astonishment, he helped to set many on the right road of scholarship, wrong as his own methods very often were. I remember his discoursing to us on the name of Hannibal, when he delivered himself thus : " Hanni = Hanno, Hanno = Johannes, ibal = bal = lord : Hannibal = Lord John." The following is, however, a better caricature of his early teaching in comparative philology. Many years after, when walking with some Oxford friends, whilst passing the palace at Lambeth, one of them said : " I wonder what is the derivation of the name of this place." The other answered and said at once : " Oh, don't you see, Lam = Lama = High Priest : Beth = house : Lambeth = House of the High Priest." His comments on the text of authors read in school were vivid and picturesque, and no lesson that he gave was ever dull. I look back to him with gratitude for what he taught me, and the way in which he taught it. Cookesley unconsciously served as a model for the well-known picture by Ward, R.A., " The Last Sleep of Argyll." Ward then lived at Slough, and was very intimate with Cookesley. Entering the study one day he found Cookesley asleep on the sofa, and sketched him for the picture then in progress.

Pickering was one whom we boys considered the most gentlemanlike of all our masters. He was always kind and just, very particular about the neatness of the boys in his form, though he bore with one of the most sordid class-rooms in the school buildings, and with a horrible drawing of a devil behind him on the wall, which a bucket of whitewash would have removed during any holiday. But he would call an untidy boy back after school, and show him how a white tie could be arranged with a neatness like his own. The boys and masters alike wore white ties then as now.

Abraham taught History in the "Remove" in such a way as to bring his High Church doctrines under the Provost's censure. Geography was so taught as to encourage the making of maps into a fine art, though the text-book then used was so bad, and the conception of the science so imperfect, that we learned little more than the ancient names of modern Italian cities. Connected with map making, however, there was a curious practice in the school, that I have elsewhere specified as illustrating the true meaning of Catholic Indulgences. I wrote : — "Some years ago, there was an usage at Eton which seemed to the present writer when only a boy of thirteen, exactly, though no doubt unintentionally, framed on the lines of ecclesiastical indulgences. The 'Remove' was a part of the school in which Geography and History were especially studied, and the making of maps was a weekly exercise, to which an importance was attached beyond their real value as a means of teaching. The masters of this form, and, as far as I remember, of this form alone, were in the habit of giving what were termed 'exemptions' for well-executed maps. A small piece of the corner of the map which deserved praise was torn off, signed with the master's initials, and handed to the artist. Perhaps a day or two afterwards the same boy was accidentally late for school, and ordered to write out fifty lines of Virgil as a punishment. When the time came for producing the lines he presented his exemption instead ; his previous merit had gained him an indulgence. I have some impression, though my memory in this serves me but imperfectly, that the transfer of exemptions was at least tacitly allowed, even if not directly sanctioned, but I speak under correction. If it so chanced that a graver fault had been committed than the more venial offence of being late for school, talking in class, or the like, and that the offender then presented an exemption, not only was it not received in lieu of punishment, but the very pleading the excuse was held to deepen the fault, and here on a lower ground was all the distinction between mortal and venial sin."

Beyond these, the masters were mainly colourless persons, with the exception of my tutor, C. O. Goodford, afterwards Head-master and Provost. He deserves a longer notice on this account, and I cannot do better than repeat in large measure the substance of the obituary notices I wrote at the time of his death in 1884 in the columns of the *Guardian* and the *Academy*.

Charles Old Goodford, born in 1812, the younger son of Mr. Goodford of Chilton Cantelo, near Yeovil, himself also an Eton man, was entered at an early age as a King's Scholar, became Fellow of King's, Cambridge, and was a master at Eton while still an under-graduate. This was, however, of no import-ance, since, as has been said, there was no selection possible of men, based on their standing in the class lists. Mr. Goodford, with many others, was unable to test in the schools the soundness of the scholarship he had gained, as full and excellent in his case as it was lacking in some others who had passed through the same training and attained the same position.

Young as Goodford was on becoming a master, and even when after a year or two he had charge of a house, succeeding his tutor,

Mr. Wilder, who survived him, he never gave his pupils the impression that he was a young man. There was about him a grave and stately dignity which his plain features and want of personal grace never impaired; there was a gentlemanlike and high-bred tone about all that he said and did, from which a strong west-country accent did not detract. Fifty years ago accent and dialect were less conformed than now to a London pattern, and it may be doubted if it be a gain to the language to have so far smoothed away linguistic differences. As a tutor Goodford had few equals. Accurate, painstaking, patient, always ready to invent or reproduce from others little aids to memory for grammatical niceties, insisting on accuracy and painstaking in his pupils, they came to know that difficulties must be faced, not shirked, and to conform in a degree to their tutor's standard. He was in the habit of stating paradoxes which at the time he meant, as when a boy made a mistake, "Did you look out that word, Jones?" "No, sir, please, sir, I thought——" "Never think till you are in the sixth form,—till then look out *every* word." This however applied to boys who had some

turn at least for work, some intellect to cultivate. No man knew better than he did that
there . were some boys who could not write
themes and make verses, for whom Latin and
Greek would ever remain dead languages, whose
only reading through life would be the sporting
papers, for whom the advantages of Eton, if
any, were that they should become less loutish
than Tony Lumpkin, the native growth in those
days of too many west - country houses. A
large proportion of his pupils came from his
own county and those adjacent. Where such
lads were under his charge, he did not attempt
the impossible, nor break his heart over their
dulness ; he let them be, minimising as best
he could their harmful example. For a respon-
sive boy he showed boundless zeal, allowed
him to borrow books from his excellent library,
explained or laid down a course of English
literature, encouraged the study of modern
languages and mathematics——in those days no
part of school work. There are many of his
pupils who feel that they owe to him their first
introduction and stimulus to whatever literary
culture they now possess.

As a form-master he was not so good. The

real work of Eton was then generally done in
the pupil-room ; the school lesson was often
treated as mere repetition to see if the work
were correctly known, illustration or explanation
being purposely left on one side. Boys used
to think that Goodford slept through most of
the lessons as fourth-form or remove-master—
he certainly always closed his eyes, but he
woke with immediate vigour and liveliness at
the sound of a mistranslation or a false quantity. It is but fair to teachers of those distant
days to record that there were other masters
who took a different view of the school work,
and that the lessons given for instance by
Carter and by Cookesley, however perverse
and erratic, were no mere hearing of tasks,
but real and brilliant teaching. And Goodford
as head-master, when he took the sixth-form
boys, who are to a large extent emancipated
from tutorial supervision, showed himself the
able and scholarly teacher, sound if not always
inspiriting, that his pupils had known him
to be.

As a house-master, Goodford was eminently
liberal and kind. He was perhaps too unsuspicious, too apt to credit all boys with the

moral excellence which had been his own as a
boy, and to hope for amendment when it was
hopeless.   He kept many a pupil in his house
when a more far - seeing and rigid kindness
would have demanded removal.   Hence there
was a time when the tone of his house was
indifferent, because he never thought that any
evils could exist beyond the trivial ones, which
he scented out with extreme vigilance, of an
occasional rubber of whist in the evening, or a
stealthy cigar behind a hedge.

In 1853 he became head-master in succession to Dr. Hawtrey, then elected Provost,
and the school at once felt the good effects of
the change.   I have already mentioned the
graceful *éloge* of Hawtrey, in Sir H. Maxwell
Lyte's *History of Eton*.   But there is another
side.   Hawtrey, who began his head-master-
ship as an eager reformer, had grown reac-
tionary after twenty years of work.   Rightly
conscious of the efficiency of his own reforms,
he could not see that more still were needed ;
his teaching had become mechanical and his
discipline lax.   He gave those who were in his
form the impression of a tired man who had
had too long a tenure of office.   But this **does**

not contradict the more enthusiastic feeling about him when he was in his prime, and an able and energetic head-master. The details of changes introduced by Goodford would not be interesting, but they were many and far reaching. He aimed at a very complete reconstruction of the system of teaching; he made discipline a reality, while he abolished many vexatious shams which had needlessly restricted liberty. If his plans were but imperfectly carried out the fault was not his but Provost Hawtrey's; for the Provost had a veto on almost everything done at Eton, while the head-master was ostensibly responsible. Goodford always maintained that in school matters the head-master should be responsible. That there was no more friction in the working of the school than really existed was owing to the new head-master's patience, persistence, and loyalty —always his most distinguishing characteristic.

The work of a head-master is unquestionably less laborious than that of a tutor, and places more time at his disposal. Dr. Goodford, as he now became, used his leisure for greater study. He was one of those fortunate persons who could rise early and go to bed late. He had two rooms which composed his library, and used them alternately, descending, as soon as he rose in the morning, to light his own fire, in the room prepared for him over-night, that it might be warmed while he was dressing. He was rarely in bed after half-past five, and for a long period timed his early rising by the step of a labourer who passed under his window at that hour on his way to work. He then warmed a cup of cocoa in an Etna, and sat down to hard work at German or Italian, both of which languages he studied thoroughly after he became head-master. Of all literature in all languages known to him, he was a diligent student, as conscientious with himself as he had been with his pupils in earlier days. Holding his own views, those of a moderate High Churchman, he had the widest toleration for the views of others, and he read with delight and acquiescence Professor Jowett's Essay on the Interpretation of Scripture in *Essays and Reviews*. In these studies he followed learning for learning's sake, and made her her own great reward, for he never wrote, or apparently desired to write, anything but his sermons, unless the edition of Terence,

which he printed to give as a "leaving book"
to his sixth-form boys, be considered an exception. The sermons were well written ; but
he was a singularly monotonous and ungrace-
ful reader ; the eloquence of Jeremy Taylor
would have failed to please had it been delivered by the head-master.

When Hawtrey died the Public School Commission was preparing ; Goodford was in the
vigour of his life, and took the greatest interest
in the work of the Commission, looking forward
to it to aid his own and other reforms. He
had no desire to quit the post he filled so
well, and his nomination by the Crown to the
Provostship was an unmitigated distress to
him. Lord Palmerston, who knew nothing of
Eton politics, had named him to the Queen,
as it afterwards appeared, solely because he
thought, erroneously, that he was following
invariable precedent ; and Goodford acquiesced
because he would not harass her Majesty,
then recently left a widow, by giving her the
trouble of another selection. His exceeding
loyalty led him to do violence to his own
feelings, and take an office which shelved him,
and he could ill afford. The death of his

elder brother, which gave him not long after the possession of the family estates, seemed then far distant, and the renunciation of about two-thirds of the income he had as head-master, was a sign of the loyal and obedient spirit which always characterised him.

His successor's rule was as narrow and pedantic as, however thwarted, his own had been large and liberal. Whatever was done by Dr. Balston to meet the demands of the time was grudgingly and unwillingly performed. So far as in him lay he undid whatever of reform had been introduced. It is, however, but fair to say that the office was forced on Dr. Balston, and that he gave it up, as he said he should, at the end of six years. He was a stop-gap, and perhaps too modest to regard himself in any other light. And no doubt great allowance must be made for a man who had already retired, and was dragged from the leisured conservatism of the Eton cloisters to take a position he did not like. The fact remains that he filled it ill.

For many years Dr. Goodford's health had been far from good. He maintained his old studious habits, but the want of a regular occupation laid on him from outside irked him, and made him less able to resist the encroachments of illness.   He would have been the first to admit, what since his day has been so abundantly clear, that a retired head-master is not the best Provost.

The teaching at the date of my entrance was entirely classical.   I believe that in the lower school the very little boys were taught writing, but the "writing-master" so called was an "extra master," and taught arithmetic, algebra, and Euclid for a special extra fee.   His name was Hexter.   He had been, I believe, a non-commissioned officer, and Cookesley, who had a genius for giving nicknames to his pupils and colleagues alike, used to call him "Old Horse-Guards."   He was very old, quite incapable of teaching, and had a chronic and distressing cough, with an equally chronic and distressing bad temper.   He used to box our ears with a slate, but was happily too feeble to inflict much damage, and after such exertion his daughter used to rush in from a neighbouring room, and shake him up in his chair like Grandfather Smallweed in Dickens.   I was one of his "extra" pupils, but learnt nothing from him, and the remainder of Hexter's pupils were in somewhat the same case. The reform in this matter came through a very flagrant job. Mr. Stephen Hawtrey, cousin of the then head-master, came as a private tutor to the school. These private tutors were occasionally sent with noblemen to board in dames' houses, and exercised a certain useless supervision, but with the exception of Selwyn, afterwards Bishop of New Zealand, they were quite out of touch with the regular school authorities. Stephen Hawtrey proposed to his cousin that the teaching of arithmetic should be placed on a different footing; and he was for a time himself the writing-master, in the same position as Hexter had been. The study was after-wards made compulsory, on far too favourable terms to "Stephen," as he was always called. The arrangement had to be modified, and the mathematical assistants took their place on the regular staff; but while they were chosen by and responsible to Stephen, the masters ap-pointed were for the most part inferior men, and the teaching quite inadequate. The extra masters were as a rule in an wholly unsatis-factory position, though Tarver, the French

master, by the excellence of his teaching, and
Evans, the drawing-master, by an overpowering
manner (which, after the publication of *Bleak
House*, gained him among the boys the name
of Mr. Turveydrop), and the bigness of his
voice, managed to hold their own fairly well.
Evans was a good water–colour painter, and his
drawings have still a certain value. Of all
these men I owe much to Goodford, Cookesley,
and Tarver, but I think to no others, and many
were far less fortunate than I. Education at
Eton in those days was thoroughly haphazard,
though it must be said that if a boy chose to
work in the way of true scholarship he found
every possible aid from some of the masters,
nor was there any discouragement in the way
of miscellaneous reading.

IV

ETON—SCHOOL LIFE

1841–1846

BESIDES the College and the masters, there was another feature of Eton which was singular enough. These were the dames, who kept many of the boarding-houses connected with the school; all now nominally at least in the hands of masters. The rate of expense was higher in a tutor's house than in a dame's, in which the accommodation was in my days much rougher. In a tutor's house all boys had a separate private room, except that two brothers were together, whilst in a dame's there were often three or four boys, not relations. This was the case with Mrs. Holt's house, where simplicity of manners lingered long after some amount of luxury had invaded other dames'. There were sanded floors, and other Spartan surroundings, which would create much astonishment in these days when an Eton boy's room is often like his sister's boudoir. Mrs. Holt had been a Miss Malthus, and the hard life of her boarders was qualified, we thought, to kill off the boys, and so check the increase of population ; but we were possibly pampered in tutors' houses. The curious part of the dame system was that the lady was the ruling power, and if she chanced to have an husband, he existed as it were on sufferance. There was a Mr. Holt, a clergyman, who had some duty in the neighbourhood, but to the boys he was a legend, and always effaced himself. There was also a Mr. Roberts, a dame's husband, at whom staircase mats were always thrown if he ventured to appear in the boys' quarters, and it was a legend that on his complaining to the head-master, Hawtrey refused to interfere, as he had intruded where he had no business to be. The dame's husband, if he were mentioned at all, was called the dominie ; but if, as in the case of Evans, the drawing-master, a dame's house was accidentally in the hands of a man, he also was called "my dame." It was impossible to imagine on what grounds some of these ladies had been appointed. Some indeed had been lady house-keepers to bachelor masters, and it was reasonable enough that when their employers married, they should as dames continue to look after boys; but some were so unfit for the work that the wildest legends grew up as to how they had come there. One old lady, no doubt always perfectly respectable, was fully believed by the boys to have been a cast-off mistress of George IV., and to have gained the post by royal favour; in other cases the charge of the house was hereditary. Each dame's house was nominally under the control of a tutor, who called "Absence" at "lock up" when the boys had to be in the house at night, and to him the dame could appeal if any disciplinary problems arose.

To Harry Dupuis, one of the most fastidious of masters, there came one evening a damp and limp brown paper parcel, out of which fell a greenish red lump, about a pound of almost raw beef, with "Miss Bareblock's compliments, and was it not quite fit for her boys' supper, though they had refused to eat it."

Though boys now and then refused their supper, they sometimes were ready to consume much more than was provided for them. If a tutor or a dame was suspected of being niggardly, it was determined to "brosier" him or her. All the house would appear at supper, whereas as a rule a well-known proportion did not usually take that meal, and steadily make their way through all that was provided, then ask for more, which was not always forthcoming at nine o'clock at night in the best regulated larders. The boys would then retire in a more or less disorderly fashion, asserting that they were starved. This only once happened in my day in my tutor's house, and he had to be summoned from a dinner-party at a friend's, because we would not leave the table, asking for more cold meat. He said to one of the ringleaders, "You are no gentleman," provoking the retort, "Sir, you are no judge!" The fact that my tutor did not "complain" of him next morning, disarmed all such hostilities for the future.

Very shortly after my entrance into the school, preparations began for the "Montem" which occurred twice within my stay at Eton, the second being the last "Montem" ever held. This was a curious survival of a mediæval festival, which has called forth a good deal of antiquarian lore, and has been connected with the installation of the boy-bishop in various places, or with such revels as Scott describes in *The Abbot*. By degrees the ceremony had come to be a means of providing the captain of the school every third year with a purse to pay his expenses at College, and the sum collected often amounted to several hundred pounds. There was, however, great uncertainty as to the recipient. For if a Fellow of King's College, Cambridge, died, resigned, or married, the vacancy created among the scholars of King's had to be filled by a scholar of Eton within so many days, and there was often a little jockeying about the vacancy. If, for instance, a man about to be married wished to help the second scholar in the school rather than the captain, he might hasten his marriage, and thwart the captain's hopes of " Montem " by calling him off to King's at once. And supposing all the play to be fair and aboveboard, there was necessarily among so many persons the chance of a death. Hence there was always great anxiety as the time approached after which it would be possible for the captain to

remain at Eton and take the proceeds of the
" Montem " even if he were summoned to King's.
This was called " Sure Montem night."   If the
captain were popular, no one went to bed, and
when twelve o'clock struck Chamber became
a scene of wild uproar, and enthusiastic con-
gratulation ; the festivities on the occasion being
winked at by the authorities.

The actual celebration of " Montem " was as
follows.   The whole school went into fancy
dress.   The sixth form, both Collegers and
Oppidans, were got up as for a fancy dress
ball—Cavaliers, Roundheads, Italian peasants
and the like.   Each sixth-form boy had one
or two pages also in fancy dress.   These
scoured the country from break of day, pene-
trating as far as they could run into the
neighbouring roads and villages.   They stopped
coaches, post-chaises, and carriages, almost like
highway robbers, asking for " Salt," the school
slang for money, and, when this was given,
presented a printed slip with the words "*mos
pro lege*" upon it, which, like a turnpike ticket—
also a thing of the past—franked the recipient
against another marauder.   By every road to
Eton arrived troops of friends to take part in

the celebration, so that the Cavalier or Planta-
genet who could go furthest to meet them gained
a larger amount of "Salt." On their return the
sum gained was handed over to the fortunate
captain.

Meanwhile the fifth-form boys had arrayed
themselves in scarlet coats, something like old-
fashioned hunting coats, but supposed to be
military, white trousers, cocked hats, yellow
waistcoats, swords and pumps, and the lower
boys in a faint imitation of a midshipman's
dress, but each carrying a white wand, and
each was for the day the servant of a fifth-
form boy, and carried the wand before him.

Between eleven and twelve a procession was
formed in the school-yard, the sixth-form boys
and pages, followed by the rest of the school
as described, and, after marching round while
"Absence" was called, they went through the
cloisters and the playing fields to Salt Hill,
ad Montem, a tumulus near Salt Hill Hotel.
Here the royal family came in semi-state, with
outriders, and smart carriages from two counties
were full of those who had contributed or were
to contribute "Salt"; the captain waved an enormous flag which he had carried at the head

of the procession, and we dispersed to dine in the gardens of Salt Hill Hotel, on a very bad dinner, with far more wine than was good for us. There was a senseless custom of cutting and slashing with our swords at the flowers and shrubs in the hotel gardens, and of generally damaging the property, for which the captain had to pay out of his " Salt," and if he were at all unpopular, the damage done was considerable.

So long as Eton was a country village, which every one had to reach in his own carriage, or in a post-chaise from London, this old-world custom was tolerable ; but a railway to Slough was felt to have destroyed the whole. Even in 1841 the crowd at Salt Hill was almost unmanageable, and in 1844 an attempt was made to confine the festivities as much as might be to the playing fields, though the flag was waved on Montem. We returned to dine in tents on the Fellows' Eyot, but the spirit of the railroad was over it all, it was difficult to masquerade, demanding "Salt" at Slough Station ; and " Montem " was no more.

On the former of the two occasions at which

I assisted at "Montem," my fag-master made sure of getting into the sixth form before the great day arrived, and wished me to be his page. This came to the ears of my tutor, who knew well that my father would be by no means prepared to meet so costly an outlay, and I have always believed that this alone prevented the number of the sixth being filled by my master, who entered it the week after "Montem," so that the expense of the fancy costumes was saved to both of us.

The cessation of "Montem" caused the regatta on June 4th to rise into greater prominence. It was made legal, whereas before it had been a surreptitious joy, and Hawtrey came in a carriage and four to the first recognised "Fourth of June." The year before, a boy named Montagu had been drowned just below the bridge, and with the recognition of the regatta, and of boating in general, watermen were stationed in punts on that part of the river which was in bounds, no boy was allowed to go in a boat till he could swim, and a committee of masters was established who took charge of the bathing places, and examined would - be swimmers in their proficiency.

To return to the boarding-house in which I found myself. My tutor, Mr. Goodford, was not married, and his house was managed by Miss Edgar, who, subsequent to his marriage, became a dame, with her sister who had been lady house - keeper to another master. Miss Edgar was a fussy and tiresome woman, and we were glad when "my tutor" married, and Mrs. Goodford presided over his house with charm and dignity. For in those days the tutor's wife did not think it beneath her position to manage her husband's home, and did it better, with the aid of good servants, than I think it has been done since. It also obliged the tutor, if his wife were young, to give his own direct superintendence to many things which otherwise would have been left to a lady, and so came nearer the ideal school in which the tutor is carefully linked at every turn and in every detail with the boys' life. Miss Edgar, as was not unnatural, considered the boys as her direst enemies, dangerous beings on whose actions she could never count; and maintained as great an aloofness as was possible. When afterwards she kept her own house, she presided at her boys' dinner, girded with an apron to carve, but took her own meal apart afterwards. At the boys' dinner she always said grace as follows : " Boys, for what *you* are about to receive, may the Lord make you truly thankful."

Under Miss Edgar there were two " boys' maids" who made our beds, swept our rooms, and laid the cloth for breakfast and tea, which we took in our own rooms in " messes " of two or three, or a lad might prefer to take those meals alone. Each maid was responsible for some twenty boys, and it was wonderful how well they managed, and with what command of temper, though of course in the actual work of the breakfast- and tea-tables, the fag system helped not a little. For the fags made tea and toast for their masters, and afterwards for themselves, bought for their masters whatever supplementary dainties were needed over and above the three rolls and butter provided, rendering the many little services of waiting which would otherwise be done by a servant. I can speak wholly in praise of the fagging system. The apportionment of two or three

younger boys to an elder, taught obedience,
punctuality, cleanliness of hands, deftness ;
while the master placed in charge held a
certain amount of responsibility towards his
fags. If he were a bully he rarely ill-used
his fags, certainly less than he would have
done without such relationship ; if he were
immoral, he rarely showed that side of himself to those who were put directly under
him. And all the fag-masters were subject
to the captain of the house, to whom was
given considerable monitorial power. Different
houses varied very much in moral tone, and
I cannot say that ours was by any means
the best, though it was perhaps average. It
certainly was in all ways immensely above
the standard of Ilminster, so that I can look
back with pleasure to Eton, and the time spent
there.

Our house was not as a rule distinguished
for hard work. Thring, afterwards head-
master of Uppingham, was indeed a pupil of
Goodford, but he was a King's Scholar, and
affected our lives in no degree ; Scott, afterwards head-master of Westminster, was in
the house, but his ungenial temper prevented

our admiring, as we might otherwise have done, his zeal for literature and his thirst for knowledge.

There were not many interesting boys in the house, and my chief friends in the school lay out of it. Strangely enough my most intimate friend in the house was Astley, afterwards so well known as Sir John Astley. We messed together, that is, took our breakfast and tea in each other's rooms for two years, till Astley minor appeared on the scene, when the two brothers naturally joined, and I left them. I have often noticed that though a man's most intimate friends in after life are his school friends, it is not because of the school companionship, but rather because the friendship is knitted again at College or elsewhere for other than schoolboy reasons. Some of my closest friends at Oxford and through my life were school friends, but only because our minds developed in the same direction, the friendship was so to speak re-made. Astley and I always continued on most cordial terms when we met at Oxford and in after life, but I remember his open - eyed amazement at the things which interested me, and at the fact that I could not even pretend to care for the sports in which he delighted.

The majority of my friends at Eton were assuredly not to be found in the more intellectual set, though Astley was perhaps the most typical instance to the contrary. But I myself read omnivorously; my tutor most kindly giving me the run of his library. I took much interest in French, not always discreetly, as "Les Mystères de Paris" was among my favourite books; and at Eton I learned to be a High Churchman.

Since I knew Eton so intimately in after life, and have always continued my close relations with it, it is not unnatural that I should be scarce aware of the changes time has wrought, so far as a boy's life is concerned, but I think that almost every one would recognise the great conservatism of the place, together with the rigid traditionalism which has prevented innovations in the short-lived generations of schoolboys. Yet certain things are different. When I first went to Eton a considerable number of boys played hockey in the winter, so that there was at least a *tertium quid* between football and mere loafing. There was a small section who dared to introduce rounders, and even prisoners' base, which had a success for a time, both excellent games, and it is a pity that the tide of fashion overwhelmed them. In summer punting was allowed, and there is much charm in the exercise. It was possible for two boys "double punting" to gain "first locks" after twelve, and get to Surley almost as soon as the boats, and those of us who were good punters, were enthusiastic in the pursuit. But on the other hand, there were those who found the backwaters and Clewer stream enticing; it was easy to conceal a can of beer in the well of a punt, though the prohibition was hard on those who had made a good and energetic use of the privilege.

I do not know how far the humble sardine and the various sorts of potted meats, almost unknown fifty years ago, have been found sufficient relish for breakfasts, and the bringing of hot dishes from without is now forbidden, but in my day, if not allowed, it was at least winked at, and the furnishing such viands was a lucrative trade. Somewhat back from the road, where the red houses opposite Upper School now stand, was a cottage occupied by

Mrs. Webber. The whole ground floor was a very large kitchen, one side of the room occupied by a gigantic grill at which Mrs. Webber cooked chops, kidneys, sausages, &c., for those who could afford to pay for them. All the space in the room that was not fire and Mrs. Webber herself, was full of fags waiting their masters' breakfast, each clamouring for his portion, kept in awe by the lady's sharp tongue and furious temper. These supplemental dishes led to much extravagance and quite needless luxury, and it was well they were suppressed. The vendors of pastry and cakes at the Wall should also have been forbidden. It was one thing to go into a shop if a boy really needed, or thought he needed, such things, another to have them thrust before him every time he went in and out of school, together with the facilities for unlimited tick. One of the men at the Wall with a tin full of puffs and jam tarts was named "Le Marchant," but always known as "Spankie" from a fancied resemblance to Mr. Serjeant Spankie, father of two boys of an earlier generation than my own. This man deserves record, because he was the most accurate and most extraordinary genealogist I ever met. The late Archdeacon Huxtable used to say that, taking in marriage connections, he would undertake to show that any given person was related to any other, and Spankie had the same marvellous power of knowing who every boy in the school was, and who were his relations to the most distant degree. I imagine him to have spent all the time he was not vending his deleterious goods on reading up Peerages, County Histories, and the like ; these with a marvellous memory both for names and faces, added to a few searching, but always civil questions, laid a boy's whole family open to his knowledge. He would say to a boy who passed him : " I saw Mr. —— go towards your tutor's a few minutes ago ; he came in a carriage from Slough, and I think he must be looking for you, as I know he is your mother's cousin," and in such things he was always correct. Some reforming and younger masters attempted to abolish him, and tried the question before the magistrates whether he was not creating an obstruction by standing where he did. He came radiant from the encounter. " The indictment is squashed, young gentlemen," he said, "the indictment is squashed." "Well, Spankie, what did you say to them?" "I said, 'Gentlemen, the road is the king's and the tin is my own.'" After this Spankie became in a measure recognised, and useful. Some boys occasionally ran away, even from so favoured a school as Eton; and Spankie was sent after them as a sort of amateur detective. I remember a boy having bolted, under circumstances which induced Hawtrey to call us all into Upper School and tell us so. "But," he said, "I have sent a trustworthy person, who will, I hope, return with the unhappy boy," and a whisper, which from many hundred lips had almost the power of a roar, uttered "Spankie."

A custom, peculiar to Eton in my day, was abolished by Dr. Goodford, so soon as he became head-master. The actual college bounds were small, and it was obviously impossible to restrict the boys to them. The river was, as I have said, declared to be within bounds. The street leading to it was nominally forbidden. Hence what had once been a reality, that a boy seen in the disallowed places should **run away, became a mere** form, under the name of "shirking," so that the masters' authority was recognised. We bolted into the nearest shop, behind the nearest hedge, and a boy was often reproved, or even punished, not because he was out of bounds, but because he did not shirk properly. I do not know that much harm was done by this patent and permitted sham, but it was difficult to convince strangers that the whole affair was a mere form, and that we were not considered to be doing wrong. For if a boy were really where he ought not to be, no amount of shirking, however well carried out, was of avail.

One of such absolutely forbidden places was the lower part of Windsor especially at the time of the annual fair. I never remember the very smallest harm which came to any boys from going there, nor how a giant, or a spotted lady, or a horse with five legs could corrupt morals, but it was assumed that the fair would be the entrance and the initiation to terrible wickedness : we were all agog to go, and as a matter of fact did see most of the wonders on show. The hot chases of the masters and the hair-breadth escapes were amusing. At my tutor's a boy, not I, arranged to get out of a window, under which was a covered water-butt. He was to scale the butt on his return, tap at the window to wake the occupant of the room, and get in by the same way. He found the fair exceedingly tame, and returned to find his friend so soundly asleep, that no battering at the window could wake him. As he prepared himself for a still more vigorous effort the top gave way, and plunged him up to the neck in water. Scrambling out he ran up and down the lane, but finally, half-frozen, he was obliged to knock meekly at the front door, to be let in by Goodford himself, who was sitting up late. His fate was a strong deterrent, his account of the worthlessness of the fair still greater. It had been, in fact, what a lady of my acquaintance called an entertainment she did not enjoy, " stupid fun."

" Tap" and " Cellar" were two public-house bars or parlours which were tacitly permitted. If a boy went to a Windsor public-house, or to Salt Hill, the offence was serious ; but these two public-houses, more mischievous because more within reach, were winked at. The masters avoided going past them at unexpected times : they saw the men who were set to keep watch looking out till they had passed, and never took steps to prevent the mischief. The matter was so well understood that when "Tap" was removed from the old Christopher Inn within the precincts of the College to a house in the town, the proprietor sent a notice of his removal to Goodford, then head-master, with "thanks for past favours and a hope of their continuance." The scandal continues to the present day.

The late Sir James Stephen has put it on record that there was at Eton, in his time, a complete absence of moral and religious enthusiasm. I am not disposed to agree with him. The wave of the Oxford movement had affected Eton, and there were certainly knots of boys whose religion was almost perfervid, who, on going to Oxford and Cambridge, at once joined the extreme sections of the High Church party, some of them stepping very soon over the bounds which separates England from Rome. Nor did the influence on religion of such men as Selwyn, Abraham, and Edward Coleridge count for nothing in the same direction. And although morals were often at a sadly low ebb, there were many sets of lads who exercised a repressive effect upon evil, which should have been the duty of their superiors, and whole houses, with perhaps a somewhat pharisaic arrogance, prided themselves on maintaining a lofty tone. At that time also, the central part of the great East window was filled with stained glass by the voluntary contributions of the boys alone. It consists of a very simple but vivid picture of the Crucifixion, and many of us found in it a striking lesson from Calvary, and, whatever was lacking in the services, knew first in that chapel what worship meant, drew strength against sin, and learnt how to suffer and to strive from the contemplation of that rood. The chapel as I first remember it was a stately and dignified Jacobean church, like many College chapels still unrestored at Oxford, and far more striking than the modern restoration. The stalls were pews, and the whole arrangement was like the old unrestored choir of St. Paul's Cathedral, in which sat the Provost and Fellows and the "noblemen," including in this term sons of Peers and Baronets.

I have elsewhere used the following words

when speaking of the change from my Ilminster to my Eton life.

At Eton, for the first time, I heard a chanted "Cathedral Service," and week-day prayers in church without the weariness of a sermon; there in 1841 such of us boys who were inclined to think and read the newspapers became conscious of the great stir which was going on at Oxford; a few of our masters were falling under the influence of the new theology, and this could not be without its effect on the boys.

It had its bearing on our minds, but to an extremely limited extent on our lives. There are lads who, by the grace of God, have in them a natural and ingrained purity of soul, and a revolt from every wrong word and deed, an instinct against evil, which preserves them in ignorant innocence through the perils of boyhood; but as a rule an average English lad is neither ignorant nor innocent. When he ceases to say his nightly prayer at his mother's knee, there is no one to force on him the connection between religion and morals; no one, except from the distant pulpit, ever speaks to him of his soul; no one deals with him individually, or helps him in his special trials. A father is as a rule shy of his son, tutors are apt to treat all trangressions as school offences, and are unwilling to see what is not forced on them, so that the boy's soul shifts for itself, and for the most part fares badly. I can truly say that for the five years I was at Eton, between the ages of thirteen and eighteen, no one ever said one word to me about my own religious life, save always my mother, but she could know nothing of a boy's dangers, and was as one that fought the air.

But as a mere matter of intellectual opinion, Church questions were extremely interesting. The *Christian Year* became known to me almost by heart; it, and still more the *Lyra Apostolica*, Miss Sewell's books, and among them especially *Margaret Percival*, put before me the Anglican Church theory, which I accepted with eagerness; nor was my pleasure and acquiescence in it disturbed even by the caricature of it which I found in *Hawkstone*, a foolish and impudent book, though written by a very able man, Miss Sewell's brother, the Rev. William Sewell, soon to be my tutor at Exeter College, Oxford.

There is little to be said of my home life during the Eton holidays. I came in contact with few or no interesting people, and no books which influenced my life or thoughts other than those of which I have spoken, except Dickens and Tennyson. My father used to read aloud each number of *Pickwick* and its successors as it appeared, in the evenings, to our great delight. Living as we did so near Bath, the scenes connected with that city were very interesting, none the less that we thought we discovered my uncle's footman, who wore red plush breeches as part of his livery, in " Blazes " of the footmen's club. There was such a club, and Dickens had penetrated there somehow as a guest.

I read Tennyson for myself, learning by heart the greater part of the original volumes, and thinking, as I still think, that for subtle workmanship no one had at all approached the same perfection since Milton. I did not then recognise how little thought is contained in that pomp and melody of verse, still less how very little of what thought there is, is the poet's own. For instance, a very large number of people are apparently unaware that Tennyson's idyll "Dora" is simply a story in Miss Mitford's *Our Village* broken up into blank verse with poetic touches added, and in later life his "Idylls of the King" are whole chapters of Malory's *Morte d'Arthur* and Lady Charlotte Guest's *Mabinogion* treated in the same way. It would be an interesting study to any one to work steadily through Tennyson and trace how often and how constantly he has touched up the work of other men. The late Mr. Woolner, the sculptor, told me both "Enoch Arden" and "Aylmer's Field" were originally stories told by him to Tennyson, who made him write them out at length, and then broke up his narrative into blank verse.

So ran the five years away till it was time for me to go to College, and I take leave of the recollections of my Eton days with something of the same regret which I quitted the place itself when the day of parting came at Easter 1846. The family conclave had often considered the question where I was to go. It was thought possible that I should obtain by nomination a Demyship at Magdalen, Oxford, but the peculiarity of that College then was that a Demy could only succeed to the Fellowship attached to the county to which he belonged. There was only one Somersetshire Fellowship, and there were already two or more Somerset Demies, so that on consultation with the one Somerset Fellow, Mr. William Robertson, an old family friend, it was decided not to send me to Magdalen, as even for a Demy it was an expensive College. Finally Exeter was selected, mainly, I think, because Mackenzie Walcott, my aunt's godson, had been there, and because Dr. Richards, the rector, was a friend of the Littlehales family into which my mother's youngest sister had married. My father went with me there to matriculate in January 1846, I having leave from Eton for three days for that purpose. At Easter I left Eton, promising myself to do a great deal of reading in the holidays, a promise which, from circumstances, I was unable to fulfil.

V

COLLEGE LIFE AT OXFORD

1846–1851

IT became necessary to do some considerable repairs at Wellow, and Mr. Harman, an old school friend of my father, lent us Hardington Park, near Frome, about ten miles from Wellow, for the summer. Hardington was an old house, with two good rooms and many bad ones. It had sunk from a mansion to a shooting-box. We were much cramped, pupils and family, and my reading was of the scantiest. I there became acquainted with Mr. Elwyn, afterwards editor of the *Quarterly*, who was curate of Hardington. He was an interesting and accomplished man, and gave me much good advice about the course of my reading. In his very poor poem "Glenaveril," Robert, Lord Lytton, the younger, has sketched Mr. Elwyn under the character of Edelrath. It is an embellished, but in many ways a truthful, portrait. In the summer I paid a visit to my tutor at Eton, going back as an old boy, and in October went up to Exeter, to enter on a new phase of my life.

It was completely new, for there were then very few Eton men at Exeter, and of the few who went up about my time, I had not happened to know any, save very slightly. Charles Parker, of whom I have since lost sight, as he lives wholly in Lincolnshire, went up from Eton with me, and we became intimate. My father, who went to start me, put into my hands a long and kind letter, in which he explained his circumstances, how little likely it was that I should ever inherit anything from him, and that a small amount settled on me from my mother's fortune was all I could ever expect, and this only at her death. Ah me ! I little thought how near that would be, which then seemed so distant that I wondered my father spoke of the contingency.

Exeter was then very full, and an objectionable arrangement was in force by which a freshman had a room out for the day, and occupied a bedroom in those sets which had

an extra bedroom, or rather closet, attached
to them, the giving up of this to a stranger
for a term being made the condition of taking
such a set of rooms. When, as in my case
a term or two afterwards, a man was able to
have a friend as his enforced lodger, the
arrangement had its advantages, but if men
were unacquainted, nothing could be less
pleasant. The man on whom I was quartered
resented the intrusion, and did nothing to
facilitate matters. My room was so small that
I had to get on my bed to undress and dress,
while washing satisfactorily had to be postponed till I reached my lodgings in New Inn
Hall Street. But the term was short, and my
troubles in that way were not of long continuance. The term was on the whole dull, for
in that amphibious state I was cut off a good
deal from College companionship, coming up
as I did without acquaintance. Thus with one
or two exceptions, the men I knew best were
those who entered in the following term after
Christmas.

Here is the place, however, to name those
friends, who for three years to come filled so
large a part of my life, and made me know how

great is the power of friendship, in many ways a nobler and higher, because a more unselfish passion than love.

First among all my friends was, and is, Richard Francis Bowles—Frank Bowles among his friends—but the affection was perhaps stronger on my side than on his. He is a most accomplished man, a good artist, a good rider, good shot, fairly read, thoughtful and high-minded. He has had an uphill game in life to play, through no fault of his own. Frank was "best man" at my marriage, and is godfather to my eldest son Louis. If we have seen but little of each other of late it is more from accident than design, though I think he has very strongly disapproved of my opinions. He is a staunch Anglican High Churchman.

George Russell, afterwards by the death of his brother Charles, Sir George, who has now himself passed away, was another of my closest intimates. Charles and I had been in the same Remove at Eton, and he transferred as it were his brother to me. There are few men about whom I feel more regret that the accidents of place and occupation severed us in after life.

Frank Du Boulay was a different man, and in a different set to these, but I saw a great deal of him, and in some ways still more intimately. He had been brought up in a school which I was only now beginning to know, the High Church, as seen in country parsonages and in actual practical life. One day, after a long conversation, he gave me a *Christian Year*, with a little inscription, hoping "that the Christian love of which this volume is a token may realise the idea of friendship entertained by us both." Frank Du Boulay invited me to his house, and I became most intimate with all his family circle. His mother, Mrs. Majendie, was for the second time a widow, and lived first at Speen, then at Torquay, with her five Du Boulay and two Majendie children. Susan Du Boulay, the eldest daughter, round whom the whole family turned, who swayed them all, became a Catholic nun. For her, while she was yet an Anglican, I took possession on my way into Cornwall of Miss Sellon's first house in Plymouth, and set up the cross of Babbicombe marble in the little oratory, the only bit of furniture then in the house, until the sisters

arrived in the evening. I dwell on this friendship with these good and kind people because
my intercourse with them was pleasant, still
more because it showed me more than anything
else the strength and the weakness of the
Anglican system. If Anglican premises are
true, Rome is the conclusion of them, and
Susan was the one logical member of her family.
I have lost sight of Frank, though when we
meet we are friendly, and I am sure he always
thinks of me as I of him with affection; but
with his principles he must look on me with
stern disapproval, and he is not a man who
ever saw two sides of a question. With
James Du Boulay, somewhat younger, and not
in those days so much my friend, my intimacy
has increased and been maintained. He is godfather to my son Maurice.

His other godfather is George David Boyle,
now Dean of Salisbury, and still my good kind
friend. He was always older than his years
at Oxford, and was better read than most of
us, who were only beginning to take a real and
intelligent delight in literature. It is a lasting
surprise to me that Boyle, though he has risen
to honourable preferment, has made no mark in

letters, or filled a more exalted place in the Church. He has always belonged to the moderately broad section of it.

James Aitken, Robert Hawtayne, Halifax Wyatt, Alan Brodrick, and many others I should like to name, are associated in my memory with those old days, but "all, all are gone, the old familiar faces." If we ever met now, much of the old affection would revive, but we are scattered abroad, and our paths in life are different.

Out of College were Frank Simmons at Lincoln, Percy Smith at Balliol, Arthur Paget at Trinity, where my cousin George Cox was a scholar, Arthur Charles Wilson, at Christ Church. With all of these I was most intimate, and through them I saw very varied and many-sided society.

Two other friends from other Colleges may be mentioned because they afterwards made their mark in literature.

George Lawrence of Balliol, author of *Guy Livingstone*, was as much the creator of the short story of his day as Stevenson or Kipling is in our time. The modern writers are purer and better, and Guy Livingstone lent himself more easily to caricature, but he at any rate was one of the forces of his time. I knew George Lawrence well before we either of us went to Oxford ; our mothers were friends, and he was much at our house during some years ; somewhat older than I, he was just one of those men who have a wonderful fascination for younger men. I mention him because all the characters in his book were careful and finished portraits of persons as he saw them, of his mother, his wife, another lady whose lot was perhaps the happier in that she did not marry him, of himself as he desired to be. Dear George Lawrence ; I have loved less many more ranged and orderly men.

Henry Kingsley was at Worcester, and was in those days remarkable for his susceptibility to mesmeric influences. We did not suspect his future brilliancy as a writer, though many of us now think that in his power as a story-teller he is greater than Charles. There was also a sister, Mrs. Chanter, who wrote a novel, *Over the Cliffs*, quite unworthy of remembrance, save for one sentence. The heroine, I think, fell " over the cliffs " and arrived at the bottom " a tangled mass of hair and brains."

Henry Kingsley was, we thought, superior to his surroundings, for Worcester had no good name amongst us. George Russell went to dine there, and said "it reminded him of the Zoological Gardens. The men growled as they ate." But George was always sarcastic.

Soon, from knowing few, I knew many, and probably was as intimately acquainted with as many phases of Oxford life as any of my contemporaries. While through Du Boulay, as I have said, I saw the working of the Tractarian movement in the country, through George Cox, mainly, I came to know the party formed by it in Oxford, so far as it existed among undergraduates. He was a year senior to me, and was in the full swing of his fervour when I went up. The whole thing was, I now think, very unreal. Newman had gone, and taken with him his mighty influence ; there was no one left in his place ; Pusey had great weight with those who sought his counsel, but they were then comparatively few, since he had not the attractive power which Newman had possessed. And while I by no means say that the young men under Tractarian teaching did not lead perfectly respectable lives, the attempt at self-denial was spasmodic, fasting, when tried, was under no rule, and the effort chiefly showed itself in a dilettante love for architecture and music, as represented by the Oxford Madrigal Society.

One man, an undergraduate at Oriel, decorated his room with texts, but that for his bedroom was so pretty in illuminated design, that he could not bring himself to put it inside, where it would have admonished him, as he lay in bed. But it certainly looked odd to see in his sitting-room, above his bedroom door, the injunction "Go to the ant, thou sluggard," as if the ant lived inside. This youth was not popular, and some other men broke into his room one evening and wrecked them, carrying casts of saints, &c., into the quadrangle. Clough, then tutor, began to speak to him on the subject next day with the words, "I am sorry, Mr. ———, that they have broken your teraphim." One day I was engaged to lunch with Hopkins of Balliol, an old Eton acquaintance, whose rooms were decorated in the most ecclesiastical manner. I found him stripping texts from the walls in wild haste, and appealing to those of his friends who had arrived to help him to shove under

the bed a large crowned figure of the Blessed
Virgin. It appeared that he had just heard
that his father, a Berkshire squire, whose
contempt for ecclesiastical millinery, &c., was
most pronounced, was in Oxford, and even
then on his way to Balliol. The transformation
was effected, and the meeting between father and
son was unbroken by storms. I was spending a few days in Berkshire with Hopkins
some years ago, and was amused to find this
very figure of the Blessed Virgin presiding
over a well in the grounds, set in a little niche
against a tree. But she is there purely for
decorative and in no degree for devotional
purposes. Of course there were many with
whom the feeling was far deeper, witness Frank
Du Boulay, Alan Brodrick and Sam Bowles,
who carried out long afterwards in their country
parishes a noble self-devotion which they had
learnt at Oxford ; but the high tide had carried
many who went with it on to Rome, and as it
retreated left short of that height a good deal of
useless wreck on the shore.

This is perhaps enough to say of my friends
and the society into which I was carried.
Apart from these peculiarities the life was like

that of an University in all times. We read—
far less than we should have done—in the
mornings, we rode and boated in the afternoons, or took long pleasant walks, pouring out
all our souls to each other, before life taught
us the need of reticence, and that daws peck
at hearts worn upon the sleeve ; we met in
each other's rooms after Hall, wasted those
evenings far too much, and read again too
seldom.

At Exeter it may fairly be said that there
was not much true encouragement to a studious
life, at least to those who were, with me, pupils
of the Rev. William Sewell. Sewell was at
that time Senior Tutor, and had been Sub-
Rector, as he again became before the end of
my stay at Oxford. He was one of the most
entertaining and clever of men, so far as
cleverness is consistent with egregious folly.
He had been a prominent member of the
Tractarian party, and was always a strong
High Churchman, but he had withdrawn himself from Newman, and preached a violent anti-
popery sermon on the text about Moses and
Aaron taking their censers to stand between
the dead and the living, so that the plague

was stayed ; the dead in his application were those who had become Catholic. Hence it was that one of the Oxford wits in those days said that his name was Sewell, *quasi suillus*, a little pig, because he would not go " the whole hog." He had held the professorship of Moral Philosophy, and in one of his lectures was said to have drawn proofs of revealed from natural religion in the manner following. After speaking of the Trinity of the Divine nature, and pointing out how there are three primary colours, three notes in a musical chord, three leaves in a trefoil, &c., he turned to the Unity and said : " There is one sun, there is one moon, there is one *multitude of stars*." Of all men I have ever known, possessing any ability at all, he was the most inaccurate, the most erratic, and he was therefore the worst possible tutor. During one term we were to read with him Aristotle's Ethics, for our degree, and came to the first lecture with a certain amount of work prepared. But before beginning to translate, Sewell gave us a short and interesting disquisition on the different ethical systems of Aristotle, St. Paul, and Shakspere. He then bid us bring to our next lecture our Bibles and

our Shaksperes, and we read no more text of
Aristotle in our Aristotle lectures during the
whole of the term.

So, too, in a Greek Testament lecture, he
took to interpreting the account of St. Paul's
voyage as a prophetic account of the fortunes
of the Church's barque. He expounded that
when St. Paul was cast "upon a certain
island" which preserved his life, this really
meant that the Church in Ireland under St.
Columba had been the preservation of the
whole Church Catholic, and he was led to this
fanciful interpretation because he and others
had recently been engaged in the foundation of
St. Columba's College in Ireland. Those who
want to see what this eccentric person really
was should read his "Diary at St. Columba,"
though it might now perhaps be difficult to
get a copy. Sewell afterwards founded and
became the second warden of Radley, in which
he was as complete a failure as in all else.

With such a man in charge of our instruction—and at Exeter the tutor had the whole
arrangement of his pupils' lectures under his
control—it was no wonder that very few of
his pupils took honours. For myself I soon

saw that it was hopeless to attempt it unless I could shake myself free from Sewell's guidance, which was not to be managed, and I turned to a great deal of private reading, which has perhaps stood me in better stead. I read History, Philosophy, and Foreign Literature, making great use of the Union library. At the Union I also became a debater, and learned considerable fluency in speech, which has since proved very useful.

In my second term I got rooms in College, garrets in the staircase opposite the porter's lodge, but afterwards excellent ones in the staircase between the lodge and the hall, on the second floor, left. They were all I could wish, and are still in my memory ideal College rooms.

Those were not days when an undergraduate made many acquaintances older than men of his own age ; Oxford society had not increased as it now has, tutors were older, and the line of separation between the Don and the pupil was very marked. I made, however, some few friends. Henry Coxe, the Librarian of the Bodleian, was one of a family with whom my mother had been very intimate as a girl, and he and his wife showed me great kindness. Who that knew Henry Coxe can ever forget him? He was very handsome, and the essence of courtesy and benevolence; his whole soul was in his work, yet he always seemed at leisure for a visit, and to give a few words of counsel to whomever sought him in his den in the Bodleian. The library floor was covered with India matting. I never smell that fresh scent of the woven reeds without thinking of the Bodleian and Henry Coxe.

Then I became intimate at another house, that of Dr. ———. The wife was extremely beautiful, and the husband was one of the kindest of men. They were thoroughly contrasted with each other—he prosaic, sensible, and somewhat dull; she clever, imaginative, religious in an hysterical kind of way, always entreating her director, Dr. Pusey, to tell her she ought to go over to Rome, but not going without the permission which he did not give, devoted to works among the poor. She always had half-a-dozen young men dangling about her, and she did us no good. Now we had to escort her late at night to some disreputable lane where she was going to sit up all night with a dying sufferer——though she was, of course, far more liable to awkward stoppages by Proctors than if she had gone unattended, or with her maid ; now she found riding necessary for her health, and we must needs ride with her ; now she insisted on our buying, at a ridiculous price, a piece of embroidery she had worked in order to sell it for a charity. She was a thoroughly good but a very foolish woman. I was never more than amused with her, nor became one of her slaves, but there were those on whom the effect was more serious, and she certainly was not a wholesome influence in the Oxford of that time.

Through her I knew Dr. Pusey. I was even in those days much disposed to think Confession a most excellent thing to any one who believes in its sacramental efficacy, and I think that it would have been good for me, who had then no doubts of any kind. But Dr. Pusey, who wished to become my Confessor, and spoke to me often on the subject, was not a person who attracted me, and even then I never separated the man from his office as the believer should, theoretically, be able to do. The opportunity was lost, and of course now that faith in sacraments has become mine again, I have sought them from Catholics and not from Anglicans.

It was, I think, in my first term that my dear mother said, in one of her wise and beautiful letters to me, that though I was always her son, she felt I was her *child* no longer. It was true, and if the change had not come quite so soon, I realised it in the following summer which I spent partly with the Du Boulays at Speen, and began to take my place in society, to be invited to dinner, to balls, &c. The Keatings came up to town every summer, and I began to join them there, making afterwards acquaintances for myself in London, in Bath, and in Somersetshire, beyond the bounds of our own circle. I came then also to know the one dear friend of my early manhood, who was not associated with Oxford or Eton, Charles Whitworth Russell, Lieut., R.N. He was a first cousin of my friend George Russell, and his mother, a widow, came to live in Bath. He was invalided from the effects of African fever, and his naval days were practically at an end. In all my vacations for some years we were inseparable, and scarce a thought of either was concealed from the other. He married Miss Maria Daubeney, and obtained an appointment as Adjutant of Volunteers at Plymouth, where he died. His photograph, in a frock coat, with clasped hands, hangs in my room. I shall be glad if one of my children will always keep it, as the portrait of a man their father dearly loved.

My life, however, was as a whole much like that of other young men who live at home and visit their friends, until my second long vacation in 1848, when came the one great and unforgotten sorrow of my life, the death of my dear mother. Six months before she had given birth to her youngest child, Edith Brooke Paul, who was born at the Keatings' house, 6 Crescent, Bath. The Rajah of Sarawak, Sir James Brooke, was her godfather. He was in England during that winter, and the last Sunday of his stay was the last that my mother was about, before her confinement. As that day was the only one available, the Keatings departed from their usual rule on Sundays, and gave a large dinner, followed by an evening party. The Rajah sat most of the evening by my mother at her sofa, only leaving her now and then to speak to an old friend, or to ask my aunt, Mrs. Littlehales, to sing. Her scruples were overborne, and I remember her magnificent singing as though it was yesterday. She had been when young a pupil of the celebrated male soprano, Veluti. The next day I went back to Oxford, the Rajah left Bath for London and Sarawak, and Edith came into the world a day or two after. She went first, as she came last, of my five sisters.

When I went home at Easter, I found my mother had made a good recovery, and at the beginning of the long vacation she was in better health and spirits than I had known her since I went to Eton. A rigid economy at home had put our finances into a somewhat more satisfactory state, and she enjoyed my driving her about in a pony carriage. She entered more than she had done since my brother's death into the society of the neighbourhood, and exerted herself to make some new acquaintances, the Parsonses especially, who had settled at Freshfield, in Sir William Napier's old house. Towards the end of July we drove one hot day to call on Mrs. Fussell at Chantry, who had just come into the neighbourhood as a bride. It turned chill and rainy as we drove home, and my mother caught a cold which developed into acute bronchitis, under which she sank rapidly, and died almost before we had realised her serious danger, on August 4, 1848.

My mother stands out to me above all women I have known in grace, beauty, wisdom, strength of character, and charm of manner. I have heard that some thought her cold, but I doubt if it ever was so, for young men turned to her as their adviser and friend, while her friendships were devoted. She made few late in life ; Lady Becher, formerly Miss O'Neil, was the one person she took to her heart in the last years. Her sweet household ways were all good ; to this day her management of an establishment, in all matters even the most trivial, are those with which all others contrast unfavourably ; she combined the housewifely qualities of the last century with the grace and refinement of modern days. Between her and her sisters was always the deepest affection, and the great love my aunt Mrs. Keating showed us was the reflected love which had been given in all its strength to her sister Fanny.

I have kept no letters on principle, but I have from time to time regretted that I have none of hers. One scrap of her writing accidentally preserved in a desk is all I have. It is a note written to me when she was in Bath and I at Wellow, asking me to see that the flowers round my brothers' grave were tended. My father put up a stone tomb after the fashion of that time, which became chipped and flaked by the action of the weather. Since his death, we, their children, have replaced it by a granite cross, over the vault which my father made to hold many, but in which she, and the two boys taken before her death, alone have found, or are likely to find, their rest.

My eldest sister was eighteen at that time, and became mistress of my father's home, for my cousins, Elizabeth and Annie Wilby, who had long lived with us, had married, the one two or three years before, and Annie, if I remember rightly, that same summer, but earlier. Elizabeth was the second wife of Frederick Curteis, a Kentish squire of some fortune ; she is now dead, but was a kind friend and sister as long as she lived. Annie married Robert Mitford, an old friend, nephew of my godfather, Edward Boodle. They live at Hampstead, and I am sorry we have wholly lost sight of each other ; but we have little in common, and I have never had the faculty of adhering to relatives simply on account of the tie of blood. I blame myself for this. My sister Fanny was too young for her new charge, all the more as we soon felt that my father was certain to marry again. The house was not a true home henceforward, though my sisters did their best under great difficulties.

The following spring, 1849, at Oxford was very important to me, as in it I formed a friendship, which coloured many years of my after life, with Charles Kingsley. He came to Oxford, having just published the *Saint's Tragedy*, to stay with Cowley Powles, one of our Exeter tutors, his old school friend. Most of my own set read the *Saint's Tragedy* as soon as it was published, and were curious to see its brilliant author. Powles asked me to breakfast, where also for the first time I met Anthony Froude, afterwards Kingsley's brother-in-law. It was, I think, their first meeting also. After breakfast I walked to Iffley with Kingsley, who wanted to see the church, and I think Percy Smith went with us. Percy was about to be ordained, and then, or soon after, it was arranged that he should go as curate to Eversley. There I visited him in the next winter, and we spent the evening at the rectory. Next morning came a note from Kingsley, characteristically dated, " Bed this morning," asking me to stay with him. I did so, and the proposed visit of a day or two became one of several weeks, the first of many such in successive years. My recollections of Kingsley are written at length in my *Biographical Sketches*, but all I have there said is far short of the impression he made on young and sensitive minds.

A large part of his character and a charming description of his life is given in the Memoir by his widow. The defect of the book is explained by the fact that it was written when the sense of her bereavement was very recent, so that the work is pervaded by a certain solemnity and gloom which were quite alien to the nature of the man as his friends knew him.

No doubt, like most persons of exuberant temperament, Kingsley had his moments of deep depression, and he was towards the end of his life a disappointed man; but at the time of which I speak he was characterised by a sunny joyousness, an abounding vitality, and a contagious energy which were most attractive. He was in no sense a learned man, nor a sound scholar, nor a deep theologian, nor a well-read historian ; he knew more of science than of all these put together, yet was not really scientific. But on almost all subjects conceivable he had read enough to talk brilliantly, without any inconvenient doubt that his equipment was entirely sufficient.

To young men still in course of formation this coruscating person, ten years older than ourselves, but young in mind, and a born leader of men, came as a kind of revelation. We had never met any one like him, nor indeed have I ever since encountered any one so impressive to the young. What was most attractive to me, and of course not to me alone, was that this man, so varied in knowledge and so brilliant in talk, athletic in habits and frame, a first-rate horseman, keen sportsman, good quoit player, was also a man of prayer and piety, filled with a personal, even passionate, love to Christ, whom he realised as his Friend and Brother in a fashion almost peculiar to the Saints.

I was at this time dissatisfied with the Tractarian theory, and such biblical criticism as I had read was inclining me to those notions which were called afterwards " Broad," and of these Kingsley was the incarnation. He stiffened later in life into a stricter orthodoxy, and found it possible to defend the Athanasian Creed ; but at that time he certainly did not use it in his church ; and his talk on biblical and dogmatic matters, while always reverent, was extremely free. In those days people actually troubled themselves—perhaps some do now—about the early chapters of Genesis, and Kingsley, Percy Smith, and I were discussing the subject as we paced up and down the garden. Kingsley, who stammered dreadfully, tossed back his head, and said with a gasp : " I've always thought that the serpent was a serpent-worshipping black tribe." We came to know that when Kingsley said, " I've *always* thought," it meant that the sometimes brilliant, always paradoxical, notion had just flashed into his head for the first time. Percy said with an air of grave puzzle: "Well! Rector! but—you know, negroes do not go on their bellies." "No," said Kingsley, not to be done, "they don't, but then snakes don't eat dirt, and niggers do." Another time, discussing the question of laughter in the divine nature, he flashed out: "What! God not laugh! What did He make a crab for then?" All this was consistent with the most passionate and personal love for Christ, as a Friend whom he knew and to whom he spoke. He was absorbed in the work of his parish—out of which he rarely stirred—and found an excellent helper in Percy. "Ah! Mr. Smith," said an old woman at Eversley to me, "he's a beautiful man! No matter what time of day or night 'tis, he whips in and puts up such a prayer."

Kingsley's reading of the Bible, whether at family prayer or in church, sounded like a true message from God; his sermons, thoroughly unconventional, written in admirable English, were vigorous, reverent, and inspiring. He knew every man, woman, and child in his scattered parish, and, with less effort than I have ever seen, with less sense of incongruity, could pass from light badinage in any casual meeting to deep religious talk on the state of his interlocutor's soul. He was, theology apart, the ideal pastor of his people, living among them and for them, wholly devoted to what he believed his divinely given work.

I remember that when the curate preached, and Kingsley's part of the service was over, he was wont to put off his surplice and take his place in his usual dress in the pew under the pulpit by his wife's side. When the sermon was ended he would stand up there in the pew and give the blessing in his cut-away coat, without vestige of ecclesiastical garment.

But the services, if unconventional, were reverent, and whatever deductions might be drawn from his omissions, Kingsley's teaching was sound on the great doctrines of the Christian faith, as expounded in the Anglican formularies. He was kind and tolerant to Nonconformists and their doctrines, and the whole vials of his wrath were reserved for Rome and the priests of Rome. On the Catholic laity he looked with compassion as foolish souls beguiled by liars. In his first novel, *Yeast*, he introduces a priest with a name which embodied this theory, Padre Bugiardo.

The great effect Kingsley had on me was that he made it possible for me to take Orders. It had always been tacitly assumed at home that I should do so, and for a long while I had no other thought. But as I grew older I disliked my father's humdrum life, and believed, as I still believe, that a country clergyman's life in the Anglican Church is either idle or fussy. He has next to nothing to do *as clergyman*, or he worries his people to death. Then for a time I was attracted by the High Church vision of constant services and sacraments, till I saw the thing did not work practically, except in large town parishes, and that the model priest and parish existed only on paper. Kingsley showed me a different ideal. A man always at work, treating his literary gifts, his schemes for social, sanitary, and political reform, as part of his priestly work ; he took a large view of things, and gave me larger ones than I had ever had before. When I felt the narrowness of the Church, the statements of dogma which fenced it from all the most attractive views of the Catholic Church on the one side and those of the Protestant Churches on the other, Kingsley had no doubt that the Church could and would be widened from within, and become more and more the religious expression of the thought of the time. And it never occurred to him—or, then, to me—to doubt that the thought of the time, the *Zeitgeist*, must be right. So after a few months of wavering, in which I thought of the Bar and of Medicine, I went back to my early intention, from which my family scarce knew, if they did know, that I had swerved.

I was moved with Kingsley's enthusiasm, and felt with his feelings; to be a parson after his pattern was my aim, and a desire to help my fellow-men seemed as a call from God. My mother had always wished to see me a clergy-man, and her death, with the deeper feelings it brought, gave me a push forward in the same direction. I accepted the curacy of Tew, in the diocese of Oxford, and was ordained deacon in the Lent of 1851.

My friendship and long residence with Kingsley brought me to know well Frederick Denison Maurice, who had been an old college friend of my father; Tom Hughes, whom I had also known as a neighbour of Mrs.

Majendie ; J. M. Ludlow, and others who were engaged in the Co-operative and Christian Socialist movements of the day, of which Kingsley's novel *Alton Locke* (to be read in its *first*, not in its later editions) is the exponent. I saw much of Maurice, but while loving him personally, as all did who came in contact with him, I am free to confess I never could make head or tail of what he taught or what he meant.

My association with Kingsley also increased the intimacy already begun at Oxford with Anthony Froude, whom I met at Eversley. Froude was Fellow and Lecturer at Exeter, and lived on terms of considerable intimacy with the senior undergraduates. He was then writing his remarkable book, *The Nemesis of Faith*, which, now almost entirely forgotten, deserves to be remembered for two or three pages describing the change which came upon the world in early Christian days at the disappearance of the old paganism. Froude was in deacon's orders, and one night, talking over his story with three or four of us, he told us he was very much puzzled to find a name for it. " Call it *The Sceptic Deacon*," said

Wiltshire Austin, and Froude was not pleased with the title, which equally well suggested the book and its author.

. On the whole my association with these men made me theologically a very broad High Churchman, broad that is in doctrine, but with a strong feeling for pomp of ritual, for music in church, paintings and symbolism of all kinds ; so that outwardly I may often have seemed to belong to the extreme section of the High Church party as it then existed, before what is now called Ritualism had arisen. Politically I became an extreme Radical — much to my uncle Mr. Keating's annoyance—a Republican and a Socialist, so far as these things can be carried out without breach of public order. In politics, at least, my creed has never changed since I became able to formulate it, while it has, on the religious side, passed through Positivism and landed me in the one true home of Faith, the Roman Church.

Before I pass away from the account of my Oxford days, I may mention that I was present at the lecture in Hall, I think a Greek Testament lecture, in the course of which Sewell burnt Anthony Froude's book, *The Nemesis of*

Faith. Another who was present has lately announced to the world that the copy burnt by Sewell was his own, and I am quite willing to defer to his recollection, though I remember that more than one of us who confessed to having the book were sent to bring it. Blomfield's was the one selected for sacrifice, and I carried my own away with triumph. It was, however, later committed to the flames by Miss M. Daubeney, who equally with Sewell disliked its teaching.

Few lectures at Oxford in my day were more than mere dry bones of scholarship, though occasionally they afforded matter for laughter afterwards. I remember a tutor at New College reproving the translation given by a man more acquainted with secular than with biblical English. He translated the word γάστηρ, stomach, to which Miller remarked, "I think, Mr. ——, that 'belly' is perhaps a more *solemn* word."

The examination for a degree was *viva voce* and public; and I heard a curious passage at arms between Frank Palgrave, afterwards Fellow of Exeter, and Jowett, who was examining. Jowett said, "What is the reason, Mr. Palgrave, that the Church of England rejects the

Apocrypha ? " " I suppose," answered Palgrave, "because there are so many odd stories in it." "Oh," said Jowett, "if that were the reason, I should think she would go further and reject a good deal more."

That fencing bout in the schools between Jowett and Palgrave was at the time the talk of all Oxford, and this was a sign that our minds were gravely stirred at any apparent deviations from orthodoxy. There were very few broad Churchmen, and those few not regarded with any favour. Men who were lax in morals and discipline were as a rule most zealous in the maintenance of the strictest verbal accuracy of Holy Scripture. "Stanley," said a man at University, who was certainly not one of the ornaments of his college, "Stanley! why, he will explain you away anything, from the whale downwards," as if the whole of Christianity depended on the acceptance of the story of Jonah.

My reading at Oxford was extensive and multifarious. Browning and Mrs. Browning are almost as much associated with my Oxford life as Tennyson was with my Eton days. Whilst staying with Kingsley on one occasion,

I had the great pleasure of making Mrs. Browning's acquaintance. She was staying with her friend Miss Mitford at Three Mile Cross, which was near Eversley, and one afternoon Miss Mitford drove over to ask if Kingsley happened to know of any one going up to London, as Mrs. Browning, then with her, did not like to travel up alone. I said I was going, and at once offered to escort Mrs. Browning. This I did, and I put her in her husband's charge at Paddington, and that was all that I ever saw of her, although I became very intimate with her husband in later years.

At this time too Carlyle became one of the great influences of my life. My friend George Boyle was an admirable reader, and constantly read aloud to his friends passages of our favourite authors, and from his lips I heard a large part of the *French Revolution*. I remember well his reading aloud in my room the narrative of the flight to Varennes, and still seem to see his hearers swaying backwards and forwards with excitement, as they heard that most dramatic episode.

In October 1849 I took my degree, a year and a half before I was of an age to take

Orders. This was a very unsatisfactory time, for I had nothing at all to do, and no particular home. Wellow was not pleasant, for my father's affairs were again in considerable difficulty, and it was clear he thought me only in the way. The Keatings' house was always a home, but I did not care to be often in Bath. I lived much at Eversley, and in the summer of 1850 went for the first time beyond London; my whole experience of the world being up to that time bounded geographically between Truro and London.

I visited my friends Eardley Knowles—now dead—at Heysham Tower on the shores of Morecambe Bay in Lancashire, and James Aitken in Scotland. His mother and uncle rented Springkell near Ecclefechan for the summer. Thence I went in September for a tour alone in the Highlands. I visited my friend George Boyle, then reading at Oban, and heard Jowett preach a sermon which has never been forgotten by those who were privileged to hear it. Sir M. E. Grant-Duff has recorded his impression of it, but not quite in the words as remembered by me. The peroration as I recorded it is as follows: "From the weakness of the sick-chamber, from the darkness and corruption of the grave, we crawl like poor worms into the light of God's presence." I spent the winter once more in Bath, where my sisters were staying with my aunt. I read fairly hard for Orders. During this time my intercourse with my dearest friend, Charlie Russell, was my great delight daily.

My father was at Wellow with the younger children, and he often came into Bath; but his relations with the Keatings were growing very strained. It was plain he intended to marry, and that he would not consult his children's interests. During the winter he announced his intention of marrying Miss Cossins, a lady we knew by name and repute, and had every reason to dislike. I admit her boldness in marrying a man of fifty with next to no means and with eight children; but this audacity was her only good quality. The Keatings did all they could to receive her courteously and to know her afterwards; but it was of no avail, she was furiously jealous of my dead mother, and quarrelled with all our old friends. The marriage took place from the house of some of Miss Cossins' old friends in London, and at my father's earnest request I went to the marriage in the early spring of 1851, returning to Wellow while they were away on the wedding tour for the few weeks before my ordination. My sisters remained in Bath, and Charlie Russell spent that time with me.

VI

CLERICAL LIFE—FIRST EXPERIENCES

1851–1854

THROUGH Charles Parker, an old Oxford friend, I had heard of the curacy of Great Tew in the North of Oxfordshire, near which his brother-in-law had lived for a time. I had visited it in the previous winter and agreed with the Rev. J. J. Campbell to become his curate. In Lent 1851 I went to Cuddesdon for the examination and subsequent ceremony. The Bishop of Oxford, Wilberforce's Life is before the world, and I need say no more of it than that I always disliked and distrusted him, and even at the ordination, which he made singularly impressive, I did not believe in him. But I thoroughly believed in *it*, and may honestly say that never a man took Orders with more sincere desire than I to do his duty in the Anglican Church to the souls that should be given to my charge. In the fervour of feeling at that time all difficulties had left me. I had passed a good examination, and was commended by the Bishop. The ordination took place in Cuddesdon Church, and was a very solemn service. I made at that time special acquaintance with Vernon Blake, now Rector of Stoke Poges, and William Jenkins, Fellow of Jesus, Oxford, who were ordained deacons at the same time, of whom I saw much in the next year or two.

After a week spent at home with my father and Mrs. Paul, my sisters also having returned, in which I too clearly saw the misery which was to come, I entered on my work at Great Tew early in April.

Great Tew is what is called a model village. There was not a cottage in it which had not been rebuilt or beautified by Mr. Boulton, the owner of the whole property and the patron of the living. It slopes on a steep hill to the north, possesses a village-green, with various ornamental fountains here and there, the whole place looking like a scene for a pastoral play. The grounds of the great house ran down the same hill, at the east of the village, and the church and rectory stood above the whole at the top. There was no house in which the curate could find a lodging, and Mr. Boulton altered and furnished for me a labourer's cottage, perhaps that which of all in the village looked the most like a theatre side-scene. The house consisted of one little parlour, a kitchen, a good bedroom above the parlour, and an attic. A woman from the village, the wife of the rector's man, undertook to do for me. She came in the morning to get my breakfast and went away when she had set my tea at night, much after the manner of a college scout. I slept as a rule in the best room, but could always give up this to a friend, or to my sisters when they came to stay with me, and the attic was terribly cold in winter.

My special duties were to help Campbell in the Sunday morning services at Great Tew, preaching on alternate Sundays, and in the evening I took a service in a school-room at Little Tew about a mile off across the fields. This was my district, and soon I knew every one in it, and most people in Great Tew, though Campbell did not wish me to visit there except casually as a friend. In the winter we had a night-school, one of the first in those parts, and it proved a great success. I set myself at once to get a church built at Little Tew, and Mr. Street, the afterwards famous architect, then beginning his career at Wantage, gave us for nothing a design for a very pretty church—chapel-like, with the roof in one span, which was built for an incredibly small sum. This, however, was not finished till I had left Tew.

The neighbourhood was not large, and consisted of the clergy chiefly; but all were very kind to me. The Bishop even then struck me as an astute and insincere man of whom a typical story may here be told, though it belongs in time to later days. Before he became a bishop he had been Archdeacon of Surrey, and his old Archdeaconry became a part of his later Bishopric of Winchester. At a meeting of the clergy at Clapham his chaplain told him that an old Dr. ——, who had been many years in the diocese, was vexed at having been forgotten. " Yes," said the Bishop, " I have not the smallest recollection of him, but I will make it all right, and will go and speak to him. Which is he ? " He was pointed out, and the Bishop made his way to him. " My dear Dr. ——, I have not had a moment for a real conversation with you.

I need not ask how *you* are after all these years. Do you still ride your grey mare ? " " Yes, my lord, how good of you to remember her," &c. &c. The chaplain, who was within earshot, said when he again came near the Bishop, " Then you *did* remember Dr. —— after all." " Not a bit of it," said the Bishop ; " I saw the grey hairs on his coat, and I *chanced the sex*."

Being so near Oxford I kept up my connection with that place, and indeed made one or two friendships with men I had not previously known, and improved some already made. Walter Short, with whom I became very intimate, was a friend of that year, whom I came to know through Henry Kingsley, and in Short's rooms I met Irving and Ormerod, who became two of my closest friends, though I had known Ormerod in a measure before.

I mention Short, Ormerod, and Kingsley here particularly, because through them I became acquainted with the phenomena of mesmerism, then so much discussed, and really so potent a power as an anæsthetic under operations, though its use in that way has been superseded by the discovery of chloroform. I found that I possessed considerable mesmeric powers, and that

Short was a singularly susceptible patient. I need not go into our experiments now, further than to say that of the phenomena generally called "mesmeric" I have no more doubt than that I am writing these words with my own hand. The powerful mesmeriser can influence his subjects at a distance when they are unconscious of his intentions, can bring about community of the sense of taste, and, in a considerable degree, of thought, can lull pain, and under certain circumstances produce organic change as in the condition of a tumour or stiff joint, and cause complete anæsthesia to surgical operations. What is called clairvoyance, which I have often seen, appears to me a combination of the thoughts transferred from the mesmeriser to his subject and ordinary dreaming, in which the patient talks in his sleep. I believe the whole affair to be purely physical, though I am unable to explain it. But I am sure the practice of it is attended with great danger, except in very careful hands. It has nothing, in my opinion, to do with any of the manifestations of "spiritualism" so called, which seem to be a mixture of imposture and hysteria.

Ormerod remains one of my dearest friends.

Short and I are very friendly when we meet, but time and distance have severed us a good deal. Harry Kingsley is dead. I rarely saw him in later life.

Martin Irving was a scholar of Balliol. He is the only son of Edward Irving, and a strong adherent to his father's opinions. With him and his family I became very intimate, and I saw much of the working of the Church to which he belonged. He is in Australia, and was for some time head of a large school at Melbourne; and though we rarely correspond, I know well that our affection each for the other is unaltered. When Mrs. Oliphant published her life of Edward Irving, Martin and his sister, Mrs. Gardiner, asked me to review the book, which I did in *Fraser's Magazine*, chiefly in order that I might counteract what she said of Mrs. Irving. Her whole notice of the lady was most disparaging. Through Martin, I had come to know his mother well. There was no house in London at which in my visits I was more warmly welcomed, and I grew to have a very cordial feeling for my friend's mother. She had adopted her husband's views in their entirety, and after her husband's death she followed every development of the doctrine and ritual of the Irvingite Church. On account of this she is represented as a woman of no intellect, who had really forced Irving to carry out an engagement made without sufficient thought, and as being altogether unworthy of him. There never was a greater mistake. It is perfectly true that an impressionable man like Irving had more than one fleeting fancy; but at the same time he was genuinely in love with his wife, a woman of very remarkable intellect, and their life was thoroughly happy. Mrs. Oliphant's disparaging view arose from the fact that her only knowledge of the lady was derived from Mrs. Carlyle, to whom, as Jane Welsh, both Irving and Carlyle had acted as tutor. Jane Welsh refused Irving and accepted Carlyle, but the lady never forgave the wife of her first love. She and Carlyle both detested all the peculiarities of the Catholic Apostolic Church, and laid the whole blame on Mrs. Irving, as can be easily noticed, so far as Carlyle is concerned, by any one who reads his beautiful biographical notice of Edward Irving. I ought in fairness, however, to add that Mrs. Procter, a keen observer, did not think Mrs. Irving at all the equal of her distinguished husband ; but that lady, sharp as she was both in eye and tongue, was seldom able to be or seem to be tolerant to others of her own sex. The Catholic Apostolic Church is an interesting experiment in church making, but is confined to a few adherents, and seems to be dying out. I cannot say I was ever attracted by the special characteristics of that Church, though its members, more than most people I have known, lived up to their principles. They really were in daily expectation of the immediate second coming of the Lord. Martin Irving is now an "Angel" or bishop of his church. He was in England in 1897, as youthful in spirit, as believing and as true a friend as ever.

I remained at Tew more than a year—a pleasant time, during which the Keatings paid me a visit, staying at the little village inn. My sisters were my guests more than once. Boyle, Short, Percy Smith, Edward Goodlake, Charlie Russell, and others paid me visits. I liked my work, and my parishioners liked me. At Easter 1852 the Bishop came to confirm at Tew, and asked me if I would take the sole charge of

Bloxham, a very large village near Banbury, and about six miles from Tew. The circumstances of the place were curious. The incumbent was over ninety, the curate over seventy. The manner in which the services had been performed had been a scandal for many years, and in days of revived interest in Church matters there was a cry for reform all through the neighbourhood. The scenes which took place in the church were almost incredible. The wine at the communion was put on the table in a black bottle, and on one occasion the cork had not been drawn. Mr. Bell, the vicar, turned to the intending communicants, as they knelt at the rails, and asked, "Has any lady or gentleman a corkscrew?" This implement having been obtained (I fancy from the public-house opposite, where stimulants were occasionally procured for the aged curate during the sermon), the service proceeded. The rite was only administered at Christmas, on Good Friday, and on Easter Day. A very worthy old woman, Mrs. Boffin, a lace-maker, went one Easter Day. When the rector drew near her at the rails, he said, "Hallo, Mrs. Boffin, you here again! Why, I gave it to you on Friday; I

am not going to give it to you again; go away!"
which the poor woman did, with many tears.
She told me the story, which I ascertained to
be quite true, as a reason for having ceased to
be a communicant. These and other scandals
which would be tedious to tell brought down
the Bishop on Mr. Bell, who to avoid legal
proceedings gave up the whole parish into the
Bishop's hands, to put in his own curate. I
asked the Bishop what were to be my relations
to Mr. Bell. "Nothing but to be civil to him,"
was the reply, and on those terms I accepted
the curacy. Mr. Sanders, the curate, was even
more infirm than Mr. Bell, and was only too
glad to resign, some small pension being secured
to him through the Bishop. I had not long
to be civil to Mr. Bell, for he caught cold,
and after a very short illness died on the
day I took possession, and the first duty I had
was to bury him.

This was an extremely awkward incident.
I had taken a small house for a year, which
I had furnished, and there was a prospect of
being turned out at once, since of course the
Bishop's arrangement was not binding on any
new incumbent. I heard, however, from Eton,

the living being in the gift of that college, that the Provost intended to offer it to a friend who was a chaplain in India, and he, if he accepted it, could not enter on it for nearly twelve months, so that even if he did not, I was to be in charge through the summer.

My work at Bloxham was singularly happy. The place had been so neglected that the people were glad to have any one to take interest in them; the few church-people left were delighted with decent services. My preaching, for I wrote my sermons with care, was at any rate fresher and more intelligible than that to which the people had been accustomed. Instead of some twenty persons, the congregation soon filled the large church. I was still a deacon, and there was some little difficulty in carrying out the Bishop's desire that I should institute monthly communions; but Mr. Wilson, the vicar of Banbury, of which town my friend Vernon Blake was curate, was extremely kind in allowing me to exchange duties on the necessary days with one of his staff.

The neighbours were very civil, and with one family in the village my relations were close and cordial. Mr. John Harman, a brewer at

Banbury, lived with his mother and sister at Bloxham, and became my intimate friend. We did not agree in church matters, he was low and I broad-high; but he knew how much depended on the church being worked decently, and he always gave me his warm support.

Among the clergy round who helped me much was the Rev. Philip Hookins, whose vigorous sermons were a refreshing change to me, who heard few other than my own. The oddities of his style came quite naturally to him; and he by no means sought for singularity, though he attained it. One sermon that he preached in aid of the schools ended thus: "And mind you, you who can must give gold, none of your paltry half-crowns for me, unless you expect what is impossible, half a crown in Heaven and half a palm branch."

I was ordained priest on Trinity Sunday, with no diminution of the fervour and eagerness with which I had been ordained deacon. I do not remember whether it was on my ordination as deacon or as priest that Kingsley made great fun of the Bishop's arrangements—a procession through the palace grounds, not as an orderly way of going from point to point, but as a service in itself, and nothing to proceed with, as Catholics carry the Host. The Bishop at that time told me the Provost now thought his friend in India would not take the living, and if not, he did not intend to exercise his right of presentation ; in which case it would fall to Mr. Bethell, and that he should be glad if Mr. Bethell could be induced to present me. My father, who was in London, went to Eton and saw Mr. Bethell, who was very favourably inclined, and for some time it seemed possible that I should stay at Bloxham. The Provost, however, once more changed his mind, and appointed his cousin, the Rev. James Hodgson, to be vicar of Bloxham. I spent the summer at Bloxham——I was there exactly six months ——and it was memorable to me from family matters. Then came the final break-up of our home at Wellow, when my elder sisters made a home with our uncle and aunt in Bath.

I was now in great doubt what was to be my next move. The Bishop, who had been kind about Bloxham, exerted himself to find me another curacy ; and by his advice I applied to Mr. Morrell, rector of Henley, for the post of senior curate, which he agreed to give me. He heard, however, of my having attended a meeting presided over by F. D. Maurice, at which Charles Kingsley was one of the speakers, and grew frightened at my opinions, or what he supposed them to be, and threw me over at the last. At this juncture I heard that a gentleman residing abroad with his family wanted a tutor in orders for his two elder boys, and as I had never been abroad, and needed change and rest, I offered myself for the post and was accepted.

I left Bloxham and Oxfordshire with much regret, and believe that if I had remained there as vicar, I might have stiffened down into a permanent high churchman, unconscious of the stir of life around. While the occupations of the clergyman of a small parish are not enough to fill his time, and I had many hours on my hands at Tew, Bloxham would have given me little leisure for reading or thought. It is an important place, and I should have probably been much absorbed in diocesan and preaching work, so that my whole course would have been different. In those two curacies I learned to know the English poor well, and to have a deep sympathy with them. They are not stolid and stupid, as is so often assumed. What they lack is book-learning, but for one who can talk their language and understand their thoughts, there is much to repay the attempt to know them better. There is scarce any limit to the influence which an unmarried clergyman, living with and for his people, may not exercise over his young men. But then the English Church does not train her parsons for celibacy, and the Roman Church alone has the secret of such training. I hope and think my time as a country curate was profitably spent : it was certainly one of great happiness. I had now settled down into that phase of thought which seemed to satisfy me. I was a latitudinarian in teaching, and a high churchman in external observances ; the controversy between the Churches had ceased to interest me, and there was no reason to suppose I should adopt other opinions than those into which I had drifted.

What is now called "Ritualism" was un- known, most of us were old-fashioned high churchmen. Very few held daily services, and a good many still preached in black gowns : even the stole was looked upon as something remarkable. I imagine that my father's mode of conducting service was the use of all the churches in the neighbourhood, though I never attended one. Hymn-books were unknown, and such singing as took place was confined to the version of the psalms at the end of the Prayer Book ; and the selection of these was as often as not left to the parish clerk. The Rev. Richard Palairet, vicar of Philip's Norton, became engaged to a lady during his holiday, and when the service was over on the Sunday morning after his return the clerk said, "I hope you were pleased, sir, with the selection of psalms this morning." "Yes," said Mr. Palairet, "I saw nothing to notice in them." "O sir, we selected them out of compliment to you, hearing as you were going to be married ; the first was—

> ' My soul with grateful thoughts of love,
>   Entirely is possessed.' "

Wilson, of Banbury, it is true, had daily service, but his father, Dr. Wilson, a clergyman also, was a pronounced Evangelical of the old school. He was Squire of Worton, and had given the living to Mr. Lancaster, an Oxford don, also of the old school, who shared with Tatham of

Lincoln the credit of the story that he wished, in the University pulpit, "that Jarman theology and Jarman philosophy were at the bottom of the Jarman Ocean."

Once at Dr. Wilson's a missionary was present who gave a very bright picture of the climes in which he had laboured. "And why should not I go too?" said old Mr. Lancaster; "I'll take a young wife, I'll renew my youth." "But what of Mrs. Lancaster?" was demanded —the old lady was quietly knitting at his side— "Oh, Nancy, poor fool, I quite forgot Nancy!" was the amazing answer. Of the Wilson family at Worton, Bishop Wilson of Calcutta was a hero and evangelical Pontiff. In after years I knew intimately many people who had lived in Calcutta during his bishopric, amongst them relatives of my own. He was a most grotesque old man, and the stories told of him would seem almost incredible, were they not so well attested. I may give one which reached me from two independent sources, both ear and eye-witnesses. Dr. M'Dougall came up to Calcutta to his consecration as Anglican bishop of Labuan. Bishop Wilson hospitably entertained a large number of the chief Indian officials at dinner the evening before, and on this occasion Dr. M'Dougall's spirits were as uproarious as usual, combining the characteristics of the medical student, which had been his previous calling, with those of a spiritual pastor. Bishop Wilson, as was his invariable custom, had family prayers before his friends left, and prayed extempore for the company present. He ended with the prayer, "That the Viceroy might properly fulfil the duties of his high office; that the Chief Justice (who was present) might administer the law righteously," &c. &c., and ended with praying, "Bless, O Lord, this our brother, on whom, after the example of the Holy Apostles, we are to-morrow to lay our hands; may he be delivered from all sins which most easily beset him, especially from that of 'inordinate jocularity.'" The prayer was interrupted by a shout of laughter from the corner where M'Dougall was kneeling, and the proceedings were brought to an untimely end.

I joined my pupils' father in London early in the autumn of 1852, and started with him via Paris and Strassburg to meet the rest of the family, including my pupils, at Carlsruhe, where we were to winter.

I am not sure that my next year was usefully spent. A governess would have done equally well for my pupils; while the life in a family, living economically abroad, and with few opportunities of mixing with intelligent people, was not so improving as it should have been.

Carlsruhe was then a terribly dull place. The Grand Duke was mad and the Prince Regent unmarried. The dynasty had not long been restored after the revolution of 1848, and the Regent had not forgotten that he had been thrown out of the barrack window in that stormy time. The town, depending on the Court as it did, was still duller than it would have been in ordinary years, for the theatre had been burnt down and was not yet rebuilt. I spoke no German, though I began at once to take lessons; and the residents were not given to much civility, had I been able to speak their tongue. There were no other English people in the place, and my employers were no companions. The father was a pompous person, absorbed in the contemplation of his own imaginary greatness; his wife a very sweet and charming woman, but afraid of him, not in strong health, and much occupied. The governess was a foolish, touchy little woman, who much resented the fact that I dined late, while she dined early with her pupils. The children made amends for a great deal. My pupils were nice boys, and the little girls delightful. There was also a family of Hoffmann, who lived in the same house on the floor above us, whom I visited a good deal, and I made a few friends in the town, notably an *attaché* from Vienna, Baron von Reichenbach, with whom I took a few walks. But for the most part my life was extremely dreary, and as the season was a very open one, we had not even the skating and sleighing which sometimes lend life and animation to a German winter. The pleasantest part of my stay in Carlsruhe is connected with the music and services in the great Catholic church. I made acquaintance with some of the priests, and was in a degree enabled to understand the rites I saw there.

At Christmas in that year I went to Wiesbaden to stay with my friends the Raymonds, and saw something of gay family German life. They were living in the house of Herr Hergenhahn, who had been Prime Minister to the Duchy of Nassau, whose family were courteous,

N

cultivated people; and there I saw my first Christmas tree, an entertainment not then naturalised and vulgarised in England. Thence I went to a village near Coblentz to spend a day or two with Colonel and Mrs. Moore, Mrs. Campbell's father and mother. She had died in childbirth soon after I left Tew, and the old people were glad to see any one who had known her. They were living in an English boarding-house, and only Trollope, or still more his mother, Mrs. Trollope, could do justice to the comic vulgarity of such an establishment.

I returned to Carlsruhe to find that with spring weather we were to go to Constance, and our move accordingly took place in April. We lived in a great house on the lake and opposite the Hecht Hotel, then kept by a very good fellow who had a villa some way off on the shore to which we used often to row on summer evenings. The stay at Constance was most pleasant, and I shall always look back on it with delight. Two acquaintances which I made there were especially pleasant, Fraülein Marie Ellenrieder, an old lady who was Hofmälerin to the Baden Court, and indeed, independently of that titular certificate, a charming painter and most interesting woman. Her work is but little known in England, and I think that a picture which the Queen has at Windsor, in the private apartments, of Saint Felicitas and her seven sons, and a little sketch in my possession, an infant Jesus with the Cross, may be the only ones in this country. But she is much appreciated in her own part of the world, and many of the churches in Baden have her works. The large martyrdom of Saint Stephen in the Catholic church at Carlsruhe, over the high altar, is by her. By the time we got to Constance I was fairly fluent in German, and I used to spend a long time with the old lady when she was painting. Our conversations almost always ended with the words, "Ah, Herr Paul, what a pity it is that you are not a Catholic."

My other friend was Colonel Johnson, of the Guards, an old Waterloo officer, at which battle he had been one of the youngest combatants. He was at that time an old bachelor, though he afterwards married a very elderly dame, Lady Eleanor Featherstonhaugh. He and I used to pace for hours at night the path overlooking

the lake, between it and a swift stream which bounded our garden, and on the old covered wooden bridge. The one is now filled up, the other destroyed by the railway. Colonel Johnson was extremely well-read, especially in poetry, and he had a good memory, so that when the conversation flagged, or anything I said set him off, he would quote Pope, Byron, or Scott literally by the canto ; and I trace my still enthusiastic admiration for Pope chiefly to the long recitations and discussions with the Colonel.

Here, too, I made the casual acquaintance of an Irishman, afterwards M.P., a man of about my own age, who was then, by no means for the first or last time, in hiding from his creditors. He was a most amusing fellow, and joined us often in our evening walks. He told one good story, which I have no reason to doubt, of his experiences at a Catholic college. I was asking him about Confession, and how far it upheld discipline. He told me that the Chaplain was the Confessor, and that when **any** sin affecting school discipline was confessed, the penance inflicted was that the penitent should **go** and admit it, *not* under the seal of **confes-**

sion, to the Rector. On one occasion he had
done something or other which would infallibly
have necessitated his removal from the college
had it come to the Rector's ears. Being therefore quite aware that any priest must hear a
confession if the penitent insists, he went
directly to the Rector, and begged him to hear
his confession, to which he consented, but with
some demur. When the grave matter in question
came out, the reason for this selection was apparent. The Rector could not know out of confession what he knew already in confession, and
there was no higher authority to whom to send
his penitent ; thus he was placed in the position
of the Lord of the Unjust Steward, who could
not but commend him because he had done so
wisely. " Go along wid ye, ye young divil,"
were the words with which the narrator said he
was dismissed, but it is probable that he unconsciously translated into Irish those which were
actually spoken.

In the early summer, through the absence
of their parents in England, I was left in sole
charge of the boys, and the governess was in
charge of the girls and younger children. The
boys and I dined at the hotel *table-d'hôte* for the

most part, but we were a good deal away on excursions in the neighbourhood. I remember with especial delight a week spent at Schaff-hausen. It was soon after our return thence, still in the early summer, that I was attacked by a serious fever, which I now believe to have been typhoid. I was very ill and had no proper doctor, for the Italian practising in Constance evidently knew nothing of the case, nor proper nursing, for the children's nurse could not neglect her charges for me, and no one dreamt, I less than any, of the need of a trained nurse. However, with days of semi-delirium and wretchedness, I got through the fever, and was left terribly weak, which made it quite necessary for me to throw up my tutorship.

At this juncture I heard from my old tutor at Eton, who had now become head-master, that a conductship or chaplaincy was vacant, to which was attached the curacy of the parish of Eton, and that he had suggested me to the Provost to fill the post.

I accepted it with pleasure, and agreed to enter on my duties in the following November, when it was convenient to Mr. Harrison, my predecessor, to leave Eton and the house, near the cemetery, which I was to occupy. I took leave of my employers with much friendliness, and being still extremely weak, adopted the way which gave me most water travel, going to Heilbronn, then down the Necker and Rhine. I was really too ill to enjoy either, and could not leave the steamer at Heidelberg. On my arrival in England I went to Weymouth, where I soon grew stronger.

In September I paid a long visit to the Harmans at Bloxham, taking the duty for a while at Mr. Harrison's new living about ten miles off, to which John Harman drove me. Hodgson was administering the parish with much High Church vigour, but by no means acceptably to the people, and was busying himself with a college founded by his curate, Mr. Hewett, which was to be a second Radley, but failed lugubriously. In other hands, and with all connection with the Parish Church severed, it is doing well enough as a secondary school. I sent my brother Willie there for a time, till I could have him with me at Eton or arrange to send him to an Eton dame's. Hodgson was maintaining a daily service single-handed, which I undertook to keep up while he took a holiday,

Harman's house being close at hand. This had
been a great tie, and Hodgson had scarce gone
beyond the bounds of the village for a year and
more. I remember the delight with which he
started on his holiday with the words, " I'm
so much obliged to you. Please God, I won't
go to church for a month." He made other
arrangements for his Sunday duty.

VII

CONDUCT OF ETON AND MASTER
IN COLLEGE

1853–1862

IT was arranged that my elder sister should come to me at Eton and keep house for me as soon as my house there was ready. My old tutor asked me to come and stay with him for as long as I pleased. I accepted his invitation, and entered on my duties at Eton on November 5th, 1853. There were then two conducts, who shared between them the whole parish work and the services in the Chapel of Ease—St. John's Church was not then built —and in the schoolroom at Eton Wick ; we took alternate weeks in the College Chapel, and had our districts in the parish. My colleague, Mr. Marshall, was easy enough to get on with, though we never became intimate. The house near the cemetery, then half the size it now is, just held us with one spare room. All the people at Eton were extremely kind, and I liked my new work well. I was near enough to see a great deal of my dear friend Charles Kingsley, and except that it was very hard to live on my small stipend of £120 a year, my time at the Cottage was a happy one. The small sum which came to me at my dear mother's death was partially spent in starting me in life, and I had also lent a considerable portion to my father. I thought all along it was a gift, and so it proved. Let it be distinctly understood, however, that I do not blame my father. He was always sanguine, and fully believed that he would be able to repay my loan. He believed, and so did I, that the sum was properly secured to me at his death; that it was not so secured was not his fault.

My next summer holidays after I went to Eton were spent in Wales. Martin Irving took a reading party with him to Aber near Bangor, and invited me to share their lodgings. Walter Short was of the party, and the stay was in every way pleasant. I was glad to have time for reading while the others were hard at work, and our afternoon excursions up the mountain, Carnedd Llewellyn, which lay immediately behind us, gave us plenty of vigorous exercise. I had then for some considerable time adopted a vegetarian diet, and was pleased to find that my powers of endurance were quite equal to those of the rest of the party. My belief in the possibilities of that diet are as great as ever, but the difficulties of carrying out such a mode of life in a flesh-eating community, unless one live a hermit life, are great. I have more than once adopted it since, once for two years; and each time I abandoned it with regret, through stress of difficulty in getting anything to eat without discomposing the habits of all around me. It has never been a matter of conscience to me, as for many years past total abstinence from strong drink has been; but I still think with Mrs. Anna Kingsford that abstinence from flesh of all kinds may be called, " The perfect way in diet."

My stay in Wales is ever memorable to me, however, from my having there read the book which did much to shake my faith in revealed religion. I do not remember what turned my attention to *Positivism*——it may have been my casual meeting with Dr. Congreve, with whom, when he was tutor at Wadham, I had been intimate at Oxford; but I was induced to study the *Philosophie Positive*, and took with me into Wales Miss Martineau's translation and abridgment of that work. It had on me a very great effect, but its leaven worked for some years without my knowing all that it had done. For nearly twenty years thereafter I believed I had accepted Comte's teaching only in politics and in social matters, that I was Positivist only as so many are at the present day, when the mode of thought which Comte formulated is in the air. It still seemed possible to be Positivist and Christian, even Christian priest, and I felt of Comte, then, what I feel now, in George Eliot's words: "that I would not submit to him my heart or my intellect." Though I still considered that the Church of England might be widened from the inside and made commensurate with English thought——though for twenty years to come I found it possible to remain within her boundaries, and that the " vivre pour autrui," Comte's great maxim, could best be carried out by me in the Church of Christ, whose principle was the same :—the study of the *Philosophie Positive* was the beginning of the end of my connection with the Established Church, and, for the time, with theology.

But if Comte's influence made me lose faith for a time, he did better for me than this. It may seem strange, but, till I did so under his direction, I had never read the *Imitation of Christ*. Comte bids all his followers meditate on this holy book, telling them to substitute humanity for God. The daily study of the *Imitation* for several years did more than aught else to bring me back to faith, and to bring faith back to me.

I had been a year at Eton when Hardisty, the master in college, who was assistant in the Lower School, took a boarding-house, and necessarily resigned his post. The head-master, with the Provost's consent, offered me the vacancy, which I accepted. This, in fact, had been his intention all along in bringing me to Eton. No salary was at first attached to it, but simply rooms in college, and a third Conduct was appointed in consequence of my withdrawal from a considerable part of my previous duties.

The mastership in college was a comparatively new appointment. Up to the year 1845, or thereabouts, when the new buildings were finished, the head-master was personally responsible for the care of the collegers. The real rule, or rather horrible tyranny, was administered by the sixth-form boys, and the head-master only occasionally appeared on the scene, preceded by a servant carrying a lantern. From certain windows his advent could be noted a minute or two before his arrival, time enough to put out of sight all that was illicit, and at one of these windows a fag was posted to keep watch. So thoroughly was this understood, that on very cold nights Dr. Keate had been known to send his compliments to the captain of the school to say he was not coming into college, in order that the poor little boy-watch might be relieved from his chilly post.

Hawtrey had rarely appeared on the scene, and when on one occasion he tasted the beer at the boys' supper and found it laced with gin, he only remarked, " Vile coachman's drink ! " and went his way without further comment. Anything more dangerous than the introduction of spirits *ad libitum* can hardly be imagined. The domestic comforts of the boys were looked after by an old woman for the little boys, and a man and his wife for the elders. These made the beds and tidied up the breakfast and tea-rooms rather less well than the same thing might be done in a workhouse ward. Each boy was apportioned to a dame, at whose house he was supposed to have a room in case of sickness; she sent his clothes to the wash, and had a general care of his health, but the dame rarely reserved the room she was bound to keep free for the use of her collegers. The sixth-form boys were allowed the use of a sitting-room " up town," a lodging, that is, for the day, over which no one whatever had the smallest control.

The state of bullying, discomfort, and misery in college was such that at the time when Hodgson stirred himself to provide new buildings for the collegers, only forty boys were found to avail themselves of the privileges meant for seventy, and those were appointed by nomination. The improvement was great, and the numbers rose. A keen competition was established for the election, and what was actually done was to give forty-nine boys each a small room as in Oppidan houses, keeping only twenty-one in the old long-chamber, all little boys. The rooms "up town" were abolished, the sixth-form boys were allowed to "stay out," that is, to be ill in their own rooms, if they were only suffering from some trivial ailment; but in all other respects the system remained the same. Abraham, who was then one of the younger masters, very generously offered to give up his boarding-house and live, or at least sleep, in college, and restore something like discipline; and no doubt some good was done, but the whole change was miserably inadequate, and it was resented by big boys who had enjoyed their lawlessness. It had come to be a tradition that "Tugs" were big and rough and brutal, and they did not like the civilising influence brought to bear on them.

Abraham after a time decided to cast in his lot with his friend Selwyn, who had become Bishop of New Zealand; he resigned his post to Marriott, who had been an old colleger and one of our lecturers at Exeter. For him rooms were made out of part of the old buildings, communicating with the college, like a rather larger set of Oxford rooms. But this was for him only a stepping-stone to a tutor's house, as it was with Hardisty, who succeeded him. The old "Tug" tradition remained in full force ; the master had no true authority, and Hardisty in going his rounds used to knock at a door before entering, and even suffered it without remonstrance to be locked against him.

The head-master, Goodford, wished that so far as possible the state of things in college should be conformed to that of an oppidan house, and therefore put me in, who knew nothing of and cared nothing for college traditions. There were considerable difficulties in my way, not the least of which was that the captain at the moment, who resented all changes, was one whose family I knew well at home. I need not, however, go into the means by which after a time discipline was restored and many grave abuses rectified, through all of which I had the general feeling of the boys with me. It is impossible to speak too gratefully of all that the boys were to me. I lived for them and with them, and thought of them only, and as a rule they were to me like

o

younger brothers and dear friends. I made some mistakes in character, but on the whole am glad to have trusted even bad boys as I did ; they were the better for being trusted, and but few abused the confidence I placed in them. Nothing could exceed the head-master's kindness to me in any difficulty ; he gave me the most constant support against any of my colleagues who thought me a dangerous innovator, and against some of the Fellows who feared I was too high a churchman.

Among the masters who gave me consistent and hearty support were Ottiwell Waterfield, Augustus Birch, and E. D. Stone. My good friend Edward Hale had not then a house, but afterwards when he had, he gave me a cordial and affectionate support. Certain lay masters, notably William Johnson and John Walford, turned over to me the preparation of their pupils for Confirmation, though a few others, namely Russell Day and Wolley Dod, considered that my religious influence was dangerous. As time went on my own collegers began to return as masters ; and one and all, I believe, administered their houses on the principle on which I had conducted college, giving me their most hearty support, notably Frank Cornish, whose friendship, begun when he was a boy in college, is among the most prized possessions of my life.

An illness which attacked a boy was among the causes which led to a reform of the arrangements in college. He was not at that time in the sixth-form, though he was only just below it ; he was feeling extremely ill, and told me how uncomfortable he was at his dame's, where no proper accommodation was provided for him, and asked my leave to stay in college. I could not give this, but obtained the head-master's permission that he should stay with me in my rooms, returning into college only at night. This was resented by his dame, who received a trifle extra for each day a boy "stayed out." When it appeared that the complaint was measles, he had of course to go to his dame's, but it brought prominently before the head-master that there were great discomforts and inconveniences attending the existing system.

It came to my knowledge that at the same dame's, in another serious case, no proper arrangement had been made for a boy of eighteen, but that when he was unable to leave

his room or even his bed, he had been placed
in the same room with a fourth-form boy, who
as best he could had to act as sick nurse. At
another boarding-house, a boy who broke his
leg had a pallet placed in the lady-housekeeper's
sitting-room, who continued to use it as such.
With the head-master's concurrence I embodied
these facts in a memorandum addressed to the
college ; and it was decided to build on the site
of the disused college stables proper rooms for
servants, to allow me to engage a housekeeper,
to provide rooms for boys staying out, and in
fact to make " college " into a proper boarding-
house. The authorities, however, with very
questionable economy, gave an exceedingly
small sum for all these arrangements, and the
class of servants we could get was not first
rate. Some of the rooms in the new buildings
were darkened by those erected for servants,
and the living arrangements for the collegers
are still susceptible of great improvement, if
indeed college as a separate institution ought
to exist at all.

I have no doubt that it would be far better
to distribute the money given in scholarships
among the school at large, and very probably

the scholars might be raised to the number of a hundred instead of seventy when the expenses of the master in college, the staff of servants, the college servants for hall, &c., were removed. This would infuse a spirit of work into the whole school, whereas at present the collegers are considered too much as a separate class, the oppidans having a certain right to be lazy. No salary was at first attached to the post I held, but I was allowed to take two private pupils, and did so. The experiment was by no means satisfactory; the boys belonged neither to me nor to their school tutor, and were a great hindrance to my work, however convenient on monetary grounds. After a while a definite though still inadequate salary was attached to the post of master in college.

Mrs. Marindin, the mother of one of my boys in college, had settled in Eton soon after her widowhood in 1851 in order to give her sons a cheaper education by removing the two eldest from the oppidan house in which they were, and keeping them at home. At her house, where I soon became very intimate, I met her sister, Margaret Agnes Colvile, who in 1856 became my wife. Before going back to Eton we paid our first and last visit to my father, who was then living at Warminster, having resigned Wellow and taken temporary duty till such time as a living in Ireland, shortly to be vacated and in the gift of a friend, should be ready for him. Mr. Keating was prepared to present me to Wellow, but that was for many reasons wholly out of the question, even had I liked Wellow, which I never did, not thinking it at all a desirable living.

We took up our work at Eton again at the beginning of the next school term, and soon afterwards were enabled to give up private pupils. Our house was most unfit for a married man's residence, especially as my wife's health proved far from strong; but we made it do for five years, and three children were born to us there. Margaret's life was not a cheerful one at Eton; she did not like the boys to whom my thought and life were so much devoted, and a wife in such a position was necessarily left much alone. I am quite convinced that an unmarried master is the fittest person to have the charge of boys in so confidential and brotherly a position as I filled with regard to mine. Mrs. Marindin left Eton when

her elder boys had done with the school, to
live at her own little property in Shropshire.
Our house was more and more unfit for a
family residence as children came ; and though
my own work had elements of delight and use-
fulness in it, far more than was the case elsewhere, it became clear that we should have to
move so soon as circumstances rendered this
possible.

My relations with the clergy in the neighbourhood were of the most cordial character,
though it became obvious to all who could
understand that my views were growing even
more liberal and less in accordance with any
of the great parties in the Church.   I suppose
that then and for many years onward they
were essentially those held by the more liberal
members of the Unitarian body.

I may here say that in my opinion the whole
theology of the almost extinct Broad Church
party is simply Unitarian.   Of course when a
distinction had to be made, it was possible to
make it by quoting Creeds and Devotions which
had been retained by the Church of England
from the old Catholic worship.   But what I
mean is that the sermons preached in Broad

Churches might have been delivered in any
Unitarian pulpits, and that Broad Churchmen
ignored as far as possible the Catholic side
of the teaching of the Church of England.
Unitarianism is, however, inconsistent and illo-
gical; the true contradictory of Catholicism is
Positivism, though I did not then see it.

The fact that my work tied me so closely at
Eton when the boys were there, and that in the
holidays Scotland and Bath had claims on us
kept me a good deal separate from Charles
Kingsley, and those of whom I saw most among
the clergy were Tom Carter, the rector of
Clewer, and Charles Eliot, the evangelical rector
of Binfield. I also saw much of Conyngham
Ellis of Brachnell. At Carter's request I was
for a time one of the Council of the House of
Mercy at Clewer, an interesting experiment,
but I have the strongest opinion, which grew
upon me from the day I was first associated
with it, that Rome alone with its organised
authority can manage religious houses of the
conventual sort. When the House of Mercy
was about to be established, Prince Albert,
who was much interested in all philanthropic
plans in the neighbourhood, sent for one of

those connected with the work and asked him
if he could account for the fact that Eton and
Windsor were said to be exceptionally bad
from a moral point of view. To this his
interlocutor had the courage to say, "I think,
sir, it is easily explained by the fact that
in those two towns there are two Barracks,
two Ecclesiastical Foundations, and a Court."
And the Prince did not resent this plain
speaking.

At Eton, as I have said, our three eldest
children were born, and during our stay there
my father and Mrs. Colvile died, so soon after
our eldest son's birth that none of my children
have ever known a grandparent. Mrs. Colvile
had long been in failing health, and we had
feared the end was near, in a visit we paid
her in Scotland during the summer of 1858.
Louis was born in the autumn, and a few days
after his birth Mrs. Colvile came up to London
extremely ill. She died about three weeks
afterwards.

On the break up of the Craigflower home,
for Sir James Colvile was on the point of
retiring from the Chief Justiceship of Bengal,
and was almost on his way to England when

his mother died, my sisters-in-law settled at Beaconsfield, within easy distance of us at Eton.

About 1860 a book was published, the fame of which was from accidental circumstances beyond its deserts, *Essays and Reviews.* For a few years past a series of Oxford essays and Cambridge essays had been published on subjects of interest to scholarly and thoughtful persons, and it was considered that a combination volume by Oxford and Cambridge men united on subjects bearing on the interpretation of Scripture would be of interest. The men who wrote were all liberals, but they had no common purpose or concert, except generally to bring out the results of modern criticism. Bishop Colenso's speculations were alarming the orthodox mind not a little, and German criticism was scarcely known in England. The book undoubtedly ran counter to many orthodox prejudices, though there is scarce a word in it which might not now be preached without fear or offence in any Protestant pulpit in England. Two essays, however, were specially singled out for attack, Mr. H. B. Wilson's and Dr. Rowland Williams', and they were made the subject of legal proceedings, with the result in both cases that the views held in them were declared tenable within the limits of the Church of England. The Convocation of the Province of Canterbury condemned the book, and all those who did not protest against it were considered heretical. The views expressed in it were in the main such as I had long held, and had been known to hold, but since I, almost alone in our clerical society, did not protest, together with the innocent fact of my buying the work at the sale of our Eton book-club, I became still more identified with those views in the sight of my neighbours and friends.

At this juncture Mr. Maurice, Tom Hughes, and others conceived the notion of starting a series of *Tracts for Priests and People* which, while putting forth liberal opinions, should yet tend to calm men's minds and show that it was possible within the Church to hold comprehensive views. Some of us met at Hughes' house, and certain subjects were assigned to those who were in sympathy with the plan. I undertook to write one on the Boundaries of the Church of England, and did so with the signature *C. K. P.* It was thought by my friends that having an official position at Eton it would be better not to put my full name, while my somewhat distinctive initials would leave no doubt as to the author on the minds of any who cared to know, and certainly the last thing I wished to do was to shirk any personal responsibility. The foolish printer, however, put *The Rev.* C. K. P., which just made it look as if I did so wish. My position in the tract was that the very minimum of dogma was required from lay members of the Church of England, that on them the Apostles' Creed only was binding, and that as interpreted by themselves ; I did not say a word to imply that was all *I* held—nor was it ; neither did I say that no more was required of the clergy, in fact, I made it very plain that from them far more was required. The tract, on looking at it now after all these years, seems to me a very harmless one to have been written by an Anglican, and in these days what is there said would be by many considered almost a truism.

But Provost Hawtrey, who was growing old and also failing in mind, was in a great fright about orthodoxy and *Essays and Reviews*, and was ready to take any alarm which was suggested to him. Roper, my colleague in the conductship, a dull, narrow, though pious man, with whom I had never been on cordial terms, thought it his duty to bring this tract before the Provost. The poor old man was in a great and immediate flurry, but it was difficult to see what he could do. He wrote to me, and I at once acknowledged the authorship of the tract ; when I asked in what it was objectionable he could only reply that he dissented from its whole tone. He called the head-master into council, who saw no reason for dismissing me ; he called a College meeting, at which the Provost was reminded that as conduct I was his curate, over whom the Fellows had no direct reponsibility, even if they cared to exercise it, and that as master in college the head-master saw no fault in me. He wrote to the Archbishop of Canterbury, to the Visitor, and to the Bishop of the Diocese, and the two first said they did not agree with the tract, but that I had a right to my opinions, and there was nothing that the Provost could do or ought to do.

The Bishop of Oxford, Wilberforce, took a very different line. Always anxious to please any one in power, he wrote to the Provost a letter full of the most unmeasured abuse of my tract. There were no words bad enough for it or for me, but he lamented that in the then state of the Church it was impossible to prosecute me, and he deeply sympathised with the Provost, who must let me alone. This letter the Bishop marked " private," evidently thinking that while he would gratify the Provost by agreeing with him, I should never know the charges of heresy and unbelief he made against me behind my back. But the Provost, whose mind was, as I have said, weakened, and whose health was failing, did not see the matter in that light; and sending for me, said, "I have received a letter from the Bishop, which, as he has marked it 'private,' I may not show you, but I am justified in reading it to you, which I will therefore do." The effect of this was of course only to manifest the Bishop's duplicity; the practical result was *nil*.

My colleagues were kind and sympathetic, and I shall always remember with gratitude that William Johnson wrote me that his purse and person were entirely at my disposal. It is of course uncertain what the Provost might ultimately have decided to do, probably the affair would have blown over, but his illness rapidly increased and he died early in 1862. Almost at the same time Mr. Heathcote, Wilder's brother-in-law, vicar of Sturminster Marshall, was promoted to a better living, and I had the offer of Sturminster from the College, a fact which shows how little the other members of it had shared in the Provost's dread of my views. The Vice Provost asked me to explain that I had not in my tract asserted that the clergy had an equal right to the latitude I had claimed for the laity, and this I had no hesitation in doing. I heard afterwards that an attempt had been made to show that this was a recantation, and I had to write and assert that it was nothing of the sort. Meanwhile the Bishop of Salisbury, who had heard of the late Provost's fears, wrote to know if it were possible to keep a heretic out of his diocese, and was assured by the College that the majority of the members had not considered me heretical. It was no doubt a trial to Bishop Hamilton that Sturminster Marshall of all places should fall to me. For Heathcote was one of the Bishop's most trusted advisers, and it was in his study that the prosecution of Dr. Rowland

Williams for heresy had been arranged. However, the College deciding to present, and the Bishop deciding not to oppose, the living, as I said, was offered to me, and I went to visit it. I joined my visit with a run to Bath to be present at the fiftieth wedding day of my uncle and aunt.

I should not have cared to leave Eton, but that the birth of a third child intensified the great discomfort of our rooms in college. Moreover, these, such as they were, would yet further be restricted. For the late Provost had allowed me to fit up a disused room for my servants under Election Chamber, really belonging to the Lodge, and this was required for the household of the new Provost. This was Goodford, late head-master, in whose place Balston was appointed, a narrow-minded person, pedantic and little read, who began at once to undo what Goodford had done, and it was clear my work under him would be far from congenial. I accepted Sturminster therefore, and determined to leave Eton at Easter.

I look back to my Eton days as those of my life in which I was of distinct use. I might have done more if I had had no parish work, but had joined to the office of conduct, as I wished and suggested, the librarianship of the college library. This was always held by one of the Fellows, and was a completely sinecure office : the library being of very little use to any one. Dr. Goodford and I were almost the only persons who ever took out books, and I, after many struggles with the late Provost, had only been grudgingly allowed to use Dr. Goodford's key. Now I believe the masters are all permitted access to the library.

During the time that I remained as master in college, after the departure of the few boys who at first resisted my authority, I had nothing but cordial assistance and loyalty from the whole of those placed under my charge. They were, as far as intellect was concerned, the pick of the school, and mostly hard workers. It seems hardly fair, when all were so kind, to pick out any for special notice, as time and place have severed me so widely from those over whom I then bore rule. But I cannot refuse myself the pleasure of naming a few of whom I did not lose sight afterwards. H. J. Nelson, afterwards a judge in India, who died at home in 1898, was one of those who, though not popular with his schoolfellows or with the masters, was always most true and courteous to me ; and among those I knew most intimately from the time I went into college, his was the most mature intellect with which I ever came into contact in a boy of his age, and there was scarcely anything he might not have done. He, Frank Warre-Cornish, now Vice Provost of Eton, Augustus Austen Leigh, Provost of King's, Felix Cobbold, and Sir William Young, Fellows of the same college, are those of whom I think with greatest regard. I was a very young master, and they—or most of them —were senior boys at the time, so that the difference between us was not so great as might seem from our respective positions.

When I left Eton the great majority of boys in college combined to give me a very handsome salver in remembrance of our long association. I knew nothing of this until it was actually presented, and therefore was unable to put a stop to it. One of the tradesmen, however, told me that it was in the minds of a number of the townspeople to give me also a testimonial, but owing to his kind offices this plan was nipped in the bud. I have a very strong feeling that such gifts are a great mistake. They either come to be almost a necessary gift to any one who vacates an office, or they pronounce a judgment between two holders of it. It is, moreover, extremely difficult for those who do not wholly approve of such a gift to disassociate themselves from it, and it is often a heavy tax on the subscribers.

Here is the place to say a few words on those of my colleagues and others with whom I had most to do as master in college. Some of them had been masters when I was a boy, others came back as masters who had been under me as collegers, some of these again became better known to me when my elder son was at Eton; I am not sure if I can always separate the judgments framed at these different times.

Of Balston, head-master, I should mention that it was he who said of Provost Hawtrey, always a great book-collector, that "when he was made Provost, he would have time to read the books he had talked about all his life." He himself will perhaps be remembered, so long as he is remembered at all, as having said before the Public School Commission that he considered French was no necessary part of a gentleman's education.

Coleridge, Cookesley, and Young had all been masters when I was a boy, and I never became intimate with any of them. Cookesley, indeed, was extremely hostile to me, thinking me an advanced High Churchman, but he did me no harm.

William Johnson, who took afterwards the name of Cory, had left Eton as a boy about the time I went to Eton, and had come there as a master after I left it. I first made his acquaintance in London, he being one of those who came about Mr. Maurice. He welcomed my coming to Eton, and was one of the most remarkable men there: full of a wide interest in literature, and a man of most encyclopædic reading. He had given up his boarding-house when I went back to Eton to his sister, Mrs. Vidal, and occupied bachelor rooms in what had been the "Old Christopher Inn," communicating with Mrs. Vidal's house. My intimacy with Johnson was at once close and fitful. He and I took very different views of some boys who were his pupils, but under my charge in college, and he thought it therefore

best that each of us should go his way independent of the other. When, however, I came
into trouble with Hawtrey on account of my
theological opinions, Johnson wrote me a most
cordial letter, in which, as I have noted, he
placed himself and his purse entirely at my
disposition. He afterwards retired from Eton on
a competence and lived on his family property
in North Devon, but beyond his means, both in
regard to expenditure on the estate and in
munificence to others. He fell into ill-health
and retired to Madeira, where he married
a very young woman, the daughter of one of
his Devon neighbours. When he was able to
return to England he lived a secluded life at
Hampstead, finding his great occupation and
delight in teaching a few young ladies, mainly
the daughters of former friends. He died
after much suffering in 1892, leaving an only
son. Mrs. Cory became a Catholic a few
years before his death. Cory, himself long a
very unorthodox man, became a moderate High
Church Anglican. Not long before his death his
wife suggested he should see one of the Domini-
can Fathers, but he said, "It is too late now,
and I must be satisfied with the religion which

was enough for my mother." His death left a void in the hearts of many who will always remember him with deep affection; but he left little to show those who did not know him what he was. A fragmentary *History of England* in the early years of this century, written for an imaginary Hindoo pupil, is full of brilliant wit and profound learning, but is known to few. He also left some of the choicest lyrics in the language, embedded among many not so good, in a little anonymous volume called "Ionica." It is difficult to say enough and not too much in regret for one so dear, so brilliant, and so incomplete.

Edward Hale, who came to Eton as assistant mathematical master, or rather, as he then was, assistant to Stephen Hawtrey, somewhat before my own return, always, till his untimely death in 1893, my great and kind friend, was the very opposite in every way of William Cory. He was known to and beloved by all, not a student, nor a man of deep knowledge, but a good talker on most subjects, and popular with every one; a gossip, but always good-natured, master of a full and favourite house, an affectionate husband and father, he was the very type of a broad Anglican clergyman, a hard worker, a good preacher, not especially orthodox, but quite satisfied with his position. He had been curate to Stephen Hawtrey at Holy Trinity Church, Windsor, and a painstaking clergyman in some of the worst districts in the town. To his friends and colleagues he was always genial and kind. He was invariably a good influence in Eton life, ever tolerant, and casting his influence on the side of right.

William Wayte was one of my constant companions. He was as learned as Johnson, but lived more with his fellows, being a sociable man, always ready for walks. His knowledge was so great and accessible that it came to be a saying in any difficulty, " We must look it out in Wayte," as though he had been a dictionary, and we always found the information required. With Wayte and C. C. James—I forget who was the fourth—I read in the evenings during my first year in college Dante's *Divina Commedia*. Wayte was a strong Whig in politics, one of the few real Whigs I have known, and a Liberal in Church matters. He retired while yet in the vigour of his age and devoted himself to active literary work in London.

With these of whom I have spoken I was in much sympathy as well as in constant intercourse; there were others of whom I saw a good deal, but who opposed me, distrusting the influence I had on their pupils. Among them Wolley Dod was perhaps the one whom I liked the best, as being always honest and outspoken. He often disapproved very strongly of sermons delivered by me in the college chapel, not on the ground that he personally disagreed with them, but because they were not in accord with the traditional tone of safe Anglicanism which he considered should be held by a teacher at Eton. His whole tone was lay rather than clerical, and except that he thought it his duty always *quieta non movere*, he had no views or enthusiasms about his work.

John Walford represented the active High Church party among the masters. After he left Eton he became a Jesuit priest. I cannot do better than repeat what I said at the request of his brethren for a collection of notes privately printed by them.

My dear friend John Thomas Walford came to

Eton as a King's Scholar just as I was leaving the school, and I only then saw him once or twice. He was a bright-eyed, fresh-coloured boy of good manners and excellent character. Dr. Goodford —his former tutor—who always watched his career with interest, brought him back to Eton, well knowing that he would carry out the methods learned from his old tutor.

In due course Walford became Scholar and Fellow of King's College, Cambridge. At Eton he had profited much by his tutor's careful and accurate scholarship, but as he lived out of the house he had not been one of that inner ring of pupils who had the run of Goodford's library and owed so much of their taste for literature and modern languages to his wide and enthusiastic culture. The same was the case at King's. Walford's scholarship was fostered and increased, but the whole tendency of the learning at King's was classical, and Walford at no time had any considerable training in general literature, nor do I think that he was at any time a great reader. After taking a good degree he became for a short time an assistant-master at Harrow, but was soon after appointed to a similar post at Eton, at the time when assistant-masters were still usually drawn from the Fellows of King's.

From that time and for about eight years I was in close and constant relation with Walford. He had I think at that early date made up his mind to a celibate life. He felt very strongly that a good schoolmaster, whether clerical or lay, could do his duty better without tie of wife or family ; that in fact such an one must live for his boys alone, who should be always first in his thought.

And having made up his mind to this he did not take a boarding-house, always a lucrative if onerous position, but lived as a boarder in a dame's house, taking as pupils only those boys who themselves boarded in dames' houses or were King's Scholars. He was a most devoted tutor, and though, as I have said, not especially literary himself, he fostered a taste for literature in others.

I remember his bringing me with delight some poems written by one who in thought, heart, and intention was a Catholic, but cut off by too early death before his intention could be carried into act ; and this early literary promise was watched with enthusiastic hope by Walford.

He went little into general society at Eton, and was intimate with few of his colleagues, living for his boys ; but of those few he was a devoted and confidential friend. One cause of his isolation, for such it may be called, was that he soon became, in principle and practice alike, an extreme High Churchman, far beyond the point then considered correct at Eton. A moderate and decorous Anglicanism was all very well, but Walford soon became convinced that for boyish needs and for boyish sins confession and frequent communion were the only safeguard and cure, and working quietly and in his own way for the souls of his boys, he could not associate much with those who would not at all have agreed with his methods or his theories.

What he inculcated for others he practised himself, and one of the causes which brought him into the Church was the inadequacy of the manner in which the Sacrament of Penance was administered in the Anglican Communion, even by those who thought they did administer it. The incompleteness of the training which two men especially, both prominent clergymen, to whom he went to confession had had, their faltering advice, their burdensome and ill-considered penances, their over-scrupulous dealing with scruples, convinced him that these were not the appointed guides of his soul.

When I left Eton in 1862 to take a college living, and parted from Walford, I had not in any degree realised that the Church would and must be his goal. It had not seemed to him expedient to tell a colleague, who at that time differed considerably from his views, precisely what they were; but in his frequent letters, when we were not working in union, he was much more open, and the end became plain to me before it was so to himself. Indeed to him it became a vague possibility long before it became a certainty.

Goodford, our old tutor, had become Provost of Eton, and Dr. Balston was head-master. Walford went to him so soon as his doubts had attained any shape, and said he thought it wise to resign his mastership, because the time might come when he would have to join the Roman Church. Balston did not accept the resignation, but with a kindness and breadth of mind which were wholly unexpected, said he trusted Walford to resign when, and only when, the end became certain and not a possibility. He went on to ask that if Walford found it necessary to resign, he would promise not to become a Catholic for one year after leaving Eton. To this Walford agreed, reserving only the case of serious illness, saying that should he leave Eton with the intention of becoming a Catholic that intention must be carried out at once if he were in danger of death. I am not prepared to say how far he was right in making even the concession he did, I know only that it was made with the best intention and loyally kept. Some months after this promise was given the time came; the mastership was resigned with grief, and a sundering as of soul from body. He prepared himself by much seclusion and a long retreat, and just one year from the time of leaving Eton he was received into the Church in a religious house in Ireland.

His first visit was paid to me and my family at our home in Dorset. His plans were quite vague, but he believed he had a vocation to the priesthood—he had not taken Anglican orders—and he hoped again to take up teaching. Cardinal Newman offered him a mastership at Edgbaston, which he accepted with alacrity, and threw himself into the new work with interest all the keener because he had been for some time idle from what was so great a delight to him—the work of teaching and guiding the young.

His letters to me were full of the difference between Catholic schools and those of which he had experience, and he was greatly struck by the simple faith of the lads with whom he was now brought into contact. I remember his delight that a rather dull boy who was going up for matriculation at Oxford sent a sovereign to the Poor Clares, asking that they would pray for his success in the examination. He was also struck with the manliness of the Edgbaston boys and the fervent piety of many, the combination not having been frequent in his previous experience. The bearing of the Sacrament of Penance, not only on individual souls, but on the discipline and purity of school life, came to him like a revelation.

While happy in his work he felt little, if any, inclination to join the Oratorian Congregation. It seemed to him that his own need was that he should be under vows of obedience, not only under a strict rule from which he might free himself at any moment. He talked over his future life with Cardinal Newman, who, while expressing his entire satisfaction with Walford's work at the Oratory, said, " I think St. Ignatius wants you," and those words decided his fate.

He accepted all that came to him in his new life with the most absolute, unquestioning, and happy obedience. An instance of this seemed very striking to me when Edward Hale and I visited him at Manresa, during his novitiate. It was some weeks after the Clerkenwell explosion, and somehow the conversation worked round to it. " Ah," said Walford, " I am interested in what you say. I heard it when I was sweeping up the weeds in the garden, and wondered what it was." The self-discipline which prevented his ever asking what the cause of the noise and shock was, even in recreation time, seemed to us at the time very strange, but to the speaker it was a matter of course.

At Beaumont, at Malta, and elsewhere he did good work for education. I visited him at Beaumont, and was struck with the way in which he had introduced there also one of his Eton reforms. An Eton " pupil-room " was as a rule a bare and cheerless room, which made work in it unattractive——where boys naturally inked the floor and furniture, and cut their names surreptitiously on the desks. Walford had made his pupil-room pleasant to the eye, with prints on the walls and curtains to the windows, and had made it a matter of pride and honour with the boys to treat it as a gentleman's sitting-room. He gained permission to do the same at Beaumont, with, as he told me, a marked effect on the manners and taste of his pupils.

After his leaving Beaumont I saw Walford at distant intervals, only to find him sinking more and more into ill-health, which led me to doubt whether he was as useful to the society as the society had been to him. The fact was that he had entered late, he aged while yet young, and the best of his life had been given elsewhere. He returned to Manresa some years since, to be laid on the shelf and wait quietly for death. In ordinary intercourse with the friends who visited him the decline of his powers was painful. He was always pleasant and cheerful, but the conversation was merely anecdotical, comprising more or less trivial reminiscences of

old Eton days. If, however, he had to con-
centrate his attention, to write a letter on
spiritual matters, to give a retreat, or hear a
confession, it was wonderful how completely he
could pull himself together and become collected,
clear, alert-minded, and wise. But the reaction
after such effort was marked.

My last visit to him was when he was quite
confined to his invalid couch, was unable to say
Mass, had, I think, received extreme unction,
and was waiting patiently and hopefully for the
end. He was more himself than I had seen
him for some time, and sent his love, with the
assurance of his constant prayers, to a friend
whose conversion had long been a matter very
near his heart. He gave me his blessing, and
asked me to make a point of attending his requiem,
which when the time came I was unable to do,
through the accidental miscarriage of a letter.

I have paid a visit to Eton since his death,
and was glad to find his memory green in the
hearts of some who differed from him widely.
In my own he will always remain as a dear
friend of old, and one whose simple faith, and
no doubt also earnest prayers, aided me to
follow him into the fold.

It was a great pleasure to. me when Cornish came back to Eton as a master. As a boy, as a colleague, and now that I have long left Eton and he is Vice Provost, he was and is one of my very dearest friends. It is quite impossible to express in any poor words of mine my sense of his worth, his charm, his learning, and his friendship.

VICAR OF STURMINSTER MARSHALL, DORSET

1862–1874

STURMINSTER MARSHALL was a living of but small value. The vicarage, or rather Bailie House, which had become the vicarage, was an old farm-house, changed and improved by many incumbents, but dating in part, as was supposed, from Elizabeth's reign. It was a very rickety structure; with the exception of two or three rooms at the east end, it was thatched, a costly covering, and had large and expensive gardens. But it was a roomy and comfortable house, in which many previous vicars had taken pupils, and it was clear that I must do so too. We left Eton therefore at Easter 1862, with keen regret.

Mr. Kingdon, now I think a Colonial Anglican bishop somewhere in Africa, and at that time

Mr. Heathcote's curate, agreed to stay on for a while, for I had promised the Bishop to keep up, at least for the present, Mr. Heathcote's daily services, and I took a house first at Bournemouth and then at Wimborne till the needful repairs and alterations were made at Bailie. Kingdon, however, was called away by Heathcote much sooner than he expected, and I, bound by my promise to the Bishop, walked over to Sturminster from Wimborne every day for the 5 P.M. daily service, generally spending the day at Bailie to make acquaintance with my parishioners. Mr. Heathcote died suddenly very soon after Mr. Kingdon had joined him, and the dilapidations on Bailie were only partially paid, so that having undertaken considerable repairs on the strength of these I began my life there a good deal crippled financially.

The parish, on a nearer inspection, had not much to recommend it. It was situated on the river level, though a mile from the water, in the great gravel plain which forms the valley of the Stour. Though beautiful country was within reach from the tops of the hills, it was not pretty, and it was relaxing. The house and garden were attractive, but the mile from church was a great addition to work. The squire and the farmers were good souls in their way and after their lights, but they were narrow and bigoted in Tory opinions, and we never really got on well, with my strong views about the rights of the labourer, especially about his right to take his labour to the best market and to improve his condition when he could. The labourers were a decent, pleasant people in many ways, and the children were as a rule particularly engaging, and so were many of the young men. There was a good deal of drunkenness, but not more than usual in country parishes, and on the whole I was lucky in the people. They gave me hearty help in choir, they came well to church, and were always loyal and good to me. My heart will always warm to a Dorset peasant.

We settled into Bailie late in the summer, and I found two pupils at once, and others came shortly. Our first intention was to take small boys preparing for school, but I was gradually offered others, and by degrees dropped the small boys and took only those who had left school and were preparing for college or the army. I will not chronicle my pupils at length, there were few who really interested me, being in this respect sadly unlike the boys whom I had left at Eton. The position of a private tutor in the country is a pre-eminently unsatisfactory one. The boys are as a rule those who have not done well at school from vice or idleness, and go to a private tutor needing just that discipline which he of all men can give least. For there is no sanction of rewards and punishments, there is no tradition, there can be but few rules. The lads are in the family without the position of sons ; they generally lack employment when the lessons of the day are over. With a few exceptions, my boys were not vicious, but they were idle and for the most part dull ; they destroyed family life sadly. Pupils enabled us to live, and to live in comfort when we could not have existed on the income of the living, but I saved nothing, and I never knew a private tutor who did. For the whole living is necessarily pitched on an expensive scale for the boys, and it is impossible to keep a check on it. The boys, I think, liked me, but I had not the hold on them that I had on my Eton lads, and my tutor days are not satisfactory in the retro-spect. Yet it is difficult to say, even apart from the question of finance, what I could have done *but* take pupils, for most assuredly the work of a small country living is not enough for an active-minded man.

Through the whole of my life my great delight has been in trying to raise boys who came under my influence in the social scale. Nothing shows the innate conservatism of an Englishman more than the fact that so few escape from their surroundings ; and very often those who seem most charming when quite young fall back only too easily into their hereditary groove. Once when an Eton master was staying with me at Sturminster one of my parish school-boys came into my study and remained for some time in frank conversation with us. After his departure the Eton master said, " Now where, except that this lad speaks broad Dorset, is the differ-ence from an Eton boy ? " He has risen in life, not indeed so remarkably as I once ex-pected, but is one of the very few examples of a complete change of life.

The one instance of entire success in this

matter was the late John Sedding, the architect, who, when I first became acquainted with him, carried about rolls in a basket for his uncle, a baker, at Eton. John's father had been a schoolmaster at Bakewell, Derbyshire, and two of his sons, another besides John, rose to be architects and men of letters. John Sedding used to borrow books from me, and I noticed that each volume that he took away was a proof of yet higher and higher culture. At last I lent him Ruskin's *Seven Lamps of Architecture*, in which one of the illustrated pages had become loose ; he brought me back the book with a copy of the illustration, and I had to look closely at it for some time before I discovered which was the original and which the copy. Mr. Street, the architect, was coming down for the day, and I showed him the drawing, telling him how much I wished to raise John Sedding from his then position. He took him into his office. John Sedding became a successful architect, and at the same time, as I knew, he became a thorough gentleman. Whilst I was at Sturminster he wrote and asked me if he might come and see me. He did so ; and his object in coming was to request me to write to the father of the lady he wished to marry to tell him the whole story. This I did, and like a sensible man the father gave his consent to the marriage, which proved in every way a happy one.

The poor people of my parish interested me personally, as I have already stated ; I was also much struck by the dialect peculiar to that part of the country, and I may as well throw together some words used in it, of which it may be said it would be well if some of them might again find place in general use.

Beal, a weazel. "One of them guinea-pigs has been bitten by a *beal.*"

Crip, to talk finely, to "talk tall." "How he do *crip.*"

Fay means to do. Query *fait* from the French *faire.* "We'll just put it up and try it (some carpenter's work), and if we can't get it to *fay,* we'll take it down again."

"*Ferrule* of a book," means the corner. "Do you mean that one with the yellow *ferrule.*"

Gridger—cake, baked on a girdle, a flat, circular plate of iron used for that purpose.

"She is always on the *grig*," "very griggy," fretful.

"The *heel* of my hand," the ball of the thumb.

Neck, throat. "I'd never pour that stuff down my neck." That is, drink it.

"He is very *plasted* a'ready," said of a dead child, which would seem to mean swollen and decomposed.

"Why do you *quirk* so?"—call out suddenly.

"She will not *sess*" or "*cess* to it," meaning take to it.

"The *smiche* nearly choked me when I was *droshin*." The chaff nearly choked me when I was thrashing.

"Bird *starving*"—bird scaring.

"To *tail* a trap," to set or bait it.

"*Vinny*," mouldy. "The last mushroom spawn you got was all *vinny*." "Blue *vinny* cheese."

"I have a *west* coming in my eye." A stye.

Our neighbours were very humdrum folk as a rule, but all civil and kind. With the clergy I got on well for some years, in spite of many differences, and the Dorset Clerical Society, under the presidency of Mr. Dayman of Shillingstone, was a really pleasant and friendly business for some time. Only a few sets of friends became more than mere acquaintances—Mr. and Mrs. Bastard, Sir Percy and Lady Shelley, Mrs. Ritchie, Mr. and Mrs. Pike, and Colonel and Mrs. Sullivan. Mr. Bastard was an old-fashioned free-thinker, and his wife shared his opinions. He was an enthusiastic educational reformer, who built and endowed a school in Blandford, of which he made it a fundamental rule that no clergyman of any denomination was ever to be a trustee, nor was any religious teaching given, and these two points set all the clergy against him. He did much by money and influence to keep the *Westminster Review* going, and was a genuine Liberal in all ways. I need hardly say that he held himself aloof from all public worship. He died a year or two ago aged over a hundred, holding all his opinions unchanged.

Sir Percy and Lady Shelley lived at Boscombe Manor, near Bournemouth. He was the only surviving son of Shelley the poet, by his second marriage, with Mary Wollstonecraft Godwin. Those who did not know him well, and thought of Shelley only as a poet, could not understand that he should have been the son of such parents, but those who were intimate with him understood that there was a great vein of fancy and no small amount of literary skill in his nature ; nor were many aware that in Shelley the poet was a strong mechanical strain, which came out in a still more marked manner in the son. I was much attached to him, and found him always interesting and agreeable. His wife had been a Mrs. St. John, left a widow at an early age ; she married Sir Percy in his mother's lifetime, and, living with her as a most affectionate daughter, adopted all the Shelley and Mary traditions in their extremest form. In a room leading out of her own sitting-room at Boscombe were collected many memorials of Shelley and his friends—a copy of the Shelley tomb at Christchurch, many of the MSS. of his works, the book he had clasped in death, locks of his and of Byron's hair—and the whole was treated as though it had been a mortuary chapel with sacred relics.

After Mrs. Shelley's death, Sir Percy and Lady Shelley asked Mr. and Mrs. Esdaile (Ianthe, Harriet's daughter) to come and see them. They accepted, but stipulated that family matters should not be discussed. The morning after the arrival the hosts were obliged to go out for all the morning, and Mr. Esdaile went for a long walk. Lady Shelley, who remembered the story of Bluebeard, gave Mrs. Esdaile the key to the MSS. case, telling her she might read all except the journals in a certain drawer. These contained the true story of Harriet, as now told, correctly, by Professor Dowden. Of course Ianthe read them, and next day was impelled to tell Lady Shelley so, and that her whole view with regard to her father's conduct was changed.

On one of my visits to Boscombe Sir Percy showed me a large cabinet full of family papers, and offered to send it over to Bailie, in order that I might look them over. They consisted of a vast number of Godwin's letters, in part arranged by Mrs. Shelley, and such of the Shelley papers as were not in the Shelley room. These formed the materials for the *Life of Godwin*, which I published in 1876 with Sir Percy's full approval.

Another family with whom I became very intimate, were Mr. and Mrs. William Pike of Wareham. They were Unitarians and strong Liberals, and therefore quite out of the county and clerical society in which we were supposed to live ; but they were clever and well-read people, and Mrs. Pike became one of my greatest friends, while I had a cordial regard for her husband. He was engaged in large clay works in the neighbourhood, paying a royalty on the china clay found near Wareham, with a little private railway from the clay pits to Poole harbour, whence it was taken to the potteries. Mr. and Mrs. Pike were friends of Miss Muloch, afterwards Mrs. Craik, the novelist, who drew them in her work, *Agatha's Husband*.

Colonel and Mrs. Sullivan settled for a short time at Upper Henbury in Sturminster parish, and I looked with some alarm at their coming, knowing that Mrs. Sullivan was of pronounced evangelical opinions and a strong teetotaller. The very day after they settled at Henbury I received a note from Mrs. Sullivan asking me what I would do for the cause she had so much at heart. I told her I should be very glad if she could convert from drink any of my drunken parishioners, and mentioned some half-dozen names which I thought might be useful to her. In about a week she came and said I had not given the names of several to whom she had spoken with effect. I said that though it was possible that they occasionally drank too much, I had no reason to think that they were habitually intemperate. " You do not think they would tell you, who are not an abstainer, their trouble ; they tell me because I am !" I found this to be so true that having lent my school for a temperance meeting I became an abstainer myself, and have never regretted it in the twenty-seven years that have passed since that date. Mrs. Sullivan became one of my best and kindest friends.

I may here repeat the story I wrote at her death of what it was given her to accomplish.

The fact that Colonel Sullivan was long on active service with the army brought his wife into various districts at different times, and, wherever she came, for many years, she was known as one who visited her poorer neighbours, unwearied in acts of kindness, and in speaking to them of religion. But it was while residing for a year or two at Dewlish House, Dorset, after her husband's retirement from the army, that her attention was more closely turned to the evils of drink. To enable others to put from them so great a snare, she abandoned herself what had seemed to her a needful stimulant in fatigue, and found, as we all find, that she was able to do much more. From Dewlish, at the end of the lease, the family removed to Henbury Park, near Wimborne, and this being less isolated than Dewlish House, Mrs. Sullivan's influence was felt beyond the bounds of the parish in which she lived.

The points in her work which most struck me were her courage, her diligence, and her extraordinary sympathy. She would speak to a drunkard of whom the neighbours or the clergyman said it was safer not to enter his house because he was so violent and insolent; would go from house to house late, and on bad days, when most persons would have thought work was over, because those whom she wished to find would be at home; she never turned impatiently from any, however weak, however fallen. She had indeed the largest sympathy with fallen women, to whom so often their own sex show themselves the most intolerant. There were many, and those not by any means only among the poor and the drunken, who might almost have applied to her the words, " To whom also I owe my own soul."

Nor did she ever forget those whose names were on her pledge-book, and this necessitated a large, ever-increasing correspondence. Her position as the mistress of a large establishment and the mother of grown-up daughters, took her much into society from time to time, nor was it among the least remarkable features in her character that one who was so thoroughly at home in the homes of the most degraded, or in speaking to " roughs " in a village school-room, was the light and life of every drawing-room she entered, though always ready to talk of the subject nearest her heart, and to testify against sensuality among high and low.

Colonel Sullivan was unable to get a long lease of Henbury, and after residing there for a year and a half removed to Hatherton Hall, Stafford. There total abstinence had at the time scarcely been heard of, and the work was all fresh to do. I need not say that it was done. As before, visits from house to house, meetings, a night-school, a bible-class, were at once set on foot, the nucleus of which were one or two steady young men taken from Dorset, and every letter for her last two years at Hatherton had spoken of hopeful though

up-hill work. But her heart had been in
Dorset, and the fact that two of their daughters
were married in that county had turned her and
her husband's thoughts towards a fixed and
permanent residence in their old neighbourhood. It was not so to be. Her Master
had called her, and the last tidings spoke of
the " peaceful, happy smile," with which she
obeyed the summons.

Besides my work in parish, church, and
schools, and my reading with private pupils, I
had some other interests to which I look back
with nothing but satisfaction. One was my
connection with the Dorset County Temperance
Association. There had been for many years
a society under that name, chiefly among the
tradespeople in Poole, Blandford, and Swanage,
and in connection with various country Dissent-
ing chapels. It had taken very little hold of
the clergy of the Church of England. It was,
however, obvious to me that no real spiritual
work could be done so long as the clergy held
aloof from so very important a work. Greatly
aided by Mrs. Sullivan, I joined this, and
soon had pleasure in associating with me
some of the clergy in the neighbourhood, one

of whom——the Rev. Owen Mansel——succeeded
me as Chairman of the Association. I am glad
to think that a large number who became tee-
totallers more than five-and-twenty years ago
are still true to their pledge ; and I am as much
convinced as ever that this movement is necessary to all social improvement in every rank of
society ; that it is possible for every man and
woman in health, is now beyond argument.

In 1872, Mr. Arch's movement for a
higher rate of wages among the labourers
reached Dorset, and he carried his agitation
into our neighbourhood with the aid of the
Hon. Auberon Herbert. I threw myself into
this movement with all my heart. Mr. Herbert
and Mr. Arch spent some days with me, during
which we visited many large meetings of
labourers, and in spite of the opposition of
farmers, squires, and clergy we had the satisfaction to know that we raised the rate of
wages at least two shillings a week all round.
The good that was then done has never been
undone ; although it is still extremely probable
that a large number of comfortable clergy are
even less persuaded of the right of the labourer
to earn decent wage than they are of the neces-

sity of keeping him from over-indulgence in strong drink, the end of the agitation will probably result in producing a yeoman class, *i.e.* men who own land and cultivate it themselves, for there seems no room for three to share the profits on land, and the middle-man must go.

Our pleasant time at Sturminster was one of good health on the whole. I mention only one exception, for its singularity, as showing the want of the most obvious hygienic precautions in country villages at that time, and probably at this time also. A village girl, who was in service in Southampton, came home with a rash and feeling very ill ; she went to bed with her mother, who was then just recovering from her confinement. The girl proved to have virulent small-pox, which the mother of course took, and died. Although the cause of death was well known, a number of neighbours from the village went to see the body, out of curiosity; and no less than thirteen deaths took place among those who went to see her, besides a very large number of cases through the parish. I went to visit the woman, in discharge of my duty, caught small-pox, and was very ill. This is curious, as I had had small-pox when a child, in spite of vaccination, and had been vaccinated but a short time before. I am the third of my own immediate family who have had small-pox twice and with whom vaccination has always taken. Besides this, one of my father's sisters died of small-pox, having had it the first time as a child by in-noculation. I do not feel the smallest doubt that I should catch small-pox again if I came within the scope of its influence, and am in-clined to doubt whether the crusade against vaccination be not thoroughly justified. It is perfectly true that the proportion is extraor-dinarily small of people marked with the small-pox to what it was when I was young, but it may be doubted whether this is not from better nursing, from better treatment of the disease, than prevailed in the first half of the century.

My residence in Dorsetshire did not bring me into very close relationship with either clergy or my neighbours. I did not feel in touch with the former and did not see much of the latter.

The Rev. D'Oyley Snow, who had resigned his living and was residing on his property near Blandford, was the only one with whom

I was in full sympathy. I saw a great deal of two Broad Church clergymen in the diocese : one the Rev. Robert Kennard of Marnhull, and the other the well-known Dr. Rowland Williams, one of the authors of *Essays and Reviews*. They were both, in fact, Unitarian in teaching, though Dr. Rowland Williams had the peculiarity, not confined to himself, of believing that his was the only orthodox form of faith, and that he was the only ex- ponent of the Church's doctrine. His books are not now nearly so well known as they should be, but two of them ought to live : one, a volume of sermon - essays called *Rational Godliness*, and another, called *Christianity and Hinduism*, on the religions in the East. Dr. Williams, though one of the most charming of men, silver tongued and kindly in speech, was one of those whose pen dripped with vitriol so soon as he began to write. He was a master of epigram, and never could resist one in a letter even at the cost of his best friends.

Through Mr. Kennard I also became intimate with the Rev. H. B. Wilson, another essayist and reviewer, and one of the four tutors who had protested at Oxford in Newman's days against Tract 90. He little thought, nor would ever have allowed, that in his writings he needed the tolerance he had refused to Newman. His Bampton Lectures at Oxford, in which he took a completely Zwinglian view of the sacraments, made a very deep impression upon me in my early clerical days ; and though I have long passed away from any shadow of his teaching, he remains to my mind one of the few masters of English style whom I should venture to place on the same level with John Henry Newman and the first Sir James Stephen.

The mention of these various persons with whom I associated on terms of so great intimacy will show that my own opinions had become gradually out of sympathy with those usually held in the Church of England ; and I had ceased to find that I took much pleasure in the parish work wherein I was expected to say that which I did not believe. It seemed to me quite possible that though I felt ministration in the Church of England was dishonest, I might remain for some time in lay communion. This, however, I found possible for a short time only.

It will serve to indicate my theological views at this time, if I quote various mottoes written on a fly-leaf of a Bible which then and for some years past I had used in the pulpit and in the preparation of my sermons.

" Hic liber est, in quo quærit sua dogmata quisque,
Invehit et pariter dogmata quisque sua."

"Among all forms of mistake, prophecy is the most gratuitous."—G. ELIOT.

" Les miracles ce sont des coups d'etat célestes."
—MASSIMO D'AZEGLIO.

" Inspiration : a clear perception of those heavenly truths which the Holy Ghost reveals to man, as the abiding thoughts of God, which ever repeat themselves in His eternal plan."—ROWLAND WILLIAMS, *Rational Godliness*, Sermon XII.

" Inspiration : the inflexible love of Truth which being inseparable from the spirit of Christianity would itself be a sufficient guarantee for fidelity and honesty."—DEAN MILMAN, *History of Christianity*.

About the year 1870, while retaining my liking for ornate services and a great deal of music in church, my opinions had, as I have already said, become practically Unitarian. I had for some time been a pretty constant contributor to the *Theological Review*—an extinct quarterly, then edited by the Rev. Charles Beard. I was quite prepared to join a society, which was in fact Unitarian, called the Free Christian Union. The intention was to promote, if possible, a general union of all persons holding Unitarian theology within the various orthodox churches and sects. It was joined by a very few clergy of the Church of England, a few French Protestant pastors, among whom the most important was the Rev. Athanase Cocquerell *fils*, and a few Congregational ministers. We were all extremely in earnest, and unable to see that there was a comic side to the whole movement. We might have been described in the words Mr. Lowell uses in his *Fable for Critics* of Theodore Parker :—

> " He went a step further without cough or hem.
> He frankly declared he believed not in them,
> And before he could be jumbled up or prevented,
> From their orthodox kind of dissent, he dissented ;
> There was heresy here you perceive, for the right
> Of privately judging means simply that light
> Has been granted to me for deciding on you,
> And in happier times, before Atheism grew,
> The deed contained clauses for cooking you too."

The Free Christian Union began and ended its operations by a service in London, at which two sermons were preached, one by Athanase Cocquerell, the other by myself. To say that

my sermon was one that I had preached at
Eton long before I went to Sturminster, with
the smallest possible alteration, is simply to
say that an Unitarian theology had long been
unconsciously mine. It made, however, more
"to-do" than might have been expected, from
the fact that a reporter from the *Pall Mall
Gazette* misheard and therefore misquoted a
sentence of mine, which made the words sound
more dangerous than they really were. This
report in the paper had no effect whatever on
my parishioners, who probably never saw it ;
but it made me a still more marked man among
the clergy of the neighbourhood, and caused the
removal of one of my pupils, though the parents
of all the others showed me the greatest possible
confidence, and did not believe that I should
teach them anything contrary to the belief of
their parents.

It is always difficult to say at what moment
an intellectual position, long held with loosening
grasp, becomes untenable ; it is so easy to
acquiesce for awhile, so hard to deny what after
all the heart continues to desire when the intellect rejects it ; but at last I had to face the
fact that I could no longer use in any honest

sense the Prayer Book of the Church of England, nor minister at her altars, nor preach a definite message when "all my mind" was "clouded with a doubt."

When entering upon my duties at Sturminster the chaotic state of parties, dogma, and discipline in the Church of England was forced at once on my attention. For many years, up to the time of my predecessor, the vicar had been non-resident, and the curate in charge was a pronounced, even extreme, Low Churchman. On the death of the vicar the living fell into the hands of a very prominent member of the ultra-Tractarian party, who at once established daily services and ornate ritual, restoring the church well, contradicting in his every word and deed the teaching and example of the former curate, who moved only to the next parish, and did all that in him lay to neutralise the work of the new vicar.

When this gentleman was preferred to a benefice in another county, the Bishop frankly told me he wished for no Broad Churchmen, and would, if it were possible, have refused to accept a man of my opinions, which had become known by various essays contributed from time to time to current literature. But as he could not help himself, he trusted I would at least continue the outward character of the services now fixed in the parish, which indeed was quite in accordance with my own intention.

It struck me, however, as most grotesque that the chief pastor of a diocese should have no voice whatever in the selection of the men appointed to serve under him, no power to inhibit what he considered false doctrine, and should have to appeal to the forbearance and good sense of his clergy to hinder a complete reversal of an established ritual approved by himself. The failure of his attempt to declare Dr. Rowland Williams an heretic, brought into still greater prominence the weakness of the Anglican Episcopate.

All through the ministrations of three clergymen—Low, High, Broad—the villagers, the farmers, and in great measure the few resident and educated gentry were scarce aware that there were any other than outward differences in the mode of conducting worship; these, and not the doctrines, were points to which objection was occasionally raised, and provided the parson went on the principle of *quieta non movere*, he might preach what he pleased, orthodoxy or heterodoxy, the doctrines of Rome, or Wittenberg, or Geneva.

Yet again, for some years, my doubts were silent. At last, however, the time came when I could no longer with any honesty continue my ministrations, and a death in the circle of my nearest relations, which called me to Bath and obliged me to take a holiday, gave me an opportunity for resigning my preferment as quietly as possible; for I was by no means anxious to make any stir about the matter.

The final decision that I must leave the Church of England was given by a word of General, now Sir Richard, Strachey, who, at the house of his and my brother-in-law, Sir James Colvile, said to me suddenly, " When are you coming out ? " This enabled me, as by a flash of light, to see myself as others saw me, and to recognise that the place I filled ought to be mine no longer.

I resigned my living and came up to London.

X

PUBLISHING—HOLIDAYS ABROAD

1874

FOR some time past I had been engaged in reading books for Mr. Henry S. King, publisher in Cornhill ; and almost coincidentally with my quitting Sturminster, he offered me a more intimate post in his business in London. I accepted this, and for five-and-twenty years thereafter was in various manners connected with the publishing business in London.

There was much in the career and the character of Mr. Henry Samuel King that was exceptional and remarkable in days which tend to reduce lives to so much of dull uniformity, and I will here say a few words about him, the pith of what I wrote of him when he died in 1878. His grandfather, Mr. King, was the senior partner of the Lewes Bank, and the family was of long standing and good position, a circumstance which stimulated Henry's efforts in no small degree when, at a very early age, he had to earn his own livelihood and to choose his own career. For his father, having realised a sufficient fortune, did not enter the bank, and lost the whole of that fortune while his children were still very young. At the age of thirteen Mr. King had to go out into the world to fight his way absolutely alone, with the proverbial half-crown in his pocket.

I have heard him describe with the greatest simplicity his eager and successful struggles to save enough out of his small earnings to help his family, to educate himself, and to get on in the world ; and the tale seemed to the hearer at once romantic and heroic, though to the narrator it was the record of mere duty, as it appeared to him, within the reach of all. At the age of twenty he and his elder brother started on their own account as booksellers at Brighton. The elder, so soon as he could afford it, left the business and took Orders ; the younger maintained the business alone.

At Brighton, and in his then occupation, he was able to carry out his self-education more satisfactorily than before. Of course his culture was and always remained deficient on some sides : he knew no language but his own ; he was only acquainted through translations with the stores of classical and foreign literature. But his knowledge of English literature was wide and accurate, his reading careful, his memory singularly retentive ; while for books — the shrines of literature— he had a real passion and a sort of personal affection. Hence he became a bookseller of a type which is getting rarer each day—one who rises far above the mere tradesman, the friend and literary associate of his customers, who look to him as, in some sense, the judge and critic of his wares. Among his Brighton friends the most conspicuous was Frederick Robertson, who lived on affectionate terms with Mr. King, and made him one of his executors.

In June 1850 Mr King married Miss Ellen Blakeway, and, becoming by this alliance brother-in-law of Mr. George Smith, he afterwards joined the firm of Smith, Elder & Co. as a partner, and moved his home to the Manor House, Chigwell, Essex.

The firm combined the various and, as it

would seem to an outsider, almost incongruous business of Indian agency, banking, and publishing; but Mr. King found himself equally at home in each branch, and the energy of the two leading partners made both successful. Every one knows that Smith, Elder & Co. were Thackeray's publishers, and started the *Cornhill Magazine* under his editorship; that they recognised the merit of the Brontës; that they gave Ruskin's earlier books to the world in a manner which satisfied even their fastidious author; that they were the publishers of Robertson's Sermons, the most wide-spread literature of that kind which has ever issued from the press. It would be impossible, and, if possible, invidious to distinguish the part played by each member of the firm in their excellent work in this or the other departments of their business.

Mr. King's one literary effort, however, must not be passed over; the arrangement and editing of the successive volumes of Robertson was his, and his alone; and it was a task of no common difficulty and delicacy. Robertson was an extempore preacher; he wrote out some of his sermons afterwards, but the MS. draft was not always so good and striking as that which had been delivered; some of his congregation took notes, and these when placed in the editor's hands were found to differ much from each other. The preacher was bold, and might seem, as Faber puts it, now and then " to stray under the shadow of condemned propositions " in expressions which it would not be always fair to repeat, since he had no opportunity of pruning his words—the publication being posthumous—while honesty demanded a faithful rescript. In all this Mr. King's rare memory and his close friendship with the preacher aided him, while his tact and literary judgment combined to produce an example of almost perfect editing. And the work was done quietly, and, as it were, in secret; no editor's name was known: Mr. King effaced himself for his friend. It is not too much to say that, but for him, Robertson's words would have been lost when the voice that uttered them ceased.

In 1868 the partners in the house of Smith, Elder & Co. separated, and Mr. King retained the Indian business in his own name, the publishing business going with the name of the firm to the senior partner. Mr. King bound himself not to engage for three years in the business carried on by the other partner. At the time of the separation Mr. King had no intention of becoming again a publisher. That each business stood better alone is plain from the extension of both when severed from the other, and from the great impulse given to Messrs. King's own trade and to the publishing business, which they sold, when these were finally divided. And at first Mr. King's attention was solely given to the extension of the banking and agency business. But books were Mr. King's delight, and books he must have as a relaxation, which proved, however, to be very hard work. As soon as he was able to do so under the terms of his agreement, he resumed business as a publisher, the first book issued being Mr. Stopford Brooke's volume, *Freedom in the Church of England.* The Robertson family soon transferred Mr. Frederick Robertson's books to their old friend, the original editor, and the business increased with rapidity and success.

The very fact of such a career shows a man of no ordinary force of character ; and few ever approached Mr. King without being aware of at least some features of it—great urbanity to all who were first introduced to him, unwearied attention to business, a large power of generalisation combined with extraordinary attention to details, an almost unexampled memory, and an iron will. And under the urbanity this iron force was very apparent; not all were able to penetrate below it. Those who did so found an extremely tender heart, a most loving and lovable nature, a high and stern sense of duty for himself and others, with great toleration prevailing over a seeming intolerance.

After I had assisted Mr. King for a few years as his literary adviser, he determined to sell his publishing business and devote himself entirely to his Indian agency. I was able to make arrangements with a partner to purchase this business, which many years afterwards was made into a company under the name of "Kegan Paul, Trench, Trübner & Co.," although I remained the managing director. It is no part of my intention to describe my life as a publisher; especially because to do so would be to mention various persons who are still alive, who would very probably not agree

in everything I might say, and would not care
that I should tell confidential matters that were
common to others. I shall therefore confine
myself to saying with regard to my office life
of those twenty-five years, that publishing is
not by any means the ready road to wealth
that many people think it, and that it is very
inexpedient for any one without a large capital
and considerable literary skill to enter such a
business. Supposing, however, any one to
have the capital and the literary skill, I can
imagine no more interesting work.

I ought to say also, after a long experience
both in publishing and editing, that every book
sent to a publisher and every article sent to a
magazine or newspaper is quite sure to be fairly
considered. It is often supposed that an introduction is necessary, but this is by no means
the case. A publisher wants authors quite as
much as these want a publisher, and they may
always be sure that the MSS. are fairly considered. That difference of opinion may take
place is no more than likely, since it cannot be
expected that an author and critic will always
take the same view of the excellence of an MS.;
but a really good book is pretty sure of accept-

ance before it has gone to many publishers. The legends of first-rate works having been the round of all the publishers in London may be fairly rejected as having an extremely small amount of truth, if any, in them. It is certain, however, that publishing in the last few years has fallen on somewhat evil days, and I am perhaps, from my age, necessarily a *laudator temporis acti*, and do not think that so many good books come in the way of publishers as was the case some years ago. Since Browning, Mrs. Browning, and Tennyson were all stars of the literary firmament at the same time no one has appeared whose verses (save a few lines now and then) could move me in any degree. There seems to me no one now worthy of being called a poet unless it be Mr. Wilfrid Blunt, Mr. Coventry Patmore, Mrs. Hamilton King, and Mr. William Morris. Since George Eliot's death and the publication of Mr. Thomas Hardy's earlier novels no great writer of fiction has come to the front, though as a writer of short stories Mr. Rudyard Kipling has made a deserved success. Scottish stories of the Kail-yard, and the snippets of tales in vogue with the publishers of the one volume novels, have not the charm of the stories of older days. But it should be remembered that at any given time the real men of letters can be counted by twos and threes, and that the literary clique is invariably composed of very second- or third-rate people, just as it was in Dr. Johnson's days, though he, a giant among the pigmies, rose superior to them all.

At a dinner-party soon after I came to London there were no less than six persons present who had published volumes of poems, and as we went in to dinner Mrs. Tom Taylor said to me, "We have all the poets here to-night, or shall we say all the Poetasters." And the second word was the truer of the two. It was a great disappointment to me as to others with a real love of poetry that the laureateship was not allowed to die out after it had been honoured by such names as Southey, Wordsworth, and Tennyson.

The principal work of Mr. Henry S. King was the "International Scientific Series," the intention of which was to bring so much of each separate science as might be thought necessary for the ordinary layman within the compass of a single volume, which, while being accurate, should also be in a "tongue understanded of the people." The initiatory movement came from America, and a distinguished scientific American came over to England to find a publisher ready to take up the venture. Mr. King, then resuming business as a publisher after his separation from Messrs. Smith and Elder, offered extremely liberal terms, too liberal indeed to make the "Series" a great financial success. Some of the most distinguished contributors gave merely old magazine articles, while others were not well known to the world in general as men of scientific importance. There were indeed some, of whom Professor Huxley was a notable example, who gave new and admirable original work, but in these cases the cost of illustration was far greater than could reasonably have been expended for the price at which these volumes were sold.

The "Series" was well under way by the time that I joined Mr. King, and my first connection with it was not fortunate. A book on "Photography" was translated from the German, and only reached my hands when the proofs were to be passed for press. Mr. King had placed the translation in the hands of a thoroughly competent man, and a considerable sum was agreed upon for translation. Shortly after it was undertaken, the translator called upon Mr. King to explain that he had really promised more than his time could allow, and begged to turn the work over to his brother-in-law, who was, he said, a most accomplished person, while he would be responsible for reading the proofs. This second translator, without leave, turned the matter over to his wife, while the first did not keep his promise of reading the proofs. The consequence was that a sentence which should have been translated " Photography by the aid of chromium compounds" appeared as " Chromo-Photography," and the proofs positively bristled with instances of equal ignorance. The whole edition of 1250 copies had to be condemned as waste-paper, and a new translation to be made by a careful chemist.

The " Series" ought to have been placed from the first in the hands of some responsible man of science. Instead of this, Mr. King asked three persons of the highest scientific reputation to become nominal editors, giving

them each a retaining fee of £100. For such
a fee they neither did, nor were expected to do,
more than give general advice about the subjects to be included, and in case of translations,
of translators ; but the real editorship remained
then, as it always has remained since, with the
publishers, and with them alone. It is fair to
say that one of these three distinguished men,
finding that he was doing nothing for his retaining fee, returned the £100 after some
years. Our discovery of the careless manner
in which translations might be done naturally
placed me on my guard. The real fact, though
little understood, is that translation is one of
the most difficult of literary feats, instead of
being, as generally considered, one of the
easiest. Every book in a foreign language
ought to be treated with the same conscien-
tiousness as a professor of Latin or Greek
brings to the editing of a classical author.

About the time that the " Series " was
begun an American firm sent a translation of
Ribot's *Sur L'Hérédité* to be taken up by
us and printed in England. I naturally examined this with some care, although the
American publishers assured us that any ex-

amination was quite unnecessary, the translator being one of the first French scholars it was possible to find. I dipped into the book quite at hazard and came on the following remarkable evidence of the translator's skill : " Un garçon armé de son arc, allait à la fête d'une commune voisine "—" A boy, armed with his bow, went to the feast of a woman in the neighbourhood." It was impossible not to remember Mrs. Gamp's apostrophe to the " Ankwerk's Package," in which she was " appearing to confound the Whale with the Prophet," on seeing how the translator confounded the lady with the village, and took away her character in doing so. It will hardly be credited that the translator demurred to our objection to his work, maintaining that as no scientific fact was involved, it really did not matter whether the boy went to visit a neighbouring woman or a neighbouring parish.

At a later time we determined to bring out a translation of *Moltke's Letters from Russia,* and I was again less wise than I should have been. I accepted the services of a lady who was reputed to be an accomplished German scholar, and paid for her translation of the book on its receipt. Before sending it to the printer, however, I opened the book quite at random and found that in a letter to his wife Moltke had described the coronation of the Emperor of Russia : " The Archbishop poured the oil on his head, *und zwei Bischöfe trockneten die Spuren ab*," " and two bishops fastened on his spurs," by which rendering the whole proceeding of the translator was laid bare. The word " *Spur* " was unknown to her, and how could it mean anything but " spurs " ? And *abtrocknen* could therefore mean nothing but " fasten on." The revision of each of these books, Ribot's *Sur L'Hérédité* and *Moltke's Letters*, occupied the better part of a well-earned holiday.

As we had paid for the latter, it was not worth while pointing out her many blunders to the translator ; for an attempt to recover the money paid would have been to imitate the elfin harper who could harp " blood out of a stone." As the lady was ignorant of her mistakes, it was not surprising to receive from her a translation of a certain *Life of Von Bismarck*. Before declining this, however, I glanced at the first page and found the curious statement that on a given night Bismarck, having "received the Holy Communion in his chambers," went off to join the emperor before Paris. This struck me as very odd, and I turned to the original to find as I expected that Bismarck started for Paris at night having had his supper. The book was accepted by another publisher, we having given no reason for declining it, and the lady's reputation as a translator being what it was, the blunder appeared. The *Times*, in reviewing the book, commented on the cynical wickedness of the German chancellor : *Punch* also alluded to it, and English readers believed the story. So true is it, as Mr. Spurgeon said, that "a lie will go half round the world while Truth is putting on her boots."

I do not think I was ever caught again publishing a translation without careful examination ; but many years afterwards a most impudent attempt was made by an ignorant woman to palm off upon us a translation of a German History. On a careful inspection of this I found that "Cardinal Cusa was the son of a mussel fisherman near Trêves," these words being supposed to be a rendering of : "War der Sohn eines Moselfischers bei Trier." The gentleman who brought me the translation from his friend was surprised to find that I considered this sentence showed at once an ignorance of German, of geography, and of natural history. That translation, I believe, has never appeared. While mentioning these blunders, it is fair to say that Mrs. Clara Bell, who did much work for us as publishers, was as unlike these ladies as it is possible to imagine. She is not only an accomplished linguist, but is possessed of admirable scientific research, patience, and skill.

The earlier of these discoveries, though not that of the Cardinal of Cusa, were made during the time of my association with Mr. King. He had before I joined him gathered around him, in addition to the writers of the "International Scientific Series," several well-known men, many of whom are now dead, whom I consider it a great privilege to have known. Among those who are gone was Mr. Walter Bagehot, who deserved all that is said of him by his friend Mr. Hutton of the *Spectator*, and whose books on economic science are likely, for a long time, to keep their place.

To Mr. King, also, we owe the publication of

the sermons of George Dawson, whom I never saw, and the works of James Hinton. He also encouraged the publication of " The Disciples," by his second wife, Mrs. Hamilton King, who survives him. A review of that poem in the *Examiner* by me was the cause of my own literary connection with Mr. King. To him also is due the discovery of the gentleman who then was known as " a new writer," Sir Lewis Morris.

All these had taken their due and fitting place in literature before I had the honour of making their acquaintance. In regard to some others, I am hardly able to say whether their books first appeared in Mr. King's days or with Mr. Trench and myself after Mr. King's mantle had fallen on our shoulders. But whether they first appeared in literature with the imprint of Henry S. King & Co. or not, they remained and remain for the most part my kind and cordial friends.

The most remarkable book published by Mr. Trench and myself, remembered for the circumstances attending its publication, as well as for the name of the author, was the *Last Journals of General Gordon*. When it was known that

these journals had been recovered and were in
the hands of his brother, Sir Henry Gordon,
much curiosity was felt as to which would be
the fortunate firm to whom Sir Henry might
offer them. A few days after they reached
England I received a note from Sir Henry
asking me to call upon him the next afternoon
at a given hour. It appears that he had asked
five publishers to call upon him at different
hours during the day, with sufficient intervals
of time to ensure our not meeting. "Now,"
said Sir Henry when I entered his study, " I
have sent for you to show you my brother's
journals, and should like you to make an offer
for them ; I can only give you a few minutes
to turn them over"—and he himself hurriedly
turned over the MS., in which he had placed
pieces of paper, giving no sufficient time for a
real inspection of any part of the work. It was
not possible even to guess the sized book that
might be made of it, or the price at which it
would be possible to sell it. In fact, the inspection accorded was of the very slightest
kind. Sir Henry said he wished an offer for
the book to be made by twelve o'clock the
next day, and intimated that in fact he was

prepared to sell the work to the highest bidder, and would give an answer immediately. After consulting with Mr. Trench, we wrote offering 5000 guineas for this pig in a poke, and ours proved the highest offer. The nearest bid to ours was £5000, and, as Sir Henry afterwards told me, the irritated nearest bidder exclaimed that "it was those damned shillings that had done it!"

At the moment that the MS. came into our hands the excitement over Gordon was at its height, and had we been able to bring it out at once, no doubt we should have realised a very large sum. Sir Henry, however, made it a condition that a relative of his should edit the work, though no such editing was at all necessary. The translation of many Arabic papers took a long time, and there were other delays. The various expenses connected with editing, translating, and printing raised the sum to £7000 before a single copy was ready. No one was to blame for this, but the delay was most vexatious. Public opinion moves so fast in England that other interests had taken the place of Gordon before the book was out, and although it was a distinct gain to us, the gain was not nearly so large as we hoped for our blind and somewhat risky venture.

Another series of publications by which the firm of Kegan Paul, Trench & Co. may still be remembered is the Parchment Library. The intention of this series was to present in thoroughly good paper and print some of the most distinguished English classics, and we certainly set the fashion of really beautiful books. No doubt many have now surpassed them, but at the time these reprints were a distinct advance.

As may be well imagined, Mr. Trench set great store by the due presentation of his father the late Archbishop of Dublin's works ; and to his determination that the most popular of these, on the " Miracles and Parables of Our Lord," should be brought within the reach of all, not only of scholars ; and to his desire, therefore, that the notes in classical language should be translated into English, I owe my friendship with Mr. Alfred Pollard of the British Museum, who performed his task admirably. I will say no more of this friendship than that it has been one of the greatest pleasures of the later period of my life.

Even more than the fact that Mr. Alfred
Trench was my partner, our literary association
with his books brought me into contact with
the Archbishop. At a very early period in our
acquaintance the question came before us as
to what attitude we should take with regard
to books against religion, such as some of the
works in the " International Scientific Series "
and others of a free-thinking or agnostic nature,
and we naturally referred the question to Archbishop Trench. He thought that the day was
long past in which the questions discussed in
those books could be shelved ; that our attitude
should be that when they were treated in a
reverent and serious spirit we should by no
means refuse to publish works of a free-thinking or agnostic type ; but that we should sternly
reject any that were merely flippant and written
for the sake of destruction. On this advice
we always acted, sometimes to the great indig-
nation of persons who wished us to publish
anti-Christian books which were as bad from
the Archbishop's literary standpoint as they
were from that of his theology.

And this brings me to the general question
of how far a publisher does well to consider

literature rather than fashion in the books he takes up. It may, I think, be laid down that a literary man is not as a rule a good publisher. He is on the one hand tempted to accept books unlikely to succeed because they fall in with his own literary tastes, and on the other, to reject those which may have a considerable sale at the time, because they are in no true sense literature. I call to mind several books, which for obvious reasons I will not specify, rejected by our firm which, in other hands, proved a great financial success, but happily will never be heard of beyond the decade which saw their production.

This leads to the further conviction, in which I shall probably run counter to the opinion of many—that literature is not in itself a profession. With perhaps the exception of Dr. Johnson and Lord Tennyson, it is difficult to name any men who, writing really good works, lived by those works and by the pensions conferred upon them on account of those works. With those exceptions, I can think of no one whose books have lived or are likely to live, who have not either had an independent fortune or a profession quite apart from literature, by which they gained at least a decent livelihood. One of the branches of her Majesty's Civil Service has been termed " a nest of singing birds," so many clerks in that office have published volumes of poetry ; and except certain newspaper writers and popular novelists, whose works will shortly be as dead as those of Mrs. Gore, so popular in my youth, the number of those who gain a livelihood by literature is extraordinarily small. An absolutely first-rate book—and the number of such in any generation may be counted on the fingers— is sure to succeed. A totally worthless book is nearly as sure of success, but the dictum of Horace still remains true in other as well as poetic literature :—

> . . . . " Mediocribus esse poetis
> Non Di, non homines, non concessere columnæ."

These have to take their chance, and the successes are far less in proportion than the failures. The author who has nothing to fall back upon is in a bad way. I ought to say, and it is a great satisfaction to me to do so, that without an exception the Catholic works published by our firm have been successful, but they are few in number, and the Catholic *monde* is not a book-buying one.

As I have already mentioned, one who lived by literature alone is Lord Tennyson, who for many years was associated with us and with whom our relations were always friendly and pleasant. He was, however, a thorough man of business, and our final parting at the end of one of our periods of agreement was that we, as publishers, and he, as author, took a different view of his pecuniary value.

Among the poets with whom we were associated and with all of whom our relations were most pleasant, were Mr. Aubrey de Vere, Archbishop Trench, and Sir Henry Taylor. I name these three poets together because they belong essentially to the same school, whose works will always be studied so long as graceful and scholarly poetry is valued ; but no one of them is likely to become in any sense popular. Mr. Andrew Lang, Mr. Frederick Locker, Mr. Edmund Gosse, and, above all, Mr. Austin Dobson were poets of a very different stamp, of lighter quality, but the last seated perhaps on a higher platform of the Hill of Helicon. Higher still by far I should place Mr. Wilfrid Blunt.

For good or evil our firm always preferred

to be literary and scholarly, and nothing was so great a delight, both to Mr. King and to ourselves, as to lend a helping hand to any young authors in whom we saw promise rather than immediate profit.

I may now mention a few of those with whom literature brought me into pleasant companionship—some such, as I have mentioned already, who had their spurs to win, others veterans in the field. Among the oldest of these was the Dorset poet, William Barnes, who, if Dorsetshire were as large as Scotland, might truly be called the Dorset Burns. His poetry will live when his philological researches, resting on unsound bases, are forgotten.

Sir Richard and Lady Burton were among those for whom we published, and Lady Burton's *Syria and Palestine* was of great interest. It was one of the few passages in her life in which she did not entirely merge herself in the personality of her distinguished husband. They both of them perhaps rated their doings and discoveries at too high a rate, but were pleasant and interesting persons. Lady Burton was anxious to assure me that her book *must* become the indispensable guide-book for every one who travelled in the Holy Land, and to this end she was extremely desirous that we should publish an edition of her work interleaved with the historical parts of the Bible, the Prophets and Gospels, because, she said, every one must take her book as a travelling companion, and it was by no means certain that they would take the Bible also. My relations with these two distinguished people were always cordial; and I wish I could persuade myself that Lady Burton's certainty that Sir Richard was received into the Catholic Church on his death-bed was correct; instead of which the verdict must be, "not proven."

We were glad to bring out a new edition of Sir George Cox's *Aryan Mythology*. He is not only a first cousin of my own, but one of my earliest friends at school. We were at Ilminster, under the Rev. John Allen, before he went to Rugby, or I to Eton. He is one of those writers whose careful research and literary talents do not perhaps reach the very highest standard of excellence; therefore, good as his books are, I should doubt whether their pecuniary has ever equalled their literary value.

With Mr. Austin Dobson, Professor Edward Dowden, and Mr. Edmund Gosse my relations were always of the most friendly kind, and all three are among those, the loss of whose companionship through illness is a great and constant regret. With Mr. Gosse, especially, I was associated privately in many pleasant tours abroad as well as in literature, and indeed literature was often discussed on these travels. In one of these tours we arranged that he should undertake the life of his father, Mr. Philip Gosse, the distinguished naturalist. "I hope," said Mr. Gosse, as we discussed his treatment of the subject, "you do not think that the natural piety of the son should entirely eclipse his sense of humour in dealing with his father's peculiarities." I assured him that I should be entirely satisfied with the treatment he might think fit to give to the *Life*, but asked him to specify an instance of what he meant. He spoke of his father, in his later years, having gone to the dedication of a chapel, at which, greatly to his dislike as a staunch Plymouth Brother, an organ accompaniment to the hymn formed part of the ritual. On his return he was asked how the service had gone off, and his only comment was, "There were harpers harping on their harps."

Robert Stephen Hawker, the Cornish High Church poet, was another with whom and his widow we were closely associated. Mr. Hawker was one of the very few persons whose modern ballad has been accepted as ancient, Sir Walter Scott being, perhaps, the only other instance.

> " Trelawney he's in keep and hold,
>   Trelawney he may die,
>   But there's fifty thousand Cornish men
>   Will know the reason why."

Trelawney was one of the seven bishops committed to the Tower by James II., and the ballad will be remembered when the controversy between Mr. Baring Gould and Mrs. Hawker, as to whether her husband was received into the Catholic Church on his death-bed, is long forgotten.

Thomas Hardy and George Meredith are the two most distinguished novel-writers with whom we ever had relations. For a true appreciation of the former it is perhaps necessary to know Dorset, or, as Mr. Hardy is pleased to call it, Wessex.

To understand George Meredith, it is perhaps necessary to belong to a somewhat esoteric circle who can enter into a literature which will

probably increase as time brings a wider
education.

One of the most popular books published
by us was the *Life of Sister Dora*, by Miss
Margaret Lonsdale. Sister Dora was as remarkable in her way as her brother, my dear
friend the Rev. Mark Pattison, was in his;
and in Miss Lonsdale she found a worthy
biographer.

It is a great satisfaction to me that we were
associated with Mr. Andrew Lang and Mr.
R. L. Stevenson, neither of whom had attained
the fame which he was afterwards to enjoy.
With regard to the first of these, it has been
always a regret to me, as to many others,
that the brilliancy of his fugitive work has
interfered with the production of some exhaus-
tive treatise on one of the many subjects in
which he is a master, worthy of a place in the
permanent literature of our time.

Some years since I was asked to deliver an
article on the production of books, which has
been reprinted in a volume of essays called
Faith and Unfaith. I may mention here
some stories which have found place therein,
and show publishing life on its more amusing

though often irritating side. A printer's **devil**, so called, is the boy who runs to and fro between the printing–office and the publishers, but·the real devil seems often to stand at the right hand of the compositor in the printing-office, and to be the cause of many astounding blunders. Messrs. Henry S. King & Co. printed an edition of Tennyson's works with the greatest possible care. The author and the printer's reader attended to every word and stop with close attention, and the work was passed to press with, as it seemed, no fault. A jog to the printer's elbow was the cause of a most ghastly misprint. When all was done, what ought to have been a faultless edition was marred by what seemed the grossest carelessness.

Some years ago a writer, intending to describe a tract of land between the base of a volcanic mountain and the sea, related that the whole of it was strewn with "erratic blocks." This appeared "that the whole plain was strewn with erotic blacks." When Louis XVIII. was dying in Paris, the bulletin one evening contained the words, "Sa Majesté se porte mieux." The next morning appeared the misprint, "Le

vieux persiste encore." It is, however, difficult
to prevent an author from regarding these things
as deliberate on the part of the printer, and
no doubt it is well that some one should be
able to justify the fact that he does well to
be angry.

As regards the publishing business, I may
venture to say that like many other businesses
it is greatly over-stocked, and that every such
business ought to be an autocracy. There
must, however, be ups and downs, and an old-
established firm may take a new lease of life, or
a new firm spring into pre-eminence so soon as
any really remarkable author needs a middle-man
between himself and the general public.

From the time that I went to Sturminster, in
1862, I adopted the plan which I never dis-
continued as long as I had health, of spending.
every possible holiday on the Continent. I
have a strong opinion that a more complete
change is to be got in this way than by any
vacation taken in England. The entire alteration of all surroundings is a clear gain, and even
a few days in France or Belgium is worth
double the time spent in holiday at home.

These tours were taken with members of my

own family or with one of my pupils when at
Sturminster. I was then a great deal at Paris;
but when my daughters were at school at
Fontainebleau and my sons had left school and
were resident in French and German families,
they were extended further. For the health of
one of my daughters, who had to spend the
winter in Madeira, I paid a short visit to settle
her in Funchal, and had the pleasure of knowing
the delight of that delightful climate. I remember waking up in the morning after I got
there, in the end of one December, drinking in
the sweet spring air and summer sunlight at
the open window. The lines of Wordsworth
came surging into my mind :—

> " Bliss was it in that Dawn to be alive,
> But to be young was very Heaven."

Not every chance visitor, however, was as
charmed with the island as I was in my short
experience of it. I met lately with the following criticism : " à Madére on existe, ou plutôt
on végète. On meurt quelquefois ; mais on ne
se marie jamais."

In Paris, in one such parson's holiday, I saw
much of Miss Charlotte Ritchie, for many years
a resident there, and a cousin of Mr. Thackeray.

She was one of those persons who so shrink from anything like publicity and live so beautiful a life unseen and almost unknown except by her friends, that to say more of her would be like rending a sacred veil asunder. But one characteristic story of her is so touching that it seems almost a duty to record it. On a cheerless wintry day a friend saw a pauper's funeral borne through one of the low quarters of Paris towards a poor suburban cemetery. Behind this walked alone through the snow and mire Miss Charlotte Ritchie. The friend went to offer his aid, and asked how she came to be there. She answered that seeing a funeral unaccompanied by any friends or attendants, she was so touched by the squalor and sadness that she had turned aside to follow the unknown pauper to his grave. The friend of course went with her and only these two, who never knew the name of the dead man they were following, attended him on his long last journey.

Through Miss Ritchie I became acquainted with M. and Mme. Mohl, and was for many years an attendant at her Salon, in the Rue du Bac, whenever I happened to be in Paris. Mme. Mohl was an Englishwoman, a Miss

Clarke, who quite late in life married the distinguished oriental scholar and gathered round her all that was most remarkable in Paris. To many of us it seemed that the only bond of union among the distinguished people at her house was hatred of the Emperor Napoleon III., and with that qualification all creeds and all politics were alike welcomed by her. On the same evening were to be seen M. Renan and M. de Montalembert. I only saw the latter once, but became intimate with M. and Mme. Renan, an intimacy never broken.

M. Renan's Autobiography is, or ought to be, known by all. I need only add what has, however, been observed by many besides myself, that he never lost the stamp impressed upon him by the seminaries in which he was educated for the priesthood, far as he wandered from the doctrines inculcated upon him. He was, however, so tolerant of the faith he had abandoned that he never could understand how it was people were so little tolerant of his own extravagations. I was sitting with him on one occasion, when he asked me how it was that Englishmen of all opinions had been so shocked with his *Vie de Jésus*, and professed himself quite unable to

understand this English standpoint. I said
that I would tell him one thing which had
revolted most English people——the passage in
which he speaks of the resurrection of Lazarus
as being probably a trick of which our Lord
might Himself have been an accomplice. M.
Renan said, with an air of considerable
astonishment, "Mais, mon ami, ce n'était
qu'une hypothèse," and remained quite unable
to see that such an hypothesis was as dis-
honouring to its holder as would have been a
direct assertion.

Although my holiday was usually spent in
France, either in Paris or the country districts,
I visited at different times and with different
companions parts of Germany before unknown
to me, Switzerland, Belgium, and Holland. I
will not attempt to describe what is so well
known to many of my readers, but I may as
well throw together what has seemed to me
worth preserving in various notes containing a
record of these tours.

In Paris, I think it was in 1865, I gained
permission to attend the emperor's Mass on
Sunday at the Tuileries, and was much scanda-
lised at all I saw, except the devotion of the

empress, which was evidently sincere. The whole performance seemed to me more a glorification of the emperor than of Him who was supposed to be worshipped. The Mass had to wait for the emperor's time, and previous to the entrance of the court, an usher, tapping his staff on the floor, marched up to the altar, turning his back to it and his face to the royal gallery, and proclaimed in loud tones and with the same sort of raps that herald the rising of the curtain at the opera, "l'Empereur!" The royal party then filed in and took their places; the priest, a Jewish gentleman who has since, I believe, reverted to the faith of his fathers, coming in and taking his place as the usher vacated it. The ceremony was a Low Mass and reduced to its shortest span.

In my tours in France I came to the conclusion that all the turmoil and fret of modern France is confined to the large towns; provincial France is quiet, orderly, conservative in the best sense, and Catholic. When I say Catholic, I remember that the Abbé Martin, in a walk I took with him through Paris, asserted that the working men even there were at heart Catholic, and he said, "They all come to us at the hour of their death." The French workman, however, is very different to the German workman, who, with scarce an exception, is proud of his education and the place taken by his country in consequence of this education. Once when in Amiens with my daughter I took a boat on the Somme, and we had a long and interesting conversation with the boatman on elementary education. He rested on his oars, and while we allowed ourselves to drift with the current, he said, "Mais, voyez-vous, Mademoiselle, plus on est instruit, plus on est bête,"—a sentiment with which many country squires in England would be found cordially to agree.

The French workman is always ready to make friends with anybody who will give himself the trouble to be interested in his occupations and pursuits. One Easter Day when staying at Dinant, I was present at a vesper service at a little village church which was filled to overflowing. The village orchestra were in the singing-gallery and performing their parts very well except on one occasion when there came a bass note in frightful discord with the rest of the voices. A village workman, who stood next to me in the aisle, turned and said to me, as trusting wholly in my sympathy : " C'est Pierre qui a fait ça."

Few congregations show such rapt devotion as those in French churches. Mr. Browning, whose sturdy Protestantism is evident throughout his books, as well as his sympathy with forms of faith not his own, once clutched the arm of a friend of his and mine at the moment of the Elevation, and said, " O Arthur, this is too good not to be true."

For several years a band of six friends, W. H. Gray, H. W. Watts, H. J. Hood, T. Hamond, E. Gosse, and I, went together for a short Easter holiday in France, and these tours are among the most delightful days of my life ; unclouded by the smallest shadow of a difference, brightened to me by incessant acts of kindness from all, and by the unfailing gaiety of Gosse.

We were often delighted with his criticisms on current literature, which we afterwards recognised in their printed form. He was particularly severe on the poems of a lady (who never had any admirers beyond her very enthusiastic husband), and had described the movements of her soul as those of a butterfly escaping from its chrysalis ; and he pretended

to believe that she was the author of an epitaph
which he had somewhere seen :—

> " She felt herself so foul within
> She broke the slough and crust of sin
> And hatched herself a cherubin."

I quote rather incongruously what I said in
1870 of the picture of the "Adoration of the
Lamb" of Ghent, in case it may lead any who
do not know it to make acquaintance with this
great work.

" Every one knows or guesses, if they have
not seen the picture, that the motive of it is
the Mystic Lamb of the Revelation, 'as it had
been slain,' and the great company of the
redeemed who came to worship him.   But
they worship in no mystic ideal heaven ; no
clouds are rolled about a throne in an unsub-
stantial sky.   A soft light from the west falls
on a sweet Rhine-land landscape, on a green
meadow studded with daisies.   Trees of foliage
and flowers strange to Germany grow indeed
in the bosquets, through which pathways lead
to the central field, but they are trees of earthly
growth, and do not seem incongruous.   The
Lamb, with a human look of life in his tender
eyes, stands on a central altar before which
plays a fountain of pure water, and all that is

idealised is the stream of blood which flows into a chalice from his pierced heart. That is ideal, for there is in it no suggestion of the shambles or of sacrifice to death ; it is a living heart that lives still, but gives of its love thus symbolised. Those who are gathered are types of men of all classes and kinds ; in front are the great saints, and patriarchs, and apostles. From the blooming thickets come those who had done for mankind great charity, who had founded abbeys of learning and of rest, and the holy women who had loved and died. There is no hint of rejection, none of the dark doctrines of sin and death. It is a bright, happy, human company gathered before the symbol of love, as it seemed to men of that day. Of the technical merits of the picture it is not for me to speak : I am no painter, no art critic— like that company, I can stand only and adore.

" The great picture is set in a disused chapel, where now no tapers flare, no Mass is said, no relics are enshrined, no censer sends up its smoke. It is not love for art as such that leaves the picture here alone, for the traveller may see the works of very great artists darkened by smoke in many a Belgian town ; it is not that the trappings of the altar would interfere with it, for it could well hang elsewhere and out of the way.

" Rather is it that into the sluggish souls of Belgian canons has penetrated some consciousness of the divinity which dwells in the great painting. An altar which is crowned by this has no need of any other presence in order to consecrate it."

Of a tour in Holland in 1876 I will quote a few lines as showing what even twenty years ago appeared to a then non-Catholic observer of the revival of the Church in Holland.

" It is of course easy to generalise from a few particulars, and it may be difficult to do so correctly, but the speakers in hotels and railway carriages who care to give information to travellers, and who show by their conversations that they are acquainted with their subjects, are no bad index to the feeling of a people. And on religion and on politics we have had several conversations with interesting men. From these it seems that the same sort of action and reaction is going on in the religious world here as in England, the same conflict between a renascent Catholicism and extreme free-thought, the same revival of

Catholic architecture, not yet here yielding to a quasi Queen Anne style, the same strife among the sects, the same growing conviction that, though existing kings and queens may be harmless and even meritorious, one shake would bring them down like the tumbling ranks which a child makes of his father's worn packs of cards.

"One of these court cards, the Crown Princess of Prussia, won all hearts at Scheveningen this summer. So said several, especially a Prussian ex-Uhlan, now a horse-dealer in Holland, with whom there came into our carriage an atmosphere as of a whole cavalry stable. He was a cheery, voluble person, likely to drive a good bargain, who consumed much cognac, 'all in the way of business,' as he told us, though it scarcely appeared how it aided his trade at that particular time. Of 'unsere Victoria' he said that she was 'eine edle, noble, gebildete, liebenswürdige Frau,' while her husband was 'echter Soldat,' and if all royal people did their trade as well as those two, the republic which must come in the end would be long postponed.

" It is no wonder that royal personages who can afford it go to Scheveningen in the season. Even now, with the shrill wind stripping the oak trees in the wood of the Hague, with a long row of disused restaurants and closed shutters, the vast stretch of firm, silver sands, and the miles of tumbling sea, the picturesque fishermen and fishwives, the great boats with their sails of ruddy brown made a pleasant picture under the bright sun and clear sky. It must be a very paradise for children, and the immediate neighbourhood of the Hague would prevent the most clubbable *père de famille* from being bored. Fancy the wildest part of the Lancashire shore, Fleetwood or Poulton-le-Sands, brought as close to Pall Mall as is St. John's Wood ! "

It may be noticed by those who are good enough to read these recollections that I have said nothing of the books which particularly moved me after my Eton days. This is because from that time onward I read everything I could, and steeped myself, so far as might be, both in English and foreign literature. It would be quite true were I to explain how large a part of myself became the poems of Clough and Matthew Arnold, the novels of George Eliot and Thomas Hardy ; but it would seem unfair to many others who perhaps affected me as much. Living as I did in Dorsetshire, I was able perhaps to understand how absolutely true to life are the pictures in Hardy's early books.

When *Far from the Madding Crowd* came out I was reading it aloud to my wife, when one of our little girls being in the room, looked up and said, " Why, mother, those people talk exactly like Mr. Singleton." Mr. Singleton was the carter whose cart stable-yard skirted our garden and constantly allowed our children to ride his great horses bare-back to watering. This unconscious criticism of a mere child was a perfect tribute to the naturalness of Hardy's descriptions and to the conversations of his peasants. At our table afterwards, when he was living in London, a lady sitting between him and me asked him where was the Egdon Heath described in *The Return of the Native*. To which he replied, " You must ask Mr. Paul, as he is the one man in England who knows Dorsetshire as well as I do." In those earlier books, even when he seems to get away to Cornwall, the real scenery remains Dorset ; and William Worm is as true a Dorset labourer as any D'Urberville of his later works.

X

FRIENDS IN LONDON

1874

NEARLY all that I have to say about my life in London falls under the recollections of various interesting persons whom I have known well, who have honoured me with their friendship during the last twenty-five years.

With few exceptions, I must speak only of those who have already passed into the hidden life, and these few will, I am sure, forgive me for mentioning what has been to me so great a pleasure.

One of the foremost of those with whom I became very intimate was Miss Thornton, who died in 1887, at the age of ninety. To her I owe the following paper of questions on Miss Austen's *Emma*, drawn up by Mr. Rose, rector of Weybridge, which is worthy to take rank with Calverley's like and well-known examination paper on *Pickwick*.

1. Indicate by a careful statement of distances in miles the exact locality of Highbury, mentioning briefly the occasions on which these distances are stated. On what coach road and on what river was it situated? Prove by exact internal evidence that it was in the vicinity of a coach road and of a river.

2. Draw a plan of Highbury Street, marking the relative positions of Randall's, Ford's, the Crown, and Miss Bates' house. Insert any other position of places which in your opinion can be determined, giving an account of the passages on which you rely.

3. State all you know about "the Sucklings"— their home, their circumstances, their accomplishments, and their neighbours.

4. Give the Christian names of James's daughter, of Frank Churchill, of Mrs. Weston, Emma's grandmother, Miss Bates, Mr. Knightley, Mr. Elton, Mr. Woodhouse, and say in what context the names of Emma's grandmother and Miss Bates occur.

5. Put down all you know about Mrs. Bates' shawl.

6. Who was the proprietor of the Crown? When do we first hear of it? Describe the ball-room and its appearance. How was it generally used? How many steps were there between it and the supper-room.

7. Give an account of all the forms of food and drink mentioned in *Emma*, and the occasions in which they respectively occur.

8. State all you know about the household of Mrs. Goddard. When she spent an evening at Hartfield how was the time passed?

9. What good service had Mr. Dixon rendered to Jane?

10. Mention the months in which the chief incidents occurred.

11. What graceful acts are recorded of Frank at his first visit?

12. What references are there in *Emma* to works of literature?

13. When was Emma first conscious that she loved Mr. Knightley?

14. What signs of love does Mr. Knightley manifest before his offer?

15. Describe Emma's complexion, eyes, and hair, stating your authority. What was her fortune?

16. Describe Harriet's vacillations at Ford's, if possible in the words of the author.

17. In the same manner write down Mrs. Elton's monologue in the strawberry beds at Donwell.

18. Describe in his own words Mr. John Knightley's views of society.

19. Describe Jane Fairfax's face and character, and say what hope you have of her future happiness, as also of the future happiness of Mr. Martin.

20. Give the chief incidents of the Cole dinner-party.

21. Give the context or the occasion of the following words :—

> "If it had been handed round once."
> "I smile because you smile."
> "They are all very different."
> "Rather he than I."
> "What do you deserve?"

I ought to speak of my friend Professor W. K. Clifford, who died after a lingering illness at Madeira in 1878. The reason for going there was not any idea of saving a life already doomed, but of making his last hours more easy. I never knew a man who was a more complete agnostic than Clifford, but it always seemed to me that, had a longer span of life been allowed him, he would have gone the whole round of disbelief and found the solution of all his difficulties in the Catholic Church. I subjoin a paper which he drew up not long before he went to Madeira to die ; it expresses views which breathe to my mind the spirit of most earnest piety, though outside the bounds of all creeds : I ought to say that I have found most deep and true indications of Christian spirit in those who seemed alien to it, and amongst these I would especially name Clifford, Dr. Congreve, and George Eliot :—

"TO LABOUR IS TO PRAY.

Let him who would raise himself by communion with what is highest and best in his own soul, or in the universe, labour for our father Man who is within us :

That his name may be counted holy among men ;

That his kingdom may come, the kingdom of the light and the right, in which there shall be no more priest or Cæsar;

That his will may be done in fact, as it is in the ideal world;

That with him we may day by day make good our daily step of progress;

That our trespasses may not be forgiven, but repaired; for there is no sin but sin against Man;

That our common efforts may lead us out of darkness and deliver us from the deceiver.

For Man's is the light, and the right, and the striving upwards, from the beginning to the end of the ages."

Another lady who attained almost the great age of Miss Thornton, but had lived far more in general society, was Mrs. Procter, formerly Miss Skepper, and stepdaughter of Basil Montagu. Like Miss Thornton, she was full of sharp sayings, but there was a certain dash of gall in them. The daughter who lived with her died, and I know well how great was the grief to her mother. She might have said of her daughter's death what Mrs. Kingsley said to me, "that only a sense of humour carried her through the dreadful weeks immediately succeeding her husband's death." With the same sense of humour, Mrs. Procter told me that another daughter, a nun, came to visit her after her daughter Edith's death, and according to the rules of her Order she could not come alone. She brought, therefore, another nun with her, who was quite unknown to Mrs. Procter. Mrs. Procter related how the first thing which gave her any hope that she might recover from the great blow she had suffered was when she and her daughter were talking and weeping over the one they had lost, " I saw the other nun, who could not have cared about my dear Edith, snivelling in the corner, and I so entered into the absurdity of it that I felt that I might regain my spirits."

I will here reprint what I wrote of her at her death, in the *Academy*, because no longer biography exists of her. By her desire all her letters and papers were burnt by her granddaughter, who lived with her for some years before her death.

" Our readers may not unnaturally have expected to see in the *Academy* last week some obituary notice of a lady so well known as Mrs. Procter, who, if not literary herself, has been closely connected with almost every eminent man and woman of letters since the beginning of the century. The present paper was not at once written, in deference to the wishes of the dead, who often expressed to the writer her feeling that obituary notices were hurried and ill-considered, and that in most cases silence was the fitting form of respect and sorrow. She had also the strongest dislike to the view, not uncommon—as it would seem—that death removes all seals of secrecy, that private letters may be read by the world, and private affairs revealed so soon as the voice which would have protested is hushed for ever. Bearing her wishes on the subject in mind, the writer only now speaks when, other notices having already appeared, some of the nearest relatives and friends wish that some further slight account of Mrs. Procter should be placed on record by one who had the honour to know her well.

"Anne Benson Procter was born at York on September 11, 1799. Her father, Mr. Skepper, was a Yorkshire squire of small landed property, but descended and deriving his name from the German Scheffer, the partner of Fust, the earliest printer. Her mother was a Miss Benson, of the same county, and aunt of the present Archbishop of Canterbury. Mrs. Skepper, early left a widow, married Mr. Basil Montagu, Q.C., the well-known reformer of the bankruptcy laws and editor of Bacon. Though he had been married twice before, he was still a young man, occupying a good social and literary position, and able to introduce his brilliant young wife to a circle in which she took a prominent part. Mr. Montagu was fourteen when Dr. Johnson, whom he knew, died; he was the intimate associate of Godwin, Coleridge, Wordsworth; he watched by Mary Wollstonecraft's deathbed; Sir James Mackintosh helped to steady those liberal principles which were growing somewhat wild under Godwin's influence; his home was the haunt not only of Londoners like Charles Lamb, but of young men from the country before they grew famous, if only they had promise in them, like Edward Irving and Carlyle.

" Thus from her early childhood Anne Skepper was surrounded by liberal and literary influences which moulded her strong and bright nature. The word liberal is used, however, only to designate her independent, vigorous thought; for in politics Mrs. Procter was, and remained, a high Tory, a Church and State woman of the old school, accepting in these later years the principles of the Primrose League, and wearing its badge with pleasure. Her recollections of those early days were most interesting ; but she was so full of life to the last, and so in touch with all that was around her, that the talk about them was quite unlike ordinary senile memories : Lamb and Godwin might have passed from us but yesterday. Not long since a letter from Lamb to Mrs. Basil Montagu found its way into the autograph market, in which he expressed contrition for having allowed himself to become the worse for liquor at her table. Mrs. Procter said, ' But they have not seen the second letter, which I have upstairs, written next day, in which he said that my mother might ask him again with safety, because he never got drunk twice in the same house.'

" She would speak as if it had been a romance of last week, of how zealously Mrs. Montagu threw herself into young people's love affairs, so that Irving's marriage with Miss Martin took place from her house ; and at the age of eighty-five, as many of Mrs. Procter's friends will remember, Mrs. Montagu's daughter engaged with inherited zeal in the arrangements for another marriage opposed by the lady's family. She was ever ready to do battle for her mother and stepfather if they were misunderstood or misrepresented in the smallest degree. It was not enough to her generous nature that their high characters and their name in the world should speak for themselves. Thus, when Carlyle's disparaging remarks on Basil Montagu's patronage and the kindness of his wife were brought to light with ill-nature and unwisdom, she printed and circulated widely early letters which showed Carlyle as a grateful suppliant for favour ; and it was with difficulty that some of her friends persuaded her to suppress a scathing motto from *Othello*, which seemed to her to fit the facts of the case.

"In 1823 Miss Skepper married Bryan Waller Procter, known in literature as 'Barry Cornwall,' who was shortly after called to the Bar. Means were small, Mr. Procter was 'a simple, sincere, shy, and delicate soul,' as Mr. Coventry Patmore calls him, and his wife's spirits often had to do for both. She retained her old literary friends, and made by degrees many more, who loved herself and her husband for their own sakes. During great part of their early married life they lived with the Montagus, so that the two circles of friends were fused into one.

" Mr. Procter's poems are probably now known but to few; but when he was a young man, in the third decade of this century, they had a vogue which would now be scarcely understood. Popular composers set his songs— much better than words to music were wont to be—and schoolboys had them by heart. Still, though more than fifty years have gone by since he saw them, the present writer could repeat a poem on London streets, which were not found to be paved with gold—' King Death,' ' The Sea,' and many others—read in school hours under the shelter of a friendly desk-lid. Nor did we schoolboys think them, as Lamb did, ' redundant.' In July 1827 Lamb wrote to Patmore: ' Procter has a wen growing out of the nape of his neck, which his wife wants him to have cut off; but I think it rather an agreeable excrescence—like his poetry —redundant.' The wen is probably as much imagination, or banter, as the next sentence: ' Godwin was taken up for picking pockets.'

"Six children, in somewhat rapid succession, left scant time for society ; but it was never dropped, and in one way or another the Procters knew most people worth knowing in London. They were, as Mr. Patmore says—we may make his words plural—' the friends of almost every person of character in art or letters. They had after a while sufficient means, Mr. Procter having been appointed in 1831 Commissioner in Lunacy—an office which he held for thirty years. Mr. Procter died in 1874, and had · reached the precise age which his wife also attained. During all those years, when as Miss Skepper in her mother's house, and afterwards in her own, so many persons passed before her, it is not to be expected that she would, or could, view all with equal liking, and in truth she piqued herself on being as good a hater as she was a friend. It would not be fair to specify later names ; but there can be no harm in telling that her pet aversion was the pedant philosopher Godwin. He was the type of the persons for whom she could feel no tolerance.

"During Mr. Procter's failing health his wife was a good deal withdrawn from the society of

all but her intimate friends——and they were
many; but for the last thirteen years few
people have been better known in London, nor
till quite within the last few months would
any one have learnt from her conversation or
manner that she had passed from middle life
to old age. What she was at fifty she was at
eighty and long past that time.

"'Our Lady of Bitterness,' one among her
friends has named her, and she did not shrink
from the title; but neither he nor any one who
knew her well would recognise it as more than
an accidental description. Her conversation
and her criticism were always tonic; and there
must be a dash of bitter in every tonic, how
pleasant and healthful soever it may be. She
always sat very upright, with her whole figure
as it were on the alert. Then, when need was,
she seemed to straighten herself still more,
and with a sparkle of mischief in her eyes,
bright to the last, she flashed out her verbal
dagger, whose blade was so keen that the interlocutor admired the weapon more than he
felt the wound. She never was prosy, though
she now and then repeated to her hearers a
good thing she had said on another occasion——

" ' I found myself, my dear,' she said, ' in such odd company last night, at Mr. ———'s. I don't know how the man came to ask me or why I went. But when I saw Lady ——— (who had just been divorced) I could not resist saying to her, " What an odd party this is ! All the men have been co-respondents, and all the women, except you and me, have lost their characters ! " '

" But this sharpness of tongue was accompanied by the greatest kindness of heart and action. When Mrs. Jameson was in need, Mrs. Procter's untiring energy gained from her friends a sufficient sum to settle on her an adequate annuity. She was even too chivalric and self-denying for the sake of those who told her a story which worked on her sympathies. And she was equally pleased to sit for an evening with an invalid or poor friend in humble lodgings as at a great entertainment where she was the life of the party. She kept herself young in a measure through the young, whose confidante and adviser she was on many occasions.

" Her reading was, with limitations, extremely various, one curious limitation being that she knew no language but her own. Some phrases of French every one must learn if they live a certain number of years in the world, but she refused to admit that she knew any; and if by chance in her presence a French story was told, or a French phrase used, her whole figure grew stony, and her countenance was as that of the deaf adder that stoppeth her ears. It might almost be thought that, as M. Renan is said to have avoided learning English lest he should injure the perfection of his French style, so Mrs. Procter avoided foreign tongues for the sake of her English. A very few weeks before her death she was speaking of the novel, *The New Antigone*, of which she had read every word, and praised it for the sake of the conversations. ' People speak in it as they were taught to speak when I was young. They use good grammar, and always finish their sentences: that is rare both in books and talk now.' It is quite true that her own words were as finished as they were incisive. There is, perhaps, no one else in recent days, with the exception of George Eliot, whose spoken words, if taken down in shorthand for a book, would have left no room for correction. But Mrs. Procter was by far the **more** rapid and conversational of the two.

"Her energy and interests were marvellous, and her physical powers great. On a day, for instance, when she was 'at home,' and received visitors all the afternoon, she would dine out, and go to an evening party, at which she rarely sat down, as fresh at midnight as at noon.

"It would be, however, a complete mistake to consider Mrs. Procter as one who lived merely for society, much as she enjoyed it. It was, she said herself, a question of temperament. There was no reason why, if she enjoyed seeing her friends abroad, she was not doing as good a work as if she had been asleep in her chair. She did not go at all on the French principle— that a man is as young as he feels, and a woman as old as she looks; feeling was to her the test in the cases of both sexes. Much the same rule applied to her entrance into society again after the deaths of husband and daughters. That those who were gone would have wished her to do so, that a pretence of not liking it better than moping alone would have been mere hypocrisy, were adequate reasons for doing as she wished; nor was there in this any want of affection. The touching way in which she was wont to speak of 'my Adelaide,' my Edith,' showed how present and vivid were the memories of those who had left her side. She could not endure the way in which many people think it a sign of reverence to change or sink their voices in talking of their dead relatives, 'as if they had done something to be ashamed of, as you would speak of a bankrupt uncle.'

" In regard to her daughters and other members of her family who followed in their steps, she showed a wise tolerance. One after another of them became Catholics, one a nun. The family union was in no way broken for this cause. The granddaughter who ministered to her last days did the same. She was free as her aunts had been to act on her honest convictions. On her own faith Mrs. Procter was reticent, no doubt believing that ' it was that of all sensible people, which sensible people never tell.' But if it be one of the signs of a mind at rest to be sunny and cheerful, then she had such a mind, the outcome of a good life.

" If Mrs. Procter was interesting as an acquaintance, she was still more valuable as a friend. Probably in later years it was only by some accident that any were admitted to this inner circle. One such friend entered into it, owing to an accidental conversation with her daughter a few weeks before her death. That the hand of death was on Miss Procter was only too evident, but the mother and the daughter each trying to spare the other, the subject was avoided. Miss Procter told a friend how near the end was, that she grieved only for the suffering it would cause her mother, how deep was her own inward peace, and how great the comfort of her faith. The end came at last suddenly ; and Mrs. Procter blamed herself with calm, unshrinking bitterness that she had not told her daughter of its near approach. The friend was able to remove the notion that death had been unexpected, and will always remember the relief to the mother's heart, the unforgetting gratitude during the remaining years for so slight a service.

"There are other old ladies living in society, clever and bright, but Mrs. Procter stood alone. She was always simple, spoke her whole mind, and was entirely herself. Any transparent artifice was never intended to conceal. If her hair was not grey, but a *blond cendré*, it was because all women of fifty years ago wore a front ;

never was false hair so completely *en evidence*. If she differed from a speaker, she said so ; and if she thought him silly it appeared in her tone, but always with a kindly tolerance.

" In her passes away one whom many have liked, and an inner circle have loved, who sat at the feet of those who talked with Johnson and Boswell, and about whose chair have gathered most of the wisest and most entertaining men who succeeded them, down to the poets and the novelists who are yet young. She wrote next to nothing herself, only bright little letters which will never be published, in a handwriting clear, precise, and lady-like as herself. If those who came about her live as long as she did, or longer yet, it will always be among their pleasantest and happiest memories——not always perhaps possible to make clear to others, since no evidence of what she was will remain——that they knew Mrs. Procter, or better still, were honoured by her friendship."

Not long before her death Mr. Browning, Mr. Matthew Arnold, and I were standing in front of the fireplace one Sunday afternoon, talking about the various incomes made by prominent persons, and Mrs. Procter was giving

her own reminiscences of barristers' and physi-**cians'** fees, and the sums obtained by literature **by** men known to her in her youth.

Mr. Browning thereupon told how at the house of a distinguished surgeon he had met an exalted personage, who to much *bonhomie* joins an inordinate curiosity. He said to the surgeon, "I should like to know, of course I do not speak of present company, what a first-rate surgeon makes in his profession." "Well, sir," said the host, "I should say that about £15,000 a year would be the mark." "What," said the prince, turning to the then acknowledged leader of the English Bar, "what does a great barrister make?" "I suppose, sir, £25,000 would hit the mark." Sir John Millais was also present, and he was the third asked. "Possibly, sir, £35,000 a year." "Oh, come, come," said the questioner. "Well, sir," said Sir John Millais, rather nettled, "as a matter of fact, last year I made £40,000, and might have made more, had I not been taking holiday longer than usual in Scotland." When he had finished speaking Mr. Browning put his arms through Mr. Arnold's and mine, and said, "We don't make that by literature, do we?"

Soon after coming to London I became acquainted with G. H. Lewes and George Eliot, who were then living at the Priory, North Bank, Regent's Park, and very soon grew extremely intimate with them. At my first visit Mrs. Paul was absent from London, and when she came home I asked her to call with me one Sunday afternoon. This she did not wish to do, but had no objection to my going alone. I did not, however, choose to visit at any house without her, and in consequence simply did not go. A few Sundays after Mrs. Paul, not wishing to shut me off from what had been so evident a pleasure, made up her mind to accompany me, and when walking home, she said, "I am convinced that she is a good and pure woman, and I will go whenever you like." I imagine that the larger number of those who were intimate at North Bank made up their minds that they were visiting altogether exceptional people, under exceptional circumstances, without being able to define to themselves wherein the exception consisted. But a few persons, who wished to seem quite consistent, affected to believe that the first Mrs. Lewes was dead and that Lewes and George Eliot had been married in Sweden.

This was an absolute fiction, in no way countenanced by themselves. I was on one occasion at their house when no one was present but Mr. and Mrs. Lewes and myself, and we were talking of social proprieties. "You know," said Lewes to her, "how completely we have set these at defiance, and how often we have doubted whether we were wise in doing so."

George Eliot's Salon on Sundays was a stately reception, in which her talk was always well worth hearing: she raised conversation on whatever subject she touched to a higher level. Miss Anna Swanwick is the only other person I know with the same immediate power of raising the conversation with apparent continuity and without seeming to force it. George Lewes used to flit about the room talking at large and brilliantly, though to many of us who were, as he described us, "pratiquants" at his house, his calling George Eliot "Polly" was rather a shock. In days when we were fortunate enough to be asked to the house when they were not at home to everybody they were both still more interesting, and when Lewes died some years before George Eliot, it was not only a grief but a surprise to many of us to find how much we had loved him. After his death my wife and I remained on most affectionate terms with George Eliot; and in the last summer of her life, after she returned from abroad with her husband, Mr. Cross, we were the only ones of her old friends who saw very much of her, as we happened to inhabit for the summer a house close to their Witley home.

I was at that time bringing out a new edition of *The Imitation of Christ*, of which she has spoken so beautifully in the *Mill on the Floss*. She wrote telling me the date at which they were to arrive in London, and I sent to her a day or two afterwards the first finished copy of the work which came into my hands. Mr. Cross wrote me a note telling me at the same time of her short illness and of her death; and also that my book only reached the house in time to be laid on her coffin. I attended her funeral, going from the house at Chelsea in the same carriage with Mrs. Browning and Mr. Blackwood, her publisher. She always took the deepest interest in my researches into the life of Mary Wollstonecraft, on which I was able to throw much light, as one who like herself set conventionalities at defiance, and triumphed over the usual feelings of society.

At the Priory I also first met, after coming up to London, Robert Browning, with whom also I became intimate. Mr. Browning, who frequently dined at the same houses with myself, always made a point of walking home, however far, at night, and on these occasions I was very often his companion. He, as can be easily understood from his letters, was a man of most varied and wide information on almost every possible subject, however unexpected. On one occasion, at the table of Mr. Leighton, the father of Lord Leighton, the conversation turned on murder, and to the surprise of everybody Mr. Browning showed himself acquainted with the minutest details of every *cause célèbre* of that kind within living memory. He quoted a ghastly stanza on Thurtell's murder of Mr. Weare—

> " His throat they cut from ear to ear,
> His brains they battered in,"

and was rather piqued that another guest was able to complete the lines with

> " His name was Mr. William Weare,
> He lived at Lyon's Inn."

Certainly no one posed less as a poet in society. On one occasion we were dining out together. He had just published one of his dramatic studies, I think it was the " Prince of Hohenstielschwangau." While passing from the dining-room to the drawing-room he said to me, " Well, do you like my new volume?" I answered, " Yes, Mr. Browning, but your old admirers, who have known you for so many years, wish that you would give us some more lyrics." Whereat he answered in a tone of contempt, " Lyrics, if you want lyrics, I can give you buckets full." In his absolute simplicity he was a great contrast to Tennyson, with whom it is almost as futile to compare him as it is in a German household to compare Goethe and Schiller. Tennyson always posed. Matthew Arnold did not pose as a poet, but he had a certain grandiose manner which he never laid aside. Browning was always the simple man of the world.

So long as Professor Huxley lived in London we were much at his house. He was an interesting and brilliant talker so long as he kept to his own studies. He was, however, totally uninteresting both in conversation and in writing when he touched on theology. This was not at all his own view, for he seemed to believe himself little short of an inspired teacher on biblical questions, just as Mr. Gladstone, to the despair of scholars who admired him, posed as a great teacher on Homer.

Though I was not in those days a Catholic, I had the honour of knowing both the great cardinals, then living, Newman and Manning, and also the man who so constantly crossed the path of both of them, Dr. Ward, the author of an *Ideal Christian Church*. I frequently met the last of these three at Mr. Tennyson's in the Isle of Wight. They were near neighbours and cordial friends. Of Manning I will only say that he struck me still more as a statesman than as a theologian. He once said to me, " Were I not Cardinal Archbishop of Westminster, I would wish to be a great demagogue." And he was then gaining the hearts of the working men of England as very few of our generation have gained them. To Newman I can only express my daily and hourly gratitude. His writings and character have been my study and my model since my earliest Oxford days, and when I came to know him, it was only to regard him with increased admiration.

The two men were very different, and perhaps a little story may serve to show how different. When about to bring out the new edition of the *Imitation*, of which I have already spoken, each of the two cardinals, at different times, asked me in what way the revised text differed from those in general use. I gave to each as a specimen a passage in which it seemed to me that Bishop Chaloner and most translators had missed the meaning. Newman answered without a moment's hesitation, " I quite agree with you, but I do not know the usual English translations, for I have never read the book in English." Cardinal Manning said to the same quotation, with his peculiar snuffle, " Yes, I agree with you, you are right ; but is it well to say it ? "

I ought to mention a friend, of just my own age, who with his wife became very dear to me—Charles Earle. There are few people during my whole life with whom I have been in more thorough sympathy ; and his sudden death by a bicycle accident has been one of the greatest sorrows of the last few years.

Through them I came to know well Mrs. Earle's brother-in-law, Robert, Lord Lytton, whose life of his father was among the books published by me. Contrary to my advice he insisted on the publication of the earlier volumes of this book without waiting for the completion of the whole ; and as so often happens, he found that he had undertaken it on too large a scale, and also that there were many details which he would not care to give to the world. It remains therefore, and will remain, only a fragment, though it is full of interest. It will be many years before the first Lord Lytton is forgotten as a novelist, though his books are little read by those who have passed their teens. For young men, however, entering into life, they will for a long time to come put into words their own unspoken yearnings after the ideal, and show that it is possible for a states-man to be also a poet and a dreamer.

Robert, the second Lord Lytton, however, was a far more interesting figure. Few men have ever been so praised by another poet as he has been by his friend Wilfrid Blunt in a sonnet called " To One in High Position," when he was Viceroy of India. Lord Lytton himself looked upon his life as rather a failure. He said to me with infinite pathos, " I gave the best of my life to India, my deepest thoughts, my most ardent anxieties, and my reward was to hear scarce anything but blame about my Indian policy. I went as ambassador to Paris, about which I did not care, and the work of which never touched my heart, to hear that I was a most admirable ambassador, and had at last found my true position." Lord Lytton was fond of his beautiful place Knebworth, although his father, whose taste was never good, had done his best to spoil it by false stucco ornaments externally, in the way of gargoyles and *quasi* Gothic pinnacles. On these time worked its inevitable revenge with even greater rapidity than might have been expected; and each frost brought down, in the life of his son, some pinnacle which (despite its composition) his father had deemed permanent. I was walking one morning with the late Lord Lytton up and down the lawn in front of the house, after a sharp night's frost, when the gardener came to tell him of the fall of another gargoyle with these words: " If you please, my lord, there is another of them bloody monkeys fallen down in the night."

While the elder Lord Lytton was far more

interesting in his books than in himself, Robert, Lord Lytton, was more interesting than his books. *Lucille* is a very clever novel in verse; *Glenaveril* is a failure, which, however, ought to be remembered for a time. The story of *Glenaveril* is one of changed children, and the one supposed to be the heir is to be nourished by a nurse after the mother's death. It is proposed to this good lady that she shall undertake to supply the needs of both children, to which she replies :—

"A wet nurse, sir, is not a *table d'hôte*,"—

a line at any rate worth preserving. The book may be remembered also for its presentment of his friend the Rev. Whitwell Elwyn, once editor of the *Edinburgh Review*, who is pictured in *Glenaveril* under the name of Edelrath. Finding him in this book took me back to my younger days again when I knew Mr. Elwyn, not at all as Edelrath, but as a very fervent preacher who used to storm in his little country curacy of Hardington as though he would take the roof off the church.

Through Lord Lytton I came to know the friend of whom I have already spoken, Wilfrid

Blunt, whom I take to be one of the two or three living poets of the present day. It may be a prejudice on my part, but among those few moderns whom my old age counts as true poets are three Catholics—Coventry Patmore, Wilfrid Blunt, and Mrs. Hamilton King.

In those years I saw a great deal more of some people I had known before, but not on the same terms of intimacy—among others, Lady Eastlake and Mrs. Oliphant. The former of these was a complete survival of a lady of the last generation. I never saw her either sitting on a sofa or in an easy chair, but she sat up at a table with a little slanting writing-desk before her, surrounded with the stiffest of furniture, although priceless works of art hung upon the walls. The mixture of these with her husband's works, to which she always showed the most touching devotion, was curious to those of a generation which had been formed rather by Ruskin than by Sir Charles Eastlake.

Mrs. Oliphant was always far more interesting than her books, and my frequent Sunday afternoons at Eton were rendered even more delightful when I paid a visit to her at Windsor. She always appeared to me to have begun her books with great enthusiasm, but to have got tired of her creations too soon ; and to me, therefore, her books seemed never worth reading to the end. But this was not so with her friends. She never tired of them, and treated them with the greatest kindness and sympathy. I seldom knew any one with such great toleration, such constant patience among many sorrows, and with such unwavering faith in a future life.

With James Anthony Froude, also, I knitted up an old Oxford acquaintance. Yet I cannot say I either trusted or believed in him. Even before I became a Catholic I loved Newman too much to feel drawn to any one who played to him a traitor's part. Froude was, I believe, the author of the " Life of Saint Bettelin," in the *Lives of the English Saints*, and was so trusted by Newman that he sent the Life to the press unread. The little postscript, in which the whole was admitted to be an ingenious fiction, really put an end to the series.

"And this is all that is known and more than all, but nothing to that which the angels know, of the life of a servant of God, who sinned and repented and did penance and washed out

his sins, and became a saint and reigns with
Christ in Heaven."

Such, however, had not always been Froude's
attitude to Newman. He was one of the in-
mates of the *quasi* monastery at Littlemore,
which played so large a part in the later
Anglican years of Cardinal Newman's life.
When Newman was at Littlemore, preparing
for the inevitable change, Cardinal Manning,
still an Anglican, preached his University
sermon on November 5th, Guy Fawkes' day,
and took occasion to fulminate against the
Church of Rome, as though by his own eloquence to reaffirm himself in his waning
allegiance to the English Church. In the
afternoon he walked over to Littlemore to call
on Newman, but the rumour of his sermon had
preceded him, and Newman refused to see him.
Sending a message to that effect by a young
novice, the two had an eager conversational
dispute at the door; and the refusal being
persistent, they walked away towards Oxford
together. So eager was their conversation that
it was not till they got close to Magdalen
Bridge that they became aware that people
were looking at them curiously, and the younger

man discovered that he had walked all the way without his hat, so vehement had he been in talk. The young novice who then took Newman's side was none other than James Anthony Froude. As though to show the truth of Mephistopheles' saying, "Du bist am Ende was du bist," Mr. Froude's attempt to smirch the memory of his second great teacher, Carlyle, is within the knowledge of us all.

At Mrs. Gordon's, Pixholme, near Dorking, I made the acquaintance of Mrs. Drummond, widow of Mr. Drummond, the Irish secretary, who soon became one of my great friends. There, too, I met and for a time saw much of Mr. George Meredith and his charming wife, whose courage and sweet temper in a long and painful illness has often come to my memory and helped me to bear my own suffering. I will here say how great a delight it was to me to know well one whom I had long regarded as among the first of living writers, whose novel, *The Ordeal of Richard Feverel*, I put on the highest level of English literature.

Of Mrs. Drummond I do not speak at length, because at her daughters' request I wrote a little Life of her. Both in her days, and own in those of her daughters, I was most kindly received at Fredley and in London.

At Mrs. Drummond's I was frequently able to meet many of her political friends ; and there had the great pleasure of an acquaintance with Mr. Bright. He was a most agreeable companion, very simple, very eloquent, but with a curious power of will and determination to be the leader. Of his simplicity I remember a very characteristic trait. He was staying in the house, and Mrs. Drummond, who thought so old a man would probably bring a servant with him, had arranged that his man should have the dressing-room attached to his bed-room. When we sat down to dinner, she said, "I hope, Mr. Bright, your man found every-thing comfortable for you." "Man," he said, "I never travel with a man." "I hope, then, that *my* man made you comfortable." "Well," he said, "I found that he had *squandered* my clothes all about my room, and that, I suppose, is what he meant to do." On the Sunday afternoon, as twilight fell, before it was time to dress, some one suggested he should read aloud. He said, "What shall I read?" One of the party handed to him a volume of Shelley which happened to be on the table. He put it aside with the simple words, " Shelley was an atheist," as though that entirely settled the question. I forget what he did read, but was struck with the beauty and the power of his voice.

Though I had known Mark Pattison at Oxford, my real acquaintance with him was in the later years of his life, during which time he became a most kind friend and adviser to my daughters, as well as a valued friend of my own. A friend of Newman's and his collaborator in the *Lives of the English Saints*, he was at one moment on the very point of reception into the Catholic Church, and had made all arrangements for this step at Birmingham. The mere accident of his missing the coach one morning gave him further time for consideration, and the opportunity neglected never was given him again. He is generally considered to have been a mere dry scholar, but he was in fact a man full of enthusiasm, and a most kind, tender friend. He always made a point of celebrating the communion in his college chapel when Rector of Lincoln, and never delegated this duty to any one, a touching instance of the hold the memory of his former convictions still had upon him.

Romanes was a man who, beginning his career in wide revolt against orthodoxy of all kinds, had gradually worked his way back to belief through science; and is one of those who, like Clifford, would, I believe, have found his way into the Church of Rome had time been allowed him.

At the invitation of one of the directors of the company in which my former firm was merged, I met at dinner at his house the notorious Madame Blavatsky, the Russian spiritist. I had for many years taken some interest in the phenomena called " occult or spiritual," and investigated them when possible before I became a Catholic. It was no surprise to me to find how deeply the Church discourages all such researches. Some years before this I had accompanied a friend to a séance at which flowers were showered on us by " spirit " hands, and was at several similar séances from time to time at the house of Mr. Priaulx in Cavendish Square, stepfather of my friend J. H. Nelson. Mrs. Priaulx was an ardent believer, Mr. Priaulx and Nelson, hard-headed materialists.

At these séances it was clear that whenever I or any other unbeliever was next the medium no phenomena occurred, while when "believers" were in immediate contact with him flowers rained, accordions played, and "spirit" forms appeared. I do not mean that such persons were in conscious collusion with the medium, but they expected what took place, and were unsuspicious of the fraud, which to me at least was often plain.

When I met Madame Blavatsky no phenomena took place, or were invited. We met only as guests at dinner, at which she ate nothing, but smoked cigarettes incessantly during dinner, and talked about spiritualism. She struck me as a vulgar woman, with an inordinate power of fiction and a vast amount of impudence. I afterwards met a high Indian official who was present in India at the celebrated picnic at which Madame Blavatsky produced a teacup said to come from some remote distance, and this, he said, was a commonplace and ordinary bit of conjuring. When she appeared in India, accompanied by an American, Colonel Olcott, a rumour got about that she was a Russian spy, and Lord Lytton, then Viceroy, thought it expedient, or was warned from home (I am not sure which), to have her watched.

Lord Lytton himself told me the following story. He sent for the proper authority, and said that Colonel Olcott and Madame Blavatsky must be under police surveillance, but with great caution, and that a private report was to be made in case of any suspicion. A day or two afterwards Lord Lytton received a formal complaint from Colonel Olcott that he and Madame Blavatsky were "shadowed," and their lives rendered intolerable. He sent for the official to whom he had given the order, and was assured that he had been obeyed with scrupulous care and discretion. "Well, tell me exactly what has been done." "My lord, wherever the suspected persons have gone they have been followed by two mounted sowars."

My deliberate view of spiritualism, long before I became a Catholic, was that the "mediums" are invariably fraudulent, but the believers not necessarily, nor perhaps often so, and that there is some truth, eked out by imposture, in the phenomena. I regarded Mr. Browning's poem, "Mr. Sludge, the Medium," as a convenient summary of my own attitude of mind. Now I go further, and am inclined to believe there is in spiritism much direct satanic agency, and that those who tamper with it are, consciously or unconsciously, in most cases working with the devil. They often start with what in skilled hands is legitimate, mesmerism to relieve pain being as harmless as anodyne drugs—but use it rashly, as they often use a beneficent drug, or a poison. From this some of those who tamper with what is forbidden by the Church fall into the detestable sins described by M. Huysmans in his novel, *Là Bas*.

The same acquaintance at whose house I saw Madame Blavatsky met at my office a Jesuit friend of mine, that they might discuss " occult " phenomena. The conversation, at first animated, resolved itself more and more into a mere harangue on the part of my acquaintance and pained silence on the part of my friend, who, as he afterwards told me, could see in it a terrible indication of spiritual pride on the part of one " given over to strong delusion to believe a lie." Such also was the impression in my own mind.

Madame Blavatsky and many of those about

her, notably the acquaintance through whom I knew her, believed in reincarnation, but the most thoroughgoing exponent of that doctrine was Miss Blackwell, who visited me at Sturminster in company with a lady who sent me her son as a pupil. Miss Blackwell not only believed that we had all been other people, and would again appear in other forms in life, but also that to her had been given the power of knowing who she and others had been ; and this she explained was indeed a rare gift. She was greatly agitated at my house because my daughter's little dog barked at her. The dog was in the child's arms, and she explained her fear by saying, "I have always been afraid of dogs since they ate me : I was once Jezebel," and she went on to say, "In none of my previous incarnations was I less than a queen." She was then appearing on earth as the correspondent of an American newspaper.

She knew who I had been, though she would not tell me, but said that Mr. Bradlaugh had asked her the same question a few days before, "And even as he spoke I saw a black cloud form itself behind his head, and on it was written in letters of a horrid grey, the name

Torquemada!" She also said that the sex was often changed in a reincarnation, and that my pupil had been in a previous life Ninon de l'Enclos.

While I am dictating the latter part of these reminiscences the papers are full of the Dreyfus case, and I confess to having very small sympathy with Jews, though Captain Dreyfus seems to me to have been convicted on very insufficient grounds. In fact, my dislike to the Jews as a race has always been strong ; though from time to time different members of the race have been among my close friends. The one who always showed me very great kindness when her own health allowed it was Lady Goldsmid, widow of Sir Francis Goldsmid. At her house I once had a curious proof of the persistence of Jewish feeling and custom even when the religion as a dogmatic theology seemed completely to have vanished. Looking round the table at a large dinner-party, I saw that my wife and I were the only non-Semitic guests. I was on one side of the hostess and Herr Richter on the other. Lady Goldsmid was speaking of the entire freedom from all Jewish customs which had come on her with advancing years. I said, "And yet in all probability all the meat which we are eating at dinner is Kosher." She said, "Of course it is, but what do you know about Kosher? I always use it not because it is ordered me as a Jew, but because it is by far the most wholesome." I felt she had really given a strong argument on my side, and so Herr Richter admitted. Hers was a house at which one was always sure of hearing the best possible music; and there were few houses more delightful to me.

At the beginning of these reminiscences I have spoken of the fire which destroyed our old premises in Paternoster Square. This was unfortunate to others besides ourselves. Not only did I lose several pieces of personal property much prized by me, but also a volume of sketches in Sicily, taken by my wife during a winter that she spent there, two of which I had used in one of our publications. These had only been returned to me the very day before the fire. A MS. of Dante, of great beauty and considerable value, which had been lent me by a friend, the late Professor Middleton, was also destroyed.

I saw much of Middleton at a time when he was more in sympathy with my Positivist views than with the Catholic creed, which was once his own. I owe to him a letter from a Coptic Patriarch in regard to some MSS. placed at his disposal, which is perhaps as good a testimony as can be imagined towards his zeal for antiquities and research. The Society for the Protection of Ancient Buildings, having heard that destruction and plunder was taking place in certain Coptic churches in Egypt, and that articles had been removed and sold by the priests of those churches, requested Middleton to write to the Patriarch of Alexandria on the subject. This was done, and as Middleton was a private friend of the Patriarch, he took occasion also to express his sympathy with the Coptic churches for the sorrow they had sustained through the war in Egypt. The following is Middleton's translation of the answer, received in December 1882 :—

"From Cyril, the Servant of God, by Grace of God Patriarch of the Churches of Christ, which are in Egypt and Abyssinia, to his friend Henrik ibn Johann, peace and all spiritual greetings, in the 7th day of the month Hator, in the year of the martyrs 1460.

"Truly, oh my son, we have received thy letter, and my heart was gladdened: we ever remember thee when the diptych is read at the Holy Office, as one who, though of the race of the Feringhees, is not without grace. And we have written these things in the name of God; let them be hidden, truly they are secret.

"Our heart is heavy and our faces are blackened. Was not Arabi ibn Achmet our friend, for whom prayers were said in every church of the Kubt, that the Lord would strengthen his hand against the accursed, the Feringhees, under whom we were grievously oppressed. Was not their yoke heavier than the yoke of Ismail ibn Ibrahmi ibn Mehemet.

"And what wrong had we, the Kubt of Misr, done to the people of your Feringhee Queen; why has she sent armies and slaughtered both the Kubt and the Muslimeen of Misr together? Verily of my people have they slain 1200 men. Surely God will requite them to the blackening of their faces in the day of doom.

"And I was grieved when I received the message from the Society of learned men, who commanded you to write to me about the Churches. To them, although Polyphysites, I send greeting and my Patriarchal benediction Es Salaam, Es Salaam Aleikum.

"Truly my heart was contracted when I heard of the robbing of the Churches, and I wrote to all the Priests of the Churches of Misr, an Encyclical Letter, and I said, O dogs! and Sons of Bitches! what is this that I hear? Can it be that the very Infidels cry out against you, that your Churches are spoiled and your Altars defiled? And if they will not hear, they shall be Anathema, and I will cut them off from their inheritance with our Father St. Mark in Paradise. Truly they are pigs—they keep Harems in the Churches and sell the treasures to the accursed ones, such as are ·——

"And behold Abon Chrysostom, Abbot of St. Macarius is with me in Kahira to-day, and he sends greetings to you and says, 'Be comforted, O my son, for of the cats there was a remnant, and they have increased exceedingly, and they fill the monastery and the rats are few. Come, O my son, and visit us, our Crypt is full of beans and oil, and we are at peace with the Bedaween, and we will kill a Camel for you, and you shall read all old books, as many as you will. And Joachim ibn Suleyman ibn Daoud had found more old books hidden under the oil vats and they are neither Arabic nor Kubt. There you shall read.' This is the message of Abon Chrysostom to you, oh my Son, and to you also I say, Come and visit us.

"Signed by one Cyril, Bahaek Keneesat Amba markos, and written by me Tadrush ibn Gregorio the Scribe. From our Palace of Mist el Kahira in Daina Sameh."

During several years of my life I was much connected with this Society for the Preservation of Ancient Buildings, and was thus brought into connection with the late Mr. William Morris. I at no time shared the extreme views of many members of the society, nor would I be understood as objecting to all restoration;

but it is well that there should always be such a society to act as "L'Avvocato del diavolo," to suggest every possible difficulty in the way of restoration, in order that none which is not thoroughly justifiable should be carried out.

On the occasion of one of our protests against the restoration of a cathedral, the dean and chapter consented to meet a deputation from the society, and Mr. Morris, Professor Middleton, and I were selected as the deputation. When the day came I was prevented going and some one else took my place, Middleton kindly writing me an account of what had occurred. He described how the dean and others had met them in the cathedral and went carefully over the whole of the edifice. He wrote, "You should have seen Mr. Morris turning from time to time into a side chapel—to swear," probably the first time that the chapel had been devoted to that purpose.

If I were to write of more friends, it would be to tell many stories of persons still living. This would not, I think, be right, as their names have not become, as the others may well be considered, public property. Enough to say that the recollection of those with whom I have lived so many years of intimacy has become "now the most precious memory of mine age." It is probable that many have noticed with me a matter·which has always seemed to me a truth, that whereas boys and young men are constantly drawing to themselves fresh and fresh friends and repairing the breaches in their circle made by time and circumstances, when middle life is once passed men make few friends of their own age, only acquaintances. These are as necessary as friends to the ordinary conduct of life and are full of pleasure; but when a man past middle age makes new friends, as distinct from mere new acquaintances, these are almost always women, or else men very much younger than themselves. My experience has been that many young men are graciously willing to make friends of older men, among the young whom they gather to themselves. Wordsworth has noticed the probabilities of friendship of those of very different ages in his lines :—

> " We talked with open heart and tongue,
>   Affectionate and true,
>   A pair of friends though I was young
>   And Matthew seventy-two."

Three exceptions in my case prove the rule. One was the late Mr. Dutton, chairman of the London and South-Western Railway, another C. W. Earle, and the third Cardinal Vaughan. With all of them I felt that I had knitted a friendship of the same kind that I was wont to make with other young men in days of old.

XI

THE END OF WANDERING

1890

WHEN I came to London I was able for the first time during many years to consider my position calmly and fairly. While doing my duties as best I could, it had not been easy to realise how completely I had fallen away from the faith. Now, as a layman, with no external obligation to use words in which it was necessary to find some meaning consistent with my opinions, the whole services of the Church of England seemed distasteful and untrue. The outward scaffolding on which I had striven to climb to God, every sacramental sign under which I had sought to find Him, had crumbled into nothingness. I was in no conscious relation to Him, God had practically no part in my life; though I did not deny Him, nor cease to believe that a First Cause existed;

simple atheism is a rare, and perhaps an impossible position. I was content not to know, and to wait.

But in the meantime certain things were abundantly clear. Human relationships exist—the family, society, our country, the race; towards all these we have duties which must be organised; some conception of history, philosophy, and science must be framed, if not depending on God, at least in relation to man. The system formulated by Auguste Comte had long attracted me on its historical and social sides; a friend who, in and since Oxford days, had swayed my life more than he knew, had found it sufficient for himself, and he placed before me the religious side also of this grave and austere philosophy.

It is not a paradox, but sober truth, to say that Positivism is Catholicism without God. And it does, after a fashion, give order and regularity to life, inculcates simplicity of manners, aims at a certain amount of discipline, and caricatures, unconsciously, and with some effect, the sacraments, the *cultus* of Saints, the place of our Lady in worship, making of humanity the ideal woman, the great mother and mistress of all.

It should in fairness be said that in this
faith, if so it may be called, men and women
live high, restrained, ascetic lives, and find in
Humanity an object, not self, for their devotion. Like the men of Athens they would
seem ignorantly, and under false names, to
worship God. And for myself I may say that
I doubt if I should have known the Faith but
for Positivism, which gave me a rule and
discipline of which I had been unaware. The
historical side of Comte's teaching still remains
in large measure true to my mind, based as it is
on the teaching of the Church. Comte had the
inestimable advantage of having been Catholic
in his youth, and could not, even when he tried,
put aside the lessons he had learnt.

So long as my Positivism lasted I brought
into it a fervour and enthusiasm to which I
had been a stranger, and I was therefore long
in discovering that these were unreal and
forced. On many Sundays, when the service
was over, I was wont to walk home with a
younger friend, whose experiences had been
largely my own, save that his loss of faith had
arisen from revolt against the extreme Calvinism
which had been presented to him in his youth.

He also had wandered out into Agnosticism, and discovered that he needed an external rule against the temptations of life, which for awhile he thought to find in the Religion of Humanity. In long walks across the the park homewards in summer and winter noons we both found that the fervour of the services evaporated, and left nothing behind them; there was none of that sense of a power abiding within us which the Catholic worshipper brings away from before the Tabernacle, even if he cannot always maintain the intensity of devotion which has been granted him during the action of Holy Mass or in the Benediction Service.

Once more I saw that my soul was stripped and bare, when it had seemed fully clothed. Such also was my friend's experience; and God has given him grace to find, as I have found, the truth after which we both were seeking. Positivism is a fair-weather creed, when men are strong, happy, untempted, or ignorant that they are tempted, and so long as a future life and its dread possibilities do not enter their thoughts; but it has no message for the sorry and the sinful, no restoration for the erring, no succour in the hour of death.

In the training of my intellect and literary faculty, such as it is, one man had always held predominant sway. Those young men who entered on their Oxford careers towards the end of the decade 1840–1850 found that one prophet at least had gained honour in his own country, even if he had experienced also scorn and rejection. John Henry Newman was a moving intellectual force along with Tennyson, Browning, Ruskin, and Carlyle. I came to know the two poets as I know my Bible, if it be not irreverent to say so, in such a way that after a time I needed no longer to read them, because the exact words surged up in memory when thought was directed to them, and there was no need of the printed page. Ruskin and Carlyle delivered their message and passed on, but Newman abode, and his intellectual influence developed into one that was moral and spiritual, preparing my soul for the great grace and revelation which God had yet in store.

Like Thomas à Kempis, so Newman, studied day by day, sank into my soul and changed it. Since Pascal none has put so plainly as he the dread alternative, all or nothing, faith or unfaith, God or the denial of God. I had not denied

Him, but had left Him on one side, and now, as it were, God took His revenge. This is no place to explain in detail how in sorrow and desolation of spirit God left His servant alone for awhile to clutch in vain for some help in temptation, for some solution of doubt, and find none, if it were not God and the old creeds. It were to lay the secrets of the soul too bare to declare minutely how each hesitation to submit to what was becoming intellectually clear was followed by some moral or spiritual fall, as though the Father would allow His child to slip in miry ways, if nothing else would teach the need of guidance.

But apart from the direct leadings of God's grace, and the general effect of the *Imitation* and Newman's writings, it may be well to specify more closely some of the arguments which weighed with me to accept the Faith I had so long set at nought.

First, and above all, was the overwhelming evidence for modern miracles, and the conclusions from their occurrence. A study of Pascal's Life, when I was engaged in translating the *Pensées*, directed my special attention to the cure of Pascal's niece, of a lachrymal fistula, by the touch of the Holy Thorn preserved at Port Royal. It is impossible to find anything of the kind better attested, and readers may judge for themselves in the narrative written of the facts by Racine, and the searching investigations by unprejudiced, and certainly not too credulous, critics, Sainte - Beuve and the late Charles Beard.

Next in importance were the miracles of Lourdes, one of which, as wrought on a friend of my own, came under my notice. I do not mean, especially in the former case, that these facts proved any doctrines ; that the miracle of the Thorn made for Jansenist teaching, or those at Lourdes for the Immaculate Conception ; but rather, that the Thorn must, from its effects, have been one that had touched the Sacred Head, that the spring at Lourdes could only have had its healing powers by the gift of God, through our Lady. It was not that miracles having been declared in the Bible made these later occurrences possible, but that these, properly attested in our own days, and in times so near our own, made the Bible miracles more credible than they were before, adding their testimony to that which the Church bears to

Holy Scripture. And it was on the testimony of a living Church that I would accept the Scripture, if I accepted it at all, for surely of all absurd figments, that of a closed revelation to be its own interpreter is the most absurd.

The books which mainly aided me at this period, when I had accepted in a more definite way than ever before the being of a God who actively, daily, and visibly interposes in His creation, were the *Grammar of Assent*, by Cardinal Newman, and *Religio Viatoris*, by Cardinal Manning. Both works postulate God and the human soul, and on that foundation build up the Catholic faith. They are very different in their method, and perhaps, as a rule, helpful to different classes of mind, but both aided me. The re-reading the *Grammar of Assent* as a theological treatise, and with the wish to believe, was quite a different matter to my earlier study of it on its publication, when I regarded it only as an intellectual effort, interesting as the revelation of a great mind, but not as yet recognising that it had any special message for me. But in these later days it proved to be the crowning gift of the many I received from that great teacher, who had been my guide through the years of my pilgrimage, little though I knew it.

It is not possible to state precisely the moment at which definite light came upon my soul, in preparation for the fuller day. As Clough says truly of earthly dawn :—

> " And not by eastern windows only,
>   When daylight comes, comes in the light ;
> In front, the sun climbs slow, how slowly,
>   But westward, look, the land is bright."

About 1888 I had light enough to attend Mass pretty frequently, but even then was not definitely Catholic in my belief and sympathies. There was one of my own family, having a right to speak, who distrusted my evident leanings, not so much from want of sympathy with religion, as from a fear that as my opinions had been so long in a state of change, this also might be a passing phase. I said to myself, whether rightly or wrongly I cannot judge, that a year should elapse before I made up my mind on the question, though I began to see which way it must be answered. This was in the spring of 1889 ; but so weak is memory that towards the end of the year I was misled by a date, and supposed it had been in the late summer.

In May 1890 I went for a short tour in France, as I had done for some years past, and a profound sense of dissatisfaction with myself filled my whole soul. In other days the cathedrals and their services, the shrines and their relics, places of pilgrimage, venerated images had all been connected with a faith in which no one who studied the workings of the human mind could fail to take an interest, but they had no relation to my own soul. Now it seemed to me that I was an alien from the family of God, unable to take a part in that which was my heritage, shut out by my own coldness of heart, my own want of will. And, as had long been the case, what attracted me most were just those things in the cult of Rome which most offended my companions.

A distinguished ecclesiastic was talking in Rome with a lady who while in England had shown some disposition towards the Church, but lamented that in the Holy City she had seen much that was to her disedifying, and quite unlike the pious practices she had known at home. He replied, " Ah, madame, il ne faut

pas regarder de si près la cuisine du Bon Dieu."
It was this which interested me and drew me
to it. At Tours the heap of crutches in the
house devoted to the *cultus* of the Holy Face,
the pathetic agony of the engraving of the same,
seen in so many churches of that diocese, ap-
pealed more to me than the celebration of High
Mass in the cathedral; the rude image of our Lady
at Chartres more than many a fairer statue.

At Beaulieu, near Loches, the end came. We
had walked there from Loches, and while my
companions were resting under the trees in the
little *Place*, and taking a photograph of a neighbouring mill, I remained in the church in conversation with the *curé*, who was superintending
some change in the arrangements of the altar.
We spoke of Tours and St. Martin, of the revived cult of the Holy Face, of M. Dupont,
"the holy man of Tours," whom the *curé* had
known, and at last he said, after a word about
English Protestantism, " Mais Monsieur est sans
doute Catholique ? " I was tempted to answer,
" À peu près," but the thought came with overwhelming force that this was a matter in which
there was " no lore of nicely-calculated less or
more "; we were Catholics or not, my interlo-

cutor was within the fold, and I without, and if without, then against knowledge, against warning, for I recognised that my full conviction had at last gone where my heart had gone before, the call of God had sounded in my ears, and I must perforce obey. But when?

The promise which I had made to myself that I would wait a year was binding on me as though made to one for whose sake I had made it, and the date at which the promise would expire seemed far off. But early in August I discovered that I had been in error as to the time, and that I was already free. On the 12th of August, at Fulham, in the Church of the Servites, an Order to which I had long felt an attraction, I made my submission to the Church, with deep thankfulness to God.

It was the day after Cardinal Newman's death, and the one bitter drop in a brimming cup of joy was that he could not know all that he had done for me, that his was the hand which had drawn me in when I sought the ark floating on the stormy seas of the world. But a few days afterwards, as I knelt by his coffin at Edgbaston and heard the Requiem Mass said for him, I felt that indeed he knew, that he was in a land where there was no need to tell him anything, for he sees all things in the heart of God.

Those who are not Catholics are apt to think and say that converts join the Roman communion in a certain exaltation of spirit, but that when it cools they regret what has been done, and would return but for very shame. It has been said of marriage that every one finds when the ceremony is over that he or she has married another, and not the bride or groom who seemed to have been won; and Clough takes the story of Jacob as a parable representing this fact. We wed Rachel, as we think, and in the morning, behold it is Leah. So the Church bears one aspect when seen from a distance, *ab extra*, another when we have given ourselves into her keeping.

But the Church is no Leah, rather a fairer Rachel than we dared to dream, her blessings are greater than we had hoped. I may say for myself that the happy tears shed at the tribunal of Penance, on that 12th of August, the fervour of my first communion, were as nothing to what I feel now. Day by day the mystery of the altar seems greater, the unseen world nearer, God more a Father, our Lady more tender, the great company of saints more friendly, if I dare use the word, my guardian angel closer to my side. All human relationships become holier, all human friends dearer, because they are explained and sanctified by the relationships and the friendships of another life. Sorrows have come to me in abundance since God gave me grace to enter His Church, but I can bear them better than of old, and the blessing He has given me outweighs them all. May He forgive me that I so long resisted Him, and lead those I love unto the fair land wherein He has brought me to dwell! It will be said, and said with truth, that I am very confident. My experience is like that of the blind man in the Gospel who also was sure. He was still ignorant of much, nor could he fully explain how Jesus opened his eyes, but this he could say with unfaltering certainty, "One thing I know, that whereas I was blind, now I see."

BIBLIOGRAPHICAL NOTE

From 1853, when I returned to England from Germany, I have been a pretty frequent writer in periodicals and of pamphlets and prefaces, but need not specify these, having collected in books all that are worth preserving. It may be well to specify those books by which I care to be known, but they will probably soon be forgotten, if they are not so already. Few books can interest men except those of their own time, and I have no reason to complain of the reception accorded to what I really wish to preserve.

They are :—

1. A *Translation of Faust*, in the metres of the original. I did this while at Sturminster, and had the kind revision of one of my pupils, Richard Brandt, of German birth, who at least preserved me from such foolish blunders as those of some former translators ; notably what Faust says of the spirits which swarmed about

him, "Und lispeln englisch wenn sie lügen," which has been turned, "And speak in English when they lie"; and "kurz gebunden," which another translator applies to the length of Gretchen's petticoats! "And oh! how short her kirtle trim." My translation, strange to say, is sold out, but is not worth reprinting.

2. *Life of Godwin.* This was undertaken with the cordial approval of his grandson, Sir Percy Shelley, who placed unreservedly at my disposal all the immense mass of papers belonging to him. I undertook it, not because I admire Godwin, but because of the society of which he was the centre, and for the light his papers threw on his time and on such people as Mary Wollstonecraft, Charles Lamb, Coleridge, Wordsworth, Bulwer, &c. &c. It had a considerable success, and I have often thought of reissuing it in a condensed form, but to do so would need so many changes and explanations to bring it into accord with my present point of view, that I shall now never do so.

3. *Letters of Mary Wollstonecraft*, edited by me with prefatory memoir, expanded from

what I had written of her in the *Life of Godwin.*

4. *Biographical Sketches.* This went through two editions and is out of print.

5. *Pascal's Thoughts*, translated. This has gone through several editions and exists in more than one form.

6. *Maria Drummond, a Sketch*, a short memoir of Mrs. Drummond, of Fredley, near Dorking, my dear and kind friend, written at the request of her surviving daughters, Mrs. Kay and Miss Drummond, who, however, allowed me an absolutely free hand in my treatment of the subject. I cannot thank them enough for their trust in me.

7. *Faith and Unfaith*, a collection of scattered essays such as seemed to me worth preserving, and by which I should wish to be remembered, if any one remember my writings at all.

8. *En Route*, translated from the work of the same name by M. Huysman, together with a preface. Ill health prevented my translating

the sequel to this, *La Cathédrale*, and I was only able to write the preface.

9. *By the Way Side*, a collection of a few verses, written from time to time, which some partial friends have desired to gather where they fell, before time has trodden them wholly under foot.

INDEX

A

ABRAHAM, Bishop, assistant-master of Eton, 91, 94, 208

Aitken, Rev. James, 141, 170

Allen, Rev. John, head-master of Ilminster School, 38
Appearance and character, 39
Musical voice, 43
Reading, 44

Allen, Mrs., appearance and character of, 44
As teacher, 46

Alton Locke, exponent of co-operative and Christian Socialist movements of the day, 165

Ancestors, West Indian, 4

Anglican system, strength and weakness of, 140

Antony and Cleopatra, reading of, 26

Arabian Nights, reading of, 22

Arch, Mr., and labourers' wages, 259

Arnold, Matthew, 33

Astley, Sir John (Bart.), boy at Eton, 120

Awdry, Sir John, ready wit of, 64

B

BALSTON, head-master of Eton, 104, 224, 227

Barnes, William, the "Dorset Burns," 295

Bastard, Mr. and Mrs., 251

Bath, custom in churches, 28
High Churchism in, 27

Beard, Rev. Charles, editor of *Theological Review*, 264

Bell, Rev., vicar of Bloxham, 183

Bethell, 79, 81, 82
Rev. —, Vice-Provost of Eton, 186

Bible, reading of, 27

Birch, Aug., assistant-master at Eton, 210

Birthplace, 2, 11

Blake, Rev. Vernon, 174

Blavatsky, Mme., 351, 352, 354

Bloxham, 182, 183, 184, 185

Blunt, Wilfred, 296, 344

Bowles, Rich. Francis, description of, 138

Bowles, Rev. Samuel, 145

Boyle, Very Rev. G. D., Dean of Salisbury, 140, 169, 170

Boys, rise in social scale of, 247

Briggs, Fellow of Eton, 84

Bright, John, 349

Brodrick, Rev. Alan, 141, 145

Brooke, Sir James, first Rajah of Sarawak, 28, 29, 153

Brooke, John Johnson, second Rajah of Sarawak, 29

Brooke, Sir Charles, third Rajah of Sarawak, 29

"Brosier," Eton custom, 111

Browning, Robert, 168, 333, 338

Browning, Mrs., 168, 169

Burton, Sir Richard and Lady, 295

C

Camilla, reading of, 21

Campbell, Rev. J. J., vicar of Tew, 173

Caribs, original inhabitants of the West Indies, 7

Carlyle, influence of, 169

Carlyle, Mrs., 180

Carter, Rev. Thomas, rector of Clewer, 216

Vice-Provost of Eton, 69, 72

Description and death of, 75

Cathedral services, 373

Cholera alarm, 33

Churches, Bath, 27, 28

Church questions, interest in, 131

Church services, manner of, 188

"Church sock," custom at Eton, 79

Church, Writhlington, 13

Clergy, influence, 187, 188

Clewer, House of Mercy, 216

Clifford, Professor W. K., 318

Cobbold, Felix, 226

Cocquerel, Rev. Athanase, member of Free Christian Union Society, 265

Coleridge, Rev. Edward, master at Eton, 85, 90, 91, 228

College, entrance on life at, 136

Colliers, Somersetshire, 20

Colvile, Margaret Agnes, 213

Mrs., death of, 217

Comforts of life, advance in the, 19

Conductship at Eton, 198, 201

Congreve, Dr., 204

Cookesley, Rev. W. G., Eton master, 92, 228

Cornish, Frank Warre, 211, 226, 242

Cossins, Miss, 171

Country neighbours, 32

Cox, Rev. Sir George (Bart.), 40, 143

Coxe, Rev. Henry Octavius, Bodleian librarian, 149

Curacy at Tew, 164, 173

D

DAMES' houses, creation of, 69, 108

Day, Rev. Russell, assistant-master at Eton, 210

Dayman, Rev. —, President of Dorset Clerical Society, 250

Dobson, Mr. Austin, 294, 296

Dod, Rev. Wolley, 210, 232

Dorset, Clerical Society, 250

County Temperance Association, 258

Dorset, movement for higher wages in, 259
Clergy, 261, 262
Dorsetshire dialect, 249
Dowden, Professor Edward, 296
Du Boulay, Rev. Frank, 139, 145
Rev. James, 140
Dupuis, Rev. G. J., Fellow of Eton, 86

E

EARLE, Charles, 341
Eastlake, Lady, 345
Eliot, George, account of, 335–338
Ellenrieder, Frl. Marie, 194
Elwyn, Rev. Whitwell, 135
Emma, questions on Miss Austen's, 316
Epigram, Bethell's sermons, 81
Hawtrey's, 65
On West Indian emancipation, 18
Plumptre's, 85
Williams, Rowland, as master of, 262
Esdaile, Mr. and Mrs., 252
Essays and Reviews, 218
Effect on Hawtrey and Wilberforce, 220, 221
Eton, assistant-masters, position of, 69
Boys, Astley, 120
Scott, 119
Thring, 119
Changes at, 121

Eton chapel, east window, 129
Choice of, 61
Church restoration, 78
Conductship, 198, 201
Roper, 221
Culloden rugs, gift of, 72
Customs, 111, 116, 118, 122, 125, 127
Dames, abuses, 108, 211
Description of, 66
Description of chapel, 76
Growth of luxury, 108
History of, by Sir H. Maxwell Lyte, 89
Inscription in Hall, 73
Long Chamber, rats, 74
Map-making in Remove, 94
Masters, support of, 210
Neighbouring clergy, 216
Reforms at, 89
Religion and morality, 128
Teaching at, 105, 107
Eton College, 61, 65, 207
Collegers and Oppidans, 212
Foundation of, 68
Fourth of June at, 116
Life, retrospect, 225
Mastership in, 205, 206
Reforms, 72, 73, 207, 208, 209, 211, 212
Residence at, 214
Evans, drawing-master at Eton, 107
Examination at Oxford, 167
Exeter College, life at, 146
Expurgated editions, concerning, 22

F

FAGGING system, 118
Father, early life of, 2, 3
   Marriage of, 11
Father Clement, influence and
   reading of, 24
Fire, destruction of premises by,
   1, 357
Floggings at Ilminster School,
   41
Foxcote, my father's curacy at,
   12
"Free Christian Union" So-
   ciety, intention of, 265
Friends at Sturminster, 251
   The making of, 362
Friendship, power of, 138
Froude, James Anthony, 157,
   165, 346
   At Littlemore, 347
   The Nemesis of Faith, 165,
      166

G

GHENT, account of picture in,
   309
Godwin, Mary, elopement of,
   32
Godwin, Life of, materials for,
   253
Goldfinch family, monuments
   and vaults of the, 15
Goldsmid, Lady, and a Jewish
   custom, 356
Goodford, Rev. C. O., D.D.,
   obituary, 96
   Head-master, 84, 100, 209,
      232

Goodford, Provost, 100, 103,
   224
   And "Church sock," 79
   And College reforms, 209
   House of, 117
*Gordon, General, Last Journals
   of*, 287
Gosse, Edmund, 296, 308
Gulliver's Travels, reading of, 21

H

HALE, Rev. Edward, account
   of, 230
   Rev. Edward, 210
Hamilton, Bishop of Salisbury,
   fears of, 223
Hardington Park, residence at,
   135
Hardisty, assistant-master at
   Eton, 205, 209
Hardy, Thomas, 298
   Novels of, 314
Harman, John, 184, 199
Hawker, Rev. Robert Stephen,
   ballad of, 298
Hawtayne, Rob., 141
Hawtrey, Rev. E. C., D.D.,
   head-master of Eton, 63,
   67
   Death of Provost, 103, 223
   Provost, 100, 227, 229
   Provost, effect of *Essays
      and Reviews* on, 220
   Retrospect of his head-
      mastership, 100
   Views on *Coningsby*, 64
   Wit of, 64, 65

Hawtrey, Rev. Stephen, private tutor at Eton, 106
Heathcote, Rev. —, vicar of Sturminster, 223, 244
Herbert, Hon. Auberon, 259
Hexter at Eton, 105
High Church at Eton, 121
Highlands, tour in the, 170
Hodgson, Rev. James, vicar of Bloxham, 186
  Work at Bloxham, 199
Hodgson, friend of Byron, 71
Hookins, Rev. Philip, his sermons, 185
Hughes, Tom, 164
Huxley, Professor, 339

I

ILMINSTER School, introduction to, 36
  Manners and lack of luxury, 45, 48
  Moral influences, 46
  Work, 41
Imitation of Christ, study of, 205
Inspiration, motto on, 264
Irving, Martin, 177, 179, 181, 202
  Mrs. Edward, 179
Irvingite Church, the, 181

J

JAMES, Rev. C. C., 231
Jenkins, Rev. William, 174
Johnson, Col., 195

Johnson, William (Cory), 210, 222
  Account of, 228
Jolliffe, Rev. Thomas, 56
Jowett, and Palgrave, 167
  Sermon by, 170

K

KEATING, Christopher, 10
  Mr. and Mrs., 171
  Mrs., 7, 156
Kegan Paul, Trench, & Co., publications, 279, 287, 288, 290, 295, 296, 299
Kennard of Marnhull, the Rev. Robert, 262
King, Henry S., career and character of, 270–76
  Purchase of his publishing business, 276
King, Mrs. Hamilton, a true poetess, 345
Kingdon, Rev. —, curate of Sturminster, 243
Kingsley, Rev. Charles, 157, 177, 179, 187, 202, 216
  As pastor, 161–63
  First visit to, 158
  His influence on my religious opinions, 160, 163
  Memoir of, 158
  Personality of, 159
  Recollections of, in *Biographical Sketches*, 158
Kingsley, Henry, 142
Knowles, Eardley, visit to, 170

L

Lang, Andrew, 299
La Souffrière, eruption of, 8
Lawrence, George, as author, 141
Lectures at Oxford, 167
Leigh, A. Austen, 226
Lent, Self-denial in, 28
Lewes, G. H., and George Eliot,
    account of, 335-38
Literature as a profession, 292
Littlehales, Mrs., 154
Ludlow, J. M., 165
Lyte's, Sir H. Maxwell, *History
    of Eton*, 89
Lytton, Edward, Lord, 353
    Robert, Earl of, 341

M

Macmullen, Very Rev. Canon,
    40
Manning, Cardinal, 340, 347
Mansel, Rev. Owen, and the
    Dorset County Tempe-
    rance Association, 259
Manuscripts, destruction by fire
    of, 1, 357
Map-making, practice at Eton,
    94
Marriage, 213
Marriott, Rev. W., assistant-
    master at Eton, 208
Marshall, Rev. S., colleague at
    Eton, 201
Maurice, Rev. Fred. Denison,
    164, 187
Meredith, George, 298, 348
Mesmerism, 177
Methodists, Primitive, 34, 35

Middleton, Professor, 358, 361
    Patriarch of Alexandria's
        letter to, 358
Miracles, 264, 369
Mohl, M. and Mme., 303
" Montem," custom at Eton, 111
    Effect of railway on, 115
Morris, William, 360, 361
Muloch, Miss (Mrs. Craik), 254

N

Negro nurse, 19
Nelson, H. J., 225
Newman, Cardinal, 340
    At Littlemore, 347
    Influence of, 368
    *The Lives of the English
        Saints*, 346
Northcote, Very Rev. Spencer,
    39

O

Oliphant, Mrs., 345
Ordination, 164, 173, 174, 185
Ormerod, Herbert, 177, 178
Orthodox, use of term, 55
Oxford movement, effect on
    Eton, 128
Oxford, society at, 149

P

Paget, Arthur, 47, 141
Palgrave, Frank, and Jowett,
    167
Parker, Charles, 136, 173
Patmore, Coventry, a true poet,
    345

Pattison, Mark, 350

Perry, Rev. Canon, 40

Philosophie Positive, Comte's influence in the, 204

Pickering, Rev. E., assistant-master at Eton, 93

Pike, Mr. and Mrs. W., 251, 253

Plumptre, 82
  Character, 86
  Eccentricities of, at Eton, 83
  Epigram, 85
  Sermons of, 85

Political opinions, 166

Pollard, Alfred W., 290

Positivism, attraction of, 365
  Attention first drawn to, 204

Powles, Rev. Cowley, 157

Procter, Mrs., 180
  Account of, 319-33

Prophecy, motto on, 264

Public-houses at Eton, 127

Publishers, attitude of, towards religious books, 291

Publishing as a career, 277

Publishing work, humours of, 299
  With Mr. H. S. King, 270

Pupils at Sturminster, 243, 245
  My father's, 52

Pusey, personal influence of, 143, 151

R

RAILWAY, first experience of, 62

Ranters' story of the devil, 34, 35

Rash, curious remedy for, 16

Reading, early, 21-27
  At Oxford, 168

Regatta, or "Fourth of June" at Eton, 116

Re-incarnation, stories of, 355

Religious opinions, 188, 364-77
  Agnosticism and Positivism, 364
  Books, religious, 371
  Broad High Churchman, 166
  Effect of Charles Kingsley's influence, 163
  Effect of Positivism, 204
  Influence of Unitarianism, 264
  Leave Church of England, 269
  Newman, influence of, 368
  The end, 374
  The faith, reasons for accepting, 369
  Want of sympathy with the Church of England, 263

Renan, M. and Mdme., 304

Ritchie, Miss Charlotte, 302
  Mrs., 251

Robertson, Rev. Frederick, 272
  His sermons, 273

Rous, Provost of Eton, 78

Routledge, Rev. Dr. ("Daddy"), 41

Russell, Charles Whitworth, 152
  Sir Charles (Bart.), 171
  Sir George (Bart.), 138

S

SANDERS, Rev. —, curate of Bloxham, 183

Sarawak, Rajahs of, 28, 29, 153

School "Dames," 33
    Friends, 47, 120
    Ilminster, 36–60
    Outfit, nightcaps, 48
    Sunday, classes, 33
    Visits and holidays, 38

Sedding, John D., architect, 248

Sellick, or "The Slug," 40

Selwyn, Bishop, private tutor at Eton, 91

Sewell, Rev. William, founder of Radley, 148
    Senior tutor at Exeter, 146, 166

Shelley, Eton boy, 90
    Memorials, 252
    Sir Percy and Lady, 251

"Shirking" at Eton, 125

Short, Rev. W. F., 177, 179, 202

Simmons, Rev. Frank Churchill, 46, 141

Slave song, old, 18

Smith, Rev. Canon Percy, 40, 46, 141, 158, 160

Snow, Rev. D'Oyley, 261

"Spankie" at Eton, 123

Spencer, Rev. Thomas, 57

Spiritualism, 351, 352, 353

Staples, Mr., 30

Stephen, Sir James, 128

Stone, Rev. E. D., assistant-master at Eton, 210

Street, Mr., 248

Stuckey, Mr., murder of, 11

Sturminster Marshall, country dialect, 249.
    Life at, 223, 224
    Living of, 243
    Neighbours and friends, 250
    Parish, 244
    Pupils at, 243, 245
    Resignation of living, 269
    Smallpox in, 260

Sullivan, Col. and Mrs., 251
    Mrs., account of, 254

Sunday, observance of, 34

T

TARVER, French master at Eton, 106

Tennyson, reading and criticism of, 132

Tew, clergy in neighbourhood, 176
    Curacy at, 164, 173, 181
    My house at, 175
    The village of, 174
    Work at, 174, 175

The Nun, reading of, 24

Theological Review, my contributions to the, 264

Theological views and mottoes, 264

Thomas, Mrs., 29

Thornton, Miss, 315

Thring, boy at Eton, 119

Tours abroad, 302, 305, 306, 308, 311, 373

Tractarian movement, 143

Tracts for Priests and People, 219

Translators, ignorance and blunders, 281–86
Travelling, modes of, 52
Trench, Archbishop of Dublin, 290
Tutorship abroad, Carlsruhe, 192
Constance, 194
Illness at Constance, 198
Leave England, 191
Schaffhausen, 198
Wiesbaden, 193
Tutor, private, position of, 246
Tweed, an usher, 40
Typhus fever, attack of, 16

U

UNITARIANISM and the Broad Church party, 215
Influence of, 264

V

VACCINATION, experience of, 261
Vegetarianism, 203

W

WALES, holiday in, 202
Walford, John Thomas, account of, 232–42
Eton master, 210
Warts, "charming" of, 49
Waterfield, Ottiwell C., Eton master, 210
Wayte, Rev. William, assistant-master at Eton, 231

Wellow, break up of home at, 186
Humorous experiences, 59
National School, 57
People at, 57
Removal to, 51
West Indies, business in the, 16
Failure of property, 51
Inhabitants of the, 7
Wilberforce, Bishop of Oxford, 173
Effect of Essays and Reviews on, 221
Wilder, Rev. John, Fellow of Eton, character of, 87
Williams, Dr. Rowland, and his books, 262
Wilson, A. C., 141
Dr., an Evangelical, 189
Rev. H. B., essayist and Bampton Lecturer, 262
Wollstonecraft, Mary, letter describing trial of king, 30
On an Eton custom, 85, 89
Wren, his work in Eton chapel, 78
Writhlington, description of, 12
My father's curacy at, 12
Wyatt, Halifax, 141

Y

YONGE, Rev. John, assistant-master at Eton, 228
Young, Sir William, 226